Teaching Haiti

TEACHING
HAITI

Strategies for Creating New Narratives

Edited by Cécile Accilien and Valérie K. Orlando

UNIVERSITY OF FLORIDA PRESS
Gainesville

Publication of this paperback edition made possible by a Sustaining the Humanities through the American Rescue Plan grant from the National Endowment for the Humanities.

Copyright 2021 by Cécile Accilien and Valérie K. Orlando
All rights reserved
Published in the United States of America

First cloth printing, 2021
First paperback printing, 2023

28 27 26 25 24 23   6 5 4 3 2 1

Library of Congress Cataloging-in-Publication Data
Names: Accilien, Cécile, 1973– editor. | Orlando, Valérie, 1963– editor.
Title: Teaching Haiti : strategies for creating new narratives / edited by Cécile Accilien and Valérie K. Orlando.
Description: 1. | Gainesville : University of Florida Press, 2021. | Includes bibliographical references and index. | Summary: "This volume provides guidance on teaching about Haiti's history and culture from a multidisciplinary perspective, offering ways of reshaping old narratives through women's and gender studies, poetry, theater, art, religion, language, politics, history, and popular culture"— Provided by publisher.
Identifiers: LCCN 2021007606 (print) | LCCN 2021007607 (ebook) | ISBN 9781683402107 (cloth) | ISBN 9781683402442 (pdf) | ISBN 9781683403999 (pbk.)
Subjects: LCSH: Haiti—Social life and customs—History. | Haiti—History.
Classification: LCC F1916 .T43 2021 (print) | LCC F1916 (ebook) | DDC 972.94—dc23
LC record available at https://lccn.loc.gov/2021007606
LC ebook record available at https://lccn.loc.gov/2021007607

University of Florida Press
2046 NE Waldo Road
Suite 2100
Gainesville, FL 32609
http://upress.ufl.edu

In memory of Carolyn Clarke Nuite (1933–2019)

In memory of Margaret Armand (1950–2016)

To Ulrick Jean-Pierre, *twoubadou*, artist, and guardian of memory, for always teaching about Haiti through his artistic wisdom

And to Zahir and Francis Accilien. May you always be curious to understand Haiti's history, which is a part of your history!

Contents

List of Illustrations ix

Ayiti se tè glise: Intersectionalities of History, Politics, and Culture 1
Cécile Accilien and Valérie K. Orlando

I. TEACHING ABOUT HAITIAN ART, LITERATURE, AND LANGUAGE

1. Getting around the Poto Mitan: Reconstructing Haitian Womanhood in the Classroom 15
   Régine Jean-Charles

2. Teaching Haiti through the Work of Rodney Saint-Éloi, écrivain *engagé* 34
   Bonnie Thomas

3. Teaching Haitian Theater: Franck Fouché's *Bouqui au Paradis* 51
   Joubert Satyre

4. Engaging Haiti through Art and Religion 68
   Cécile Accilien

5. Creating Interdisciplinary Knowledge about Haiti's Creole Language 92
   Don E. Walicek

II. TEACHING ABOUT HAITIAN HISTORY AND POLITICS

6. Haiti in the Presidencies of John Adams and John Quincy Adams: Lesson Plans and Course Modules 119
   Darren Staloff and Alessandra Benedicty-Kokken

7. Teaching the 2004 Coup in Haiti from a French Perspective: Insights into France's Neocolonial Culture and Practices 137
   Sophie Watt

8. Peck's *Fatal Assistance*: A Filmic Lesson on the Failures of Aid 166
   Agnès Peysson-Zeiss

III. TEACHING ABOUT HAITI IN AMERICAN STUDIES, LATIN AMERICAN STUDIES, AND GENERAL STUDIES CONTEXTS

9. Rendering Haiti Visible in an Introductory American Studies Course 183
   Elizabeth Langley

10. Race and Culture on the Thrift Store Shift: Teaching about Haiti Inside and Outside the Academy 201
    Jessica Adams

11. Rethinking Latinx Studies from Hispaniola's Borderlands 221
    John Ribó

12. Teaching Haiti and the Dominican Republic: Cultural Representations of Haitian Immigrant Experiences 239
    Anne M. François

List of Contributors 249
Index 255

Illustrations

Figures

0.1. Pre-Columbian map of Haiti 3
4.1. Malcolm X is Ogoun X, the warrior god 78
4.2. Image of the Vodou lwa Grann Brigitte 79
4.3. "Marassa Separé," who represents two Èzili 81
4.4. Abstract art by Colette Brésilla 82
4.5. *Crucified Liberty*, a painting by Ulrick Jean-Pierre 84
5.1. Idea map to be used for essay writing 114
6.1. Colonial-era map of Saint-Domingue and Louisiana 121

Tables

6.1. Sources readily available to instructors 132
9.1. American Studies or American Cultural Studies 196

Ayiti se tè glise

Intersectionalities of History, Politics, and Culture

CÉCILE ACCILIEN AND VALÉRIE K. ORLANDO

Ayiti se tè glise. "Haiti is a slippery land." This proverb is often used to refer to Haiti's complexity in terms of its historic and present challenges. It also invites those who think they know the country on the surface to search deeper in order to discover the complexities inherent in its culture, history, and geography. Our experience of teaching about Haiti is that many students come to class with the baggage of Western mediatized images that associate the country with disaster, poverty, and negative concepts of Vodou. Therefore, in response, the contributing scholars to this volume recommend various concrete ways for instructors and students to extend their inquiry beyond simplistic representations that repeatedly cast Haiti as "the poorest country in the Western Hemisphere."

This volume seeks to contextualize Haiti outside the stereotypes that have labeled it for over a century. We envision this island nation "in relation," as Martinican theorist Edouard Glissant would say, to the rest of the Caribbean and, more broadly, to the extensive hemisphere of the Americas, and to the globe. As these chapters demonstrate, Haiti in relation with and to others—their histories and their cultures—is part of the "Tout-Monde," which Glissant defines as "un monde qui [fait] bouger choses et gens" (a world that makes people and things move) (Glissant, *Tout-Monde* 35). Glissant's conception of "relation" is understood as "à l'opposé" (in opposition) to "enfermement" (closed; literally, imprisonment). "*Relation est ici entendue comme la quantité réalisée de toutes les différences du monde, sans qu'on puisse en excepter une seule*" [Relation is here understood as the sum quality of all the differences of the world, without a single exception] (Glissant, *Philosophie* 42).[1] Haiti, part of Glissant's Tout-Monde, is a dynamic place in a world in motion that promotes fruitful encounters among "les cultures humaines . . . mises en contact et en effervescence de réaction les unes avec les autres" [human cultures . . . put in contact with the effervescent reactions of one another] (Glissant, *Traité du Tout-Monde* 23). Recognizing the importance of relationships and encounters with others as contributing to Haitian identity today is an essential goal in this volume. As Guadeloupean author Simone Schwarz-Bart notes, "encounters," even the most painful, are the reasons for today's vibrant creole cultures across the Caribbean: "*Nous sommes le fruit de la rencontre des mondes, géographiquement et historiquement. Des rencontres violentes, mais des rencontres tout de même. Nous sommes le monde en marche.*" [We are the fruit of the encounter of worlds, geographically and historically. Violent encounters, but encounters all the same. We are the world in motion.][2]

Positioning Haiti in the vibrant Tout-Monde, "*le monde en marche*," our contributors reveal a country whose artistic and literary creators are contributing to a multi-faceted culture with a rich literary tradition in multiple languages. Also demonstrated is Haiti's captivating cinematic oeuvre, promoted by filmmakers from the island nation and its diaspora. Haiti is not obscured in a void of silence, but is rather part of the world's stage. To contextualize the country's contributions and challenges, our contributors' syllabi and classroom experiences offer valuable lessons about Haiti's past and present as they relate to immigration, migration, locality, and globality. These are subjects that are pertinent not only to Haiti, but also to our common humanity in an era in which scholars and teachers are increasingly called upon to find ways to address the defining challenges of our age. These include neoliberalist views and practices, fascist rhetoric, and isolationist politics.

In order to place Haiti "in relation" to numerous sociocultural, political, and linguistic facets of today's world, each chapter is comparable to a well-traveled proverb. Our goal in this format is to encourage the instructor and the student to explore Haiti through a particular topic or lens. Proverbs play a fundamental role in Haitian culture and daily life, and it seems as if there is one for every situation. Proverbs are utilized to encourage people as they face struggles and difficult situations as well as the joys and celebrations of daily life. They are also a way to teach lessons and offer wisdom from one generation to the next.

With the multiple Haitian spaces of relation in mind, we emphasize that the main objective of this volume is to map pathways for instructors to teach about Haiti and to help create new windows through which to see it because, as scholar and activist Gina Athena Ulysse affirms, "Haiti needs new narratives."[3] Many of our contributors take up this challenge explicitly, pointing the way to new narratives that challenge and go beyond stereotypical, neocolonial, imperialist, racist, and simplistic discourses about Haiti and Haitian culture.

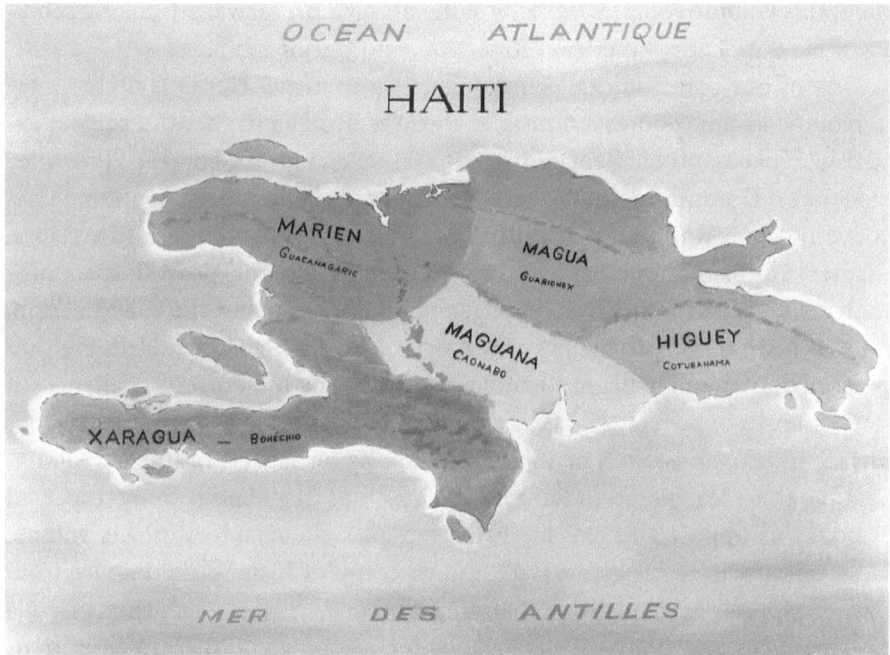

Figure 0.1. Pre-Columbian map of Haiti. Ulrick Jean-Pierre, *Precolumbian Map of Haiti*. 1984. Oil on canvas. 36 × 36 inches. Collection of the late Dr. and Mrs. Yves Jérôme.

Over the past two decades, we have seen a wealth of research and scholarship centered on teaching and learning, as well as a focus on the importance of intellectual exchange across disciplines through critical pedagogy. Scholars in the field of Caribbean Studies have worked assiduously to defend the idea that teaching is "significant intellectual work in the academy" (121).[4] If we understand how our intellectual work informs teaching "in relation," it becomes a means of helping students develop critical thinking in order to express their passions and goals for the world in which they live. Such inquiry helps students engage in their communities, understand others, and recognize that they are also "other" as they consider their own privilege, power, and positionality. Relational pedagogy reinforces what bell hooks notes in *Teaching to Transgress: Education as the Practice of Freedom* must happen in the classroom space: that is, it must become "the most radical space of possibility . . . a communal place that enhances the likelihood of collective effort in creating and sustaining a learning community" (8). In our effort to create "the most radical space of possibility," celebrating the relations among disciplines, points of view, geographical locations, and philosophical treatises and theories that are evoked when studying

Haiti, this volume contains work by some of the most forward-thinking scholars of Haitian, Latin American, American, and Caribbean Studies.

One of our contributors' primary goals is to dispel Haiti's contemporary stereotype as the "poorest country in the Western Hemisphere," a subject explicitly evoked and challenged in poet Danielle Legros Georges's "Poem for the Poorest Country in the Western Hemisphere": "Oh poorest country, this is not your name/You should be called beacon, and flame" (Georges). Therefore, chapters in this volume depict a multi-faceted Haiti and provide spaces for students and instructors to hold engaging dialogues about the island nation, from its birth in 1804 to the present. As our scholars note, often Haiti is either venerated as the first Black Republic, or pitied for the current challenges it faces in terms of poverty and geographical catastrophes. When its history does surface in texts, it is often mythologized, taking on aspects of the surreal. Expressing this idea, historian Philippe Zacaïr notes that Haiti is "only respected in books as opposed to real life."[5] In response, the chapters in this volume focus on how to teach about Haiti and its complex history and culture from transdisciplinary perspectives that are grounded in "real life." They provide best practices and practical suggestions for teaching about Haiti from multiple angles, including art, theater, linguistics, literature, cultural studies, film, gender, and history, with the goal of offering students more nuanced views of the nation as a whole.

This volume is geared toward students and instructors in Caribbean Studies, Francophone Studies, Cultural Studies, literature, history, and art who are seeking new, transnational, multidisciplinary ways to engage with Haiti. The growing interest in Haiti is reflected in the large number of books published over the last decade, particularly since the 2010 earthquake. These include, but are by no means limited to, *Haiti and the Haitian Diaspora in the Wider Caribbean*, edited by Philippe Zacaïr (2010); *Tropics of Haiti: Race and the Literary History of the Haitian Revolution in the Atlantic World, 1789–1865*, by Marlene Daut (2015); *Humanitarian Aftershocks in Haiti*, by Mark Schuller (2016); *Istwa across the Water: Haitian History, Memory, and the Cultural Imagination*, by Toni Pressley-Sanon (2017); *Contrary Destinies: A Century of America's Occupation, Deoccupation, and Reoccupation of Haiti*, by Léon Pamphile (2017); *Between Two Worlds: Jean-Price Mars, Haiti and Africa*, edited by Celucien L. Joseph, Jean-Eddy Saint Paul, and Glodel Mezilas (2018); and *Who Owns Haiti? People, Power, and Sovereignty*, edited by Robert Maguire and Scott Freeman (2017). Our volume—the first to focus on teaching about Haiti—builds on works such as these, giving instructors across a spectrum of departments who are interested in teaching about Haiti the resources, methodologies, and strategies to do so.

We hope this collection will impart to students in the US in particular a sense of the US's role in shaping the history of Haiti, as well as that of nations across Latin America and the Caribbean. American imperialism is often challenging for US students to confront because it pushes them to problematize capitalism, globalism, and neocolonialism in ways that may become very personal. For example, encouraging students to question service learning abroad and to understand the complexity of voluntourism and disaster tourism can lead to fraught discussions. However, as our contributors note, many students appreciate a classroom that is a transformative, "radical" space, in bell hooks's terms, one that allows them to share their questions, confront assumptions, and work together to create new knowledge. This volume reflects hooks's challenge to instructors to create an environment in which all learners can be pedagogically engaged. As hooks stresses, these learners can also be teachers: "Engaged pedagogy does not seek simply to empower students. Any classroom that employs a holistic model of learning will also be a place where teachers grow, and are empowered in the process" (21). These skills help students to build a sense of community in their classrooms, and to feel that they are an integral part of the learning process. This volume therefore actively supports the creation of such spaces of interactive and peer-based learning.

Because many instructors who will use this book are teaching in predominantly white institutions (PWI), their students may be unfamiliar with, or even resistant to, recognizing the US's imperial mission in Haiti. However, it is our feeling that we must find ways to engage them in this kind of learning, even if it can, on some level, be painful and uncomfortable to expose positions of privilege and power that students might not be aware they possess. As institutions of higher learning become more profit-driven and caught in the yoke of terms such as "buy-ins," "profit margin," "deliverables," and "clients/consumers," and as the bottom line is linked to class size, keeping our students interested and engaged while helping them to be critical thinkers is more difficult than ever. In response, these chapters provide avenues to address these challenges, to enable students to think critically about issues of power, privilege, and positionality, and the ways in which their identities are layered in terms of class, culture, gender, religion, sexual orientation, and race, for example. We draw readers' attention to the importance of focusing on ways that we "can begin as teachers, scholars and critical thinkers to cross boundaries, the barriers that may or may not be erected by race, gender, class, professional standing, and a host of other differences" (hooks 130).

A central theme across these chapters is the mythologization of the Haitian

Revolution, which remains a constant trope for contemporary Haitian writers and critics in the Americas. Yet as several contributors note, paradoxically, Latin American and American Studies curricula in US universities often sideline Haiti altogether. These curricular anomalies confirm what anthropologist Michel-Rolph Trouillot argues in his seminal work *Silencing the Past*—that the "production of . . . historical narrative" affects our understanding and perception of history and culture (26).

The volume is divided into three sections, based on the general pedagogical focus of the chapters they contain. Each chapter includes practical teaching suggestions in the form of sample syllabi and/or lesson plans. Section I considers innovative ways of "Teaching about Haitian Art, Literature, and Language." In "Getting around the Poto Mitan: Reconstructing Haitian Womanhood in the Classroom," Régine Jean-Charles proposes a perspective that moves beyond the *poto mitan* (center pole) image often used to represent the social role of Haitian women. A poto mitan is "a central pillar in the middle of a room around which the majority of the action of a Vodou ceremony unfolds," and Jean-Charles discusses ways in which her literature-focused course on Haitian women considers and complicates this image. She uses a range of texts that accommodate strikingly divergent representations, including Yanick Lahens's *Guillaume et Nathalie*, Edwidge Danticat's *Claire of the Sea Light*, Roxane Gay's *An Untamed State*, and Myriam Chancy's *Framing Silence: Revolutionary Novels by Haitian Women*.

Bonnie Thomas's "Teaching Haiti through the Work of Rodney Saint-Éloi, écrivain *engagé*" focuses on a lesser-known writer from Haiti whose work beautifully encapsulates the complexities of Haiti. Rodney Saint-Éloi (b. 1963) is a distinguished Haitian poet and writer as well as the founder of two publishing houses, Les Éditions Mémoire (founded in Port-au-Prince in 1991), and Mémoire d'encrier (founded in Montreal in 2003). Through a study of Saint-Éloi's recent texts, including *Haïti kenbe la* (2010), *Jacques Roche, je t'écris cette lettre* (2013), and *Je suis la fille du baobab brûlé* (2015), this chapter provides insights into the politics and poetics of one of Haiti's most important writers.

Joubert Satyre emphasizes theater as an extremely effective yet underappreciated way to teach about Haiti in "Teaching Haitian Theater: Franck Fouché's *Bouqui au Paradis*." "For the sake of mimesis," he writes, "Haitian theater has always been interested in all aspects of Haitian society in order to unveil its foundations. While staging the Haitian world, plays offer a journey of discovery into Haitian imagination and culture." After reviewing the history of theater in Haiti, Satyre considers its renewal, "thanks to the use of Creole as a language of expression and the dramatization of the myths of Vodou and of folklore." He then examines Fouché's play *Bouqui au Paradis* and offers suggestions for how to teach the work in undergraduate settings.

In "Engaging Haiti through Art and Religion," Cécile Accilien proposes concrete methods for teaching about Haiti through the combined lenses of art and Vodou religious practices, two fundamental aspects of Haitian culture. Accilien shows how popular misconceptions of Haitian art as non-threatening, and Vodou as terrifying, are both misguided as she looks at how the two go hand in hand in Haitian culture. As she demonstrates, "considering the relationships between them can generate creative and transformative avenues through which students gain more profound understandings of Haitian society and culture." For the benefit of instructors who may be unfamiliar with these topics, she provides overviews of Haitian Vodou and Haitian painting (focusing on its connections to religion) as well as analyzing the works of contemporary Haitian artists for whom Vodou is central.

Don E. Walicek concentrates on language in Haiti in "Creating Interdisciplinary Knowledge about Haiti's Creole Language." Walicek shows how important it is to understand issues of language from an interdisciplinary perspective as he explores the structure of the Haitian language itself, the sociopolitical context from which it emerged, and its significance in contemporary Haitian life. He offers information and strategies that instructors who are not specialists in linguistics can use to help their students understand the relationship between language and social life in Haiti.

Section II focuses on "Teaching about Haitian History and Politics," including Haiti's connections with hemispheric political issues beginning in the era of the Haitian Revolution. Darren Staloff and Alessandra Benedicty-Kokken's chapter, "Haiti in the Presidencies of John Adams and John Quincy Adams: Lesson Plans and Course Modules," argues that it is impossible to fully understand the political careers of these men without understanding their relationships to the Haitian struggle for independence. This chapter serves as the historical foundation for a lesson plan whose primary learning outcome is to underscore how specific political decisions by individual US leaders came to define not only political realities, but also the political imaginaries that still dominate the histories told about Haiti.

Furthering the study of Haitian history and politics in this section, Sophie Watt's "Teaching the 2004 Coup in Haiti from a French Perspective: Insight into France's Neocolonial Culture and Practices" presents a module on teaching Haiti entitled "Haiti: Tragedy, History, Politics, and Literature from the Colonial Period until Today." Watt emphasizes that it is essential to discuss the coup within the framework of French history and politics. She explores Jean-

Bertrand Aristide's demands to France for reparations and retribution for the financial impact of colonial slavery, and shows how after these official demands were made, clear changes of tone occurred in French press coverage of Aristide's government.

Agnès Peysson-Zeiss's "Peck's *Fatal Assistance*: A Filmic Lesson on the Failures of Aid" analyzes Peck's post-earthquake film depicting the pitfalls of aid. As Peysson-Zeiss describes, Peck probes the different stakeholders—states, NGOs, non-profit organizations, and individuals who went to "rescue" Haiti—coalescing after January 12, 2010. Through interviews, footage, and voice-overs, Peck shows why, "despite the billions of dollars flushed into [Haiti]," the help was chaotic, disorganized, and disproportionate. Peysson-Zeiss emphasizes Peck's desire to depart from traditional victims' perspectives in order to "reverse" the gaze.

Section III, "Teaching about Haiti in American Studies, Latin American Studies, and General Studies Contexts," foregrounds interdisciplinary approaches. In "Rendering Haiti Visible in an Introductory American Studies Course," Elizabeth Langley explains how a "keyword approach" to analyzing particular texts pertinent to the Haitian/Haitian American experience can help students develop a richer understanding of the transnational relationship between Haiti and the United States. She analyses three texts that address different Haitian experiences: Edouard Duval-Carrié's *Imagined Landscapes* (an art exhibit that treats the broad Caribbean and its relationship to imperialism, expansion and tourism); Alex Stepick's "Just Comes and Cover-Ups: Haitians in High School," an academic article that explores the Haitian/Haitian American experience in Miami in the 80s and 90s; and excerpts from Edwidge Danticat's *Create Dangerously*.

Jessica Adams's "Race and Culture on the Thrift Store Shift: Teaching about Haiti Inside and Outside the Academy" describes her observations of *antihaitianismo* and racism toward Haitians in the Dominican Republic and St. Thomas and meditates on ways to shift pervasive objectification and devaluation with respect to Haiti. Through a pedagogy that blends the personal and the academic, including strategies from Performance Studies, she encourages students in her General Studies writing courses to become aware of the labels and wider racism that persist with respect to Haitians, both on the island and in the larger diaspora.

John Ribó's "Rethinking Latinx Studies from Hispaniola's Borderlands" argues for the inclusion of Haiti and its history as part of the global histories of empire, race, slavery, and abolition. "Despite [the] groundswell of Dominican Studies scholarship approaching Hispaniola transnationally and arguing for the island's centrality in global histories of empire, race, slavery, and abolition," he writes, "Latinx Studies has been slow to include Haiti." Ribó aims to correct this in his chapter focusing on the "Power Suit" episode of *Orange Is the New Black* (2016), and *Forget* (2010) the first album by the Dominican American rock musician George Lewis, Jr., a.k.a. Twin Shadow. Ribó uses descriptions of his innovative, student-centered pedagogy to help demonstrate how transnational approaches to Hispaniola encourage us to rethink Latinx Studies.

In the final chapter, "Teaching Haiti and the Dominican Republic: Cultural Representations of Haitian Immigrant Experiences," Anne François also considers relationships between Haiti and the Dominican Republic to describe a course that complicates the often one-dimensional portrayal of Haitian im/migrants in popular media. François focuses on fiction and visual art by Dominican and Haitian writers and artists, as well as music, as she describes a pedagogical approach that promotes empathy, understanding, and a sense of shared humanity in the face of ever more rigid borders.

As walls are built and national boundaries are redefined, we must seek ways to construct our own counter-narratives and spaces for rational learning so that new Glissantian relations can be forged to bolster students' knowledge of Haiti, and the Caribbean more broadly, in an era of global capitalism and hyper-connectivity. It is up to us as teachers to insist on the importance of the "world of relation" as one in constant motion and flux, a Tout-Monde of multilingualism, exploration, and travel across borders in and from nations where all are welcomed to deterritorialize and reterritorialize. We must "[é]coutons le cri du monde" [listen to the cry of the world] in order to "tisser [un] réseau . . . dans le Tout-Monde" [braid a network . . . in the Tout-Monde] (*Traité du Tout-Monde* 251).

Dèyè mòn gen mòn. "Behind the mountains are more mountains." As this proverb vividly expresses, there is always more to learn about Haiti. We hope this volume will inspire instructors and students alike to think in new and ever-evolving ways about a place that is fundamental not only to the history of the west, but to the history of the world.

Acknowledgments

Writing a book is a journey that includes several destinations. Jessica Gerschultz and Anne François initially encouraged the idea for this collection when Cécile lamented not finding materials to teach her Haitian culture course, compiling articles from books and other sources to be able to present a complex image of Haiti. This is the lacuna we hope this book will fill. Our heartfelt thanks to the contributors to this volume, who have undertaken this journey with us. We appreciate their patience, and their generosity in sharing their wonderful and wide-ranging strategies for teaching about Haiti. We thank Caesar Akuetey for his long-standing support, which included traveling to Cap-Haïtien in 2016 to help spread the word about this project. Many thanks also to Stephanye Hunter, our editor at the University of Florida Press, who believed in this project from the beginning. Jessica Adams's skills as a developmental editor are superb. She is very much a birthing editor of this book, and we say *Ayibobo* to her!

We will always be grateful for the support of artists Colette Bresilla, Vladimir Cybil Charlier, and Ulrick Jean-Pierre, who have generously shared their work with us and with the world.

To the anonymous readers who gave us essential feedback and helped us to achieve our vision of a book in which instructors will find new ways to help their students listen to and engage with the "new narratives" of Haiti, we say *mèsi*!

Valérie Orlando would like to thank Carolyn Clarke Nuite and Philipe Orlando.

Cécile Accilien would like to thank colleagues at the University of Kansas with whom she had the pleasure of working in different settings, and especially via writing groups and seminars from 2015–2020: Giselle Anatol, Santa Arias, Tony Bolden, Anne Dotter, Betsy Esch, Angela Gist-Mackey, Maryemma Graham, Sara Gregg, Jennifer Hamer, Ayesha Hardison, Randal M. Jelks, Joo Ok Kim, Jowel Laguerre, Clarence Lang, Cassandra Messick Braun, Anna Neill, Peter Ojiambo, Chris Perreira, Betsaida Reyes, Celka Straughn, Brenda Wawire, and Antje Ziethen. Thank you also to friends and family members Paulette Cezil Pogue, Véronique Accilien, and Zahir Accilien for their ongoing support.

Mèsi anpil!!!

Notes

1. The italics are Glissant's.
2. https://la1ere.francetvinfo.fr/8-mars-nous-sommes-fruit-rencontre-mondes-dit-romanciere-guadeloupeenne-simone-schwarz-bart-450583.html
3. For more information, see *Why Haiti Needs New Narratives: A Post-Quake Chronicle*.
4. For more information on the scholarship of teaching and learning, see Peter Felten's "Principles of Good Practice in SoTL."
5. This is an issue that Philippe Zacaïr has often mentioned in personal conversations with Cécile Accilien focused on Haiti and how it is represented in the larger Caribbean. Zacaïr is the editor of *Haiti and the Haitian Diaspora in the Wider Caribbean*.

Works Cited

Daut, Marlene. *Tropics of Haiti: Race and the Literary History of the Haitian Revolution in the Atlantic World, 1789–1865*. Liverpool University Press, 2015.

Felten, Peter. "Principles of Good Practice in SoTL." *Teaching & Learning Inquiry*, vol. 1, no. 1, 2013, pp. 121-125.

Georges, Danielle Legros. "Poem for the Poorest Country in the Western Hemisphere." poets.org/poem/poem-poorest-country-western-hemisphere. Accessed on 1 July 2019.

Glissant, Edouard. *Tout-Monde*. Gallimard, 1993.

———. *Traité du Tout-Monde*. Gallimard, 1997.

———. *Philosophie de la relation*. Gallimard, 2009.

hooks, bell. *Teaching to Transgress: Education as the Practice of Freedom*. Routledge, 1994.

Joseph, Celucien L., Jean-Eddy Saint Paul, and Glodel Mezilas, editors. *Between Two Worlds: Jean-Price Mars, Haiti and Africa*. Lexington Books, 2018.

Maguire, Robert, and Scott Freeman, editors. *Who Owns Haiti? People, Power and Sovereignty*. University Press of Florida, 2017.

Pamphile, Léon. *Contrary Destinies: A Century of America's Occupation, Deoccupation and Reoccupation of Haiti*. University Press of Florida, 2015.

Pressley-Sanon, Toni. *Istwa Across the Water: Haitian History, Memory, and the Cultural Imagination*. University Press of Florida, 2017.

Schuller, Mark. *Humanitarian Aftershocks in Haiti*. Rutgers University Press, 2016.

Trouillot, Michel-Rolph. *Silencing the Past*. Penguin, 1995.

Ulysse, Gina Athena. *Why Haiti Needs New Narratives: A Post-Quake Chronicle*. Wesleyan University Press, 2015.

Zacaïr, Philippe. *Haiti and the Haitian Diaspora in the Wider Caribbean*. University Press of Florida, 2010.

I

Teaching about Haitian Art, Literature, and Language

1

Getting around the Poto Mitan

Reconstructing Haitian Womanhood in the Classroom

RÉGINE JEAN-CHARLES

Fanm se poto mitan. This Kreyòl expression is well known throughout Haiti and the diaspora; it means that the woman is the pillar or pole in the middle of a room that holds it up. The term poto mitan translates literally to "post in the middle," a central pillar in the middle of a room around which the majority of the action of a Vodou ceremony unfolds. Equating Haitian women with the poto mitan is another way to indicate their centrality in society; it points to the indispensable role they occupy in the family. The title of poto mitan also suggests a number of character traits, like strength, tenacity, and resilience, with which Haitian women are often associated. In her essay "Papa, Patriarchy, and Power: Snapshots of a Good Haitian Girl, Feminism, & Dyasporic Dreams," feminist anthropologist and performance artist Gina Ulysse writes, "I grew up with the knowledge that women in my culture were the poto-mitan of their families. I was choosing another way" (35). Ulysse's anti–poto mitan stance can be understood as longing for a de-essentialization of Haitian womanhood that nuances the fixed idea of the central pillar. The alternative to the poto mitan that Ulysse would favor is a model of Black feminism that is deeply intersectional and constantly in negotiation. Ulysse's discomfort with the poto mitan can be attributed to its fixity—a rigid central pillar that speaks to the ways in which women shoulder various burdens in society, the pillar is intransigent, set in stone, and firmly entrenched.

This essay proposes one path for teaching Haitian womanhood from a perspective that moves beyond the poto mitan model, or, rather, around it, which is to acknowledge its centrality but also account for its limitations. To do so I propose my class entitled "Reconstructing Haitian Womanhood" as a teaching model that incorporates a range of texts accommodating strikingly divergent representations: Marie Chauvet's *Dance on the Volcano* (*La Danse sur le volcan* 1957, 2016), Evelyne Trouillot's *The Infamous Rosalie* (*Rosalie l'infâme* 2003, 2013), Kettly Mars's *Savage Seasons* (*Saisons sauvages* 2010, 2015), Edwidge Danticat's *Claire of the Sea Light* (2013); the films *Woch Nan Soley* (2012) and *Poto Mitan: Haitian Women, Pillars of the Global Economy* (2009); and essays by feminist scholars in the fields of anthropology, literary studies, media studies, and sociology.[1] (See the sample syllabus at the end of this chapter.) Taken together, these novels, films, and essays help to create a more dynamic picture of Haitian womanhood that allows students to seriously interrogate rigid notions of what it means to be a Haitian woman.

My approach to this class is born out of three important teaching encounters I have had with students and scholars. The first was a teaching moment in which *I* played the role of *student*. During a conversation with feminist scholar Carolle Charles about studies of women in tent cities after the earthquake, she stated emphatically, "Haitian women cannot be reduced to their status as rape victims." Having just published a book on rape representation in which I argue for more complex ways of understanding rape as a cultural trope as well as rape victim-survivors themselves, I was especially struck by Professor Charles's words.[2] That our conversation took place a few years after the earthquake in 2010 was also important because in the aftermath of the earthquake a number of reports about the rape of Haitian women in tent cities surfaced, some of which took on astonishingly reductive and essentialist approaches to rape representation. Perhaps the best example of this tendency was the journalist Mac McClelland's deeply disturbing coverage for the popular news magazine *Mother Jones* in which she deployed myths of Haitian culture as synonymous with rape culture to animate her reflections on post-earthquake Haiti. Often visual, spoken, and written representations of sexual violence exploit both the spectacle of suffering and the spectacular nature of suffering in post-earthquake Haiti. The combined lexicon of suffering and the spectacular mirrors neo-imperial, neoliberal, and humanitarian scripts of subject formation that have characterized the relationship between the United States and Haiti since as early as the Haitian Revolution. Rape plays an operative role in the iconography of Haitian suffering, not necessarily because of the urgency of the crisis and the people subjected to it, but rather because it reaffirms a set of dominant narratives that reflect the long-standing use of gendered ideologies to signify national and international agendas.[3] Instances such as these underscore the necessity of narrative autonomy because, as anthropologist Erica Caple James explains in

Democratic Insecurities: Violence, Trauma, and Intervention in Haiti, Haitian activists can also deploy the logics of the spectacular to advance their own human rights claims and appeals for recognition in the context of international human rights advocacy. So the idea of the spectacular can serve multiple functions, but what matters as much as how the story is told, then, is who tells the story. Following this logic, an important part of the poto mitan construction is how it further underscores the idea of the strong Black woman who can endure all things. When suffering only operates as spectacle it can point to the resilience of Haitian women, which too often reduces their subjecthood to a single frame.

The second teaching moment was when I taught the documentary *Poto Mitan: Haitian Women, Pillars of the Global Economy* in an interdisciplinary seminar entitled "Haiti and Globalization" several years ago. The day before class discussion, a student born in Haiti who had attended two years of high school in the United States prior to coming to university came to my office hours to share her concerns about the film. She was apprehensive about discussing the film in class because the people "lived in such squalor," and she was afraid that her classmates would make assumptions about how all Haitians live as a result. As a Haitian student she was worried that the film would simply reinforce the stereotypical image of Haiti as "the poorest country in the Western Hemisphere," what Joel Dreyfuss has aptly called "the phrase in a box" and "a metaphorical prison" (Dreyfuss 57). What followed was a lengthy discussion with my student in which I explained the importance of presenting multiple stories about class in Haiti—not ignoring poverty altogether but not making it the only story.

The third teaching moment was during an oral presentation by students in my advanced seminar on Francophone women writers in which the students juxtaposed two images: one of a run-down shack on a dirt road and the other of the Montreal skyline. For this presentation on Marie-Célie Agnant's *La dot de Sara* they focused on the idea of *ici* (here) versus *là-bas* (there). In the novel, the author uses the ici versus là-bas construction to describe how the protagonist experiences the differences between her two countries. For example, the protagonist contrasts the bitter cold in Montreal while she is here (ici) to the all-encompassing heat she remembers from her life in Haiti (là-bas). Throughout the novel these comparisons help the reader to perceive the differences between the two places through the eyes of a woman longing to return to her home in Haiti. Again the visual images that the students used in their presentation highlighted the persistence of the poverty trope, despite the fact that in the book the comparisons were structured around weather, language, food, and social norms. Their use of a broken-down shack in an unspecified location to serve as the sign for Haiti was problematic, reductive, and alarming. These moments highlight a need for vigilance on the part of the scholar and the teacher.

One of the main objectives of this proposed course is to utilize an interdisciplinary approach that draws from scholarship in different fields as well as cultural production in different forms (including fiction, poetry, and film) to offer a critical perspective on the construction of Haitian womanhood. In addition to being interdisciplinary, this kind of multidimensional view is grounded in an intersectional (feminist) framework. An intersectional approach to studying Haitian womanhood should account for how the various locations of race, class, gender, and sexuality, as well as citizenship status, influence the lived experiences of Haitian women. Ultimately my goal is to provide a pedagogical tool for teaching Haitian womanhood that will simultaneously interrogate why certain narratives have developed and explore how scholars and cultural workers have responded to these discourses.

Perhaps the first question to consider is: What is the problem with the title of poto mitan? My view is that when the poto mitan serves as shorthand for everything that Haitian womanhood represents in its entirety, it quickly becomes a stereotype that can flatten the human aspects of Haitian women's lives. Like the resilience trope, the poto mitan can empty women of their humanity by focusing on their strength and their ability to overcome rather than on the different registers of emotion that texture their daily lives. In order to avoid perpetuating this view with students, it is important to teach works about Haitian women that prominently feature different kinds of experiences across class, privilege, and emotional modalities. Of utmost importance in this practice is showing Haitian women from different class backgrounds, with varying degrees of education, access, and relationships to the diaspora.

At the beginning of the semester, students view the TED talk by Nigerian writer Chimamanda Ngozi Adichie entitled *The Danger of a Single Story*. Following Adichie, I use "the single story" as a framing device to inform the study of Haitian women because they too have been assigned a stereotypical designation. As such, another way to consider the main objective of this course is that we are to teach about Haitian women beyond "the single story." Doing so requires asking students: What is the single story, or dominant narrative, of Haiti that we have seen in the US-dominated media? Students should be asked to interrogate the images of Haiti and Haitians that circulate most prominently in the United States context. First, what are the images of Haiti with which they are most familiar? For many these will relate to the ubiquitous poverty trope. The question to consider after reflecting on those images is: How does gender play into our view of Haiti? How are Haitian women configured within this framework? These questions serve as a point of departure for some of the questions we will ask throughout the course of the semester.

The TED talk serves as a primer for students when they read the article "Deconstructing Portrayals of Haitian Women in the Media" by María José Rendón and Guerda Nicolas, which falls within the field of Media Studies. Based on a study that these authors conducted in which they examined photographs of Haitian women between the years 1994 and 2009, this article provides ample evidence for the kinds of images of Haitian women that dominate mainstream media. What this article helps to demonstrate is that images of Haitian women have been fraught since long before the earthquake of 2010.

Rendón and Nicolas's "Deconstructing the Portrayals of Haitian Women in the Media" highlights the different ways in which Haitian women are identified according to a set of dominant images that flatten their subjectivities. The authors' focus on how the media portrays women is an important pedagogical tool because students can be asked to do their own research into images of Haitian women and then bring those to class to add to the discussion. Using the article as a framework, students will be asked to group the images that they bring to class according to the broader categories of poverty, disaster, disease, and political instability. The images that students find on their own serve to complement and underscore the arguments of the authors. As the authors point out, "media coverage that includes Haitian women seems to interweave an invisible discourse about this group as the media recycle old narratives about Haiti as a 'failed state'" (Rendón and Nicolas 228). The article is also instructive because it helps students to think through the significance of narrative construction (how stories are told) in relation to power dynamics.

Poto Mitan: Definition and Foundational Texts

A course on Haitian women beyond the poto mitan would necessarily begin with an introduction to the term itself. By way of introducing the idea and definition of the poto mitan, I pair the documentary *Poto Mitan: Haitian Women, Pillars of the Global Economy* by René Bergan and Mark Schuller alongside the article "Fanm Se Poto Mitan: Haitian Woman, the Pillar of Society" by literary scholar Marie-José N'Zengou-Tayo. The latter traces a social history of Haitian women in which the author explains how they operate according to this role, whereas the former exposes the negative effects of globalization on the lives of poor urban Haitian women. In her article, N'Zengou-Tayo affirms a number of dominant images of Haitian women that are in circulation; for example, "the black peasant woman represents the nation's resilience" (134). The article is divided into two parts as N'Zengou-Tayo first provides an overview of Haitian womanhood from the nineteenth century to the present day. In the article she draws on historic, contemporary, and literary sources, reflecting a methodology similar to the pedagogy for developing this class. The social history of Haitian women that N'Zengou-Tayo provides draws from historical and anthropological sources as well as testimonies by Haitian women in their own words. In the second half of the article she focuses on how these themes emerge in literature. By turning to the literary representation of Haitian women by both male and female writers, N'Zengou-Tayo is able to demonstrate how literature reflects history and society. This will allow for a discussion of what theorists such as Erich Auerbach have long observed to be the crisis of representation, the fraught relationship between reality and representation: the inability of texts to fully convey the social realities they depict, also referred to as mimesis. A discussion of this question of the relationship between representation and reality will allow students to think critically about the social role of literature. The article also provides an opportunity for students to begin considering how narratives are constructed prior to reading the first work of fiction. N'Zengou-Tayo ends her article with an analysis of Haitian women writers in which she concludes,

> Coming from a tradition in which women always had to summon their forces in silence and hold firm in the face of adversity, they have developed narrative strategies intertwining double discourse, double entendre, silence and words. They have tried to redefine themselves, subverting the dominant male discourse that sought to silence them. The new narrative strategies they crafted have enriched the body of Haitian literature. (138)

While the course is interdisciplinary, it is structured around four novels that serve as key anchor texts, which is why it is important for students to reflect on what it means to study literature in the context of constructions of Haitian womanhood. To this end, essays on women's writing such as those in Myriam Chancy's *Framing Silence: Revolutionary Novels by Haitian Women* and Marie-Denise Shelton's article "Haitian Women's Fiction" are also useful. As Shelton pointed out in her article, published over 20 years ago,

> The woman writer in Haiti has cracked open the doors of literature and is searching for her voice. While she, too often, speaks through alienating ideologies and fails to capture the common experiences of most Haitian women, she can question the culture in some fundamental ways. (776)

What I am calling "getting around the poto mitan" requires this kind of attention to voice and critique. How can we construct Haitian womanhood in relation to social realities and nonetheless account for how women throughout history as well as in literature have resisted these norms? Furthermore, how do we avoid stories that focus only on marginalization and degradation as a point of departure for Haitian women?

Another key text for definitions of poto mitan is the documentary of the same name, *Poto Mitan: Haitian Women, Pillars of the Global Economy*. The documentary focuses on five different Haitian women living in Port-au-Prince in order to take on themes such as poverty, hardship, struggle, and injustice. Throughout the film, topics such as the rampant abuse of factory workers, the political repression following the first coup against Aristide, the enormous chasm between Haiti's rich and poor, and the United States' negative role in Haitian agriculture from rice production to pig farming reveal the structural and social inequalities faced by poor women. As a counterpoint to this grim reality, the film scatters the natural beauty of the landscape and the richness of Haitian culture throughout. For example, in each section the storytelling of Edwidge Danticat is featured along with a woman braiding her daughter's hair, which is meant to underscore the importance of different generations of women. The music of Emeline Michel and Boukman Eksperyans also helps to introduce viewers to different aspects of Haitian culture. Students should be asked to identify other ways in which Haitian culture is made visible throughout the film and reflect on the point that, as many scholars have noted, Haiti is economically poor, but culturally rich. Additionally, asking students to look for such examples does the work of focusing their minds on the narrative and counter-narrative structure of the class. There are also interviews with public figures such as the former Minister of Women's Rights Marie-Laurence Lassègue. The film describes Solange, Marie-Jeanne, Frisline, Hélène, and Thérèse as the "five brave *poto mitan* who requested to have their stories told" (*Poto Mitan*), and their stories reveal how women do more than struggle. Throughout the film, we witness how these women resolve their problems, offer political critique and analysis, lead their families, and empower the young women of their communities. Thus, despite difficult images and sad stories, the film's message is that Haitian women are agents of transformation. Historical figures such as Anacaona, Defilée, and Catherine Flon demonstrate this salient fact. Such agents of positive transformation also exist in the present, as the documentary's protagonists attest, and they will be in the future despite the immeasurable losses caused by the earthquake's devastation. "Women used to think that they were second-class people. But women are important. Women are the bouillon, without them there would be no taste. We are an essential ingredient," remarks Thérèse at one moment in the film. *Poto Mitan* ensures that the importance of Haitian women's contributions to the world economy will not be forgotten. It is also a critical visual example of the different ways Haitian women contribute to society as well as the social factors that constrain them.

Gina Ulysse, *Why Haiti Needs New Narratives*

Immediately after teaching students the concept of the poto mitan through the articles and the film, the syllabus moves on to Gina Ulysse's *Why Haiti Needs New Narratives: A Post-Earthquake Chronicle* as a theoretical framing for the idea of moving beyond dominant discourses surrounding Haiti. Like the TED talk by Adichie, *Why Haiti Needs New Narratives* presents the idea of a single story about Haiti and carefully explains why moving beyond it is essential not only in terms of epistemology but also in terms of policy. These essays will constantly be referred to throughout the course in order to help students interrogate what the traditional narrative is and which counter-narratives are being constructed in response to those. Structuring the class in this way (narrative/counter-narrative) encourages more critical thinking as students are asked to develop an analysis as to why prevailing narratives exist and then are pushed to move beyond those.

Why Haiti Needs New Narratives takes an intersectional approach to chronicling the aftermath of the earthquake, and is especially useful for teaching students what Black feminism looks like in the Haitian context. In the essays Ulysse pays meticulous attention to how race, class, gender, nationality, religious practice, sexuality, and language influence responses to and reactions to the earthquake. In terms of race, she describes how the mainstream media coverage of Haiti is usually informed by its position as a Black nation. She writes,

> in media coverage of the quake and its aftermath [a] dehumanization narrative—portraying traumatized Haitians as indifferent and even callous—took off on what I call the sub-humanity strand, which was particularly trendy. It stems from the dominant idea that Haitians are irrational, devil worshipping, progress-resistant, uneducated accursed black natives overpopulating their godforsaken island. There is of course here a subtext about race. Haiti and Haitians remain a manifestation of blackness in its worst form because, simply put, the unruly *enfant terrible* of the Americans defied all European odds and created a disorder of things colonial. Haiti had to become colonialism's *bête noire* if the sanctity of whiteness were to remain unquestioned. (28)

The above quote highlights how race and religious practice in particular combine to determine how Haiti gets inscribed into a dominant narrative that is unabashedly dehumanizing.

Ulysse further explores the dynamics of such invisibility at length, and writes,

> The world has watched Haiti's most vulnerable women survive quake, flood, cholera and homelessness in the last year—yet those women still feel invisible. What will it take for them to be seen and heard? "Nou pa gen visibilite." We don't have visibility, Mary-Kettley Jean said to me. (53)

The author continues, describing this visibility in further detail by explaining,

> Her words are ironic, considering the ubiquitous images of Haitian women covered with concrete dust after the devastating earthquake a year ago. Or considering how the global media was plastered with photos of Haiti's women six months later as they remained in tent camps that replaced their broken homes. (53)

This tension between visibility and invisibility is also an important part of how to teach Haitian womanhood because it returns to the key concept of subject formation—how women are permitted to tell their own stories as subjects in control of their own narratives, rather than objects to be studied.

Ulysse's focus on gender is especially evident in the second section of *Why Haiti Needs New Narratives*, "Reassessing My Response," in which she foregrounds the stories, lives, and work of several different women: Myrlande Constant, who is a self-taught maker of Vodou flags (77); Yolette Jeanty, advocate and supporter of Haitian women and girls and executive director for Kay Fanm; and the Haitian feminist Paulette Poujol-Oriol (1926–2011). This section is helpful for elaborating a version of Haitian womanhood that accommodates a range of differences. In the case of Myrlande Constant, who was less known than some of the other women mentioned, Ulysse emphasizes what is unique about Constant's creative work: her innovation in using a new technique to make Vodou flags. But even this example can be linked to the Black feminist imperative of social justice because it is contextualized by the social perception of Vodou. As Ulysse notes, "Given the historic ways that vodou has been demonized and remains a scapegoat for Haiti's problems, Myrlande Constant's artistry and communion with the spirits through her flags is [sic] an education unto itself" (79). Overall, *Haiti Needs New Narratives* is an essential book for the class in terms of both how it actively questions perceptions of Haiti and the analyses it offers of Haitian women writers, activists, and organizers.

The Infamous Rosalie by Evelyne Trouillot

The first novel taught in the course, *Rosalie l'infâme/The Infamous Rosalie* by Evelyne Trouillot, is a fitting point of departure for literature about Haitian women because it begins prior to the Haitian Revolution. The novel is set in 1789 Saint-Domingue on the Fayot Plantation. The title refers to the name of the transatlantic slave ship that transported the ancestors of the novel's protagonist, Lisette. *The Infamous Rosalie* charts Lisette's story as a young woman on the plantation living in the midst of unrelenting violence, constant death, and maroon plots of resistance. Storytelling is central to the novel as Lisette implores her grandmother and godmother to tell her about life before she was born. These stories are crucial as they begin Lisette's radicalization.

Introducing a novel that takes place before the Revolution allows us to move away from some of the grand master narratives of Haitian history by thinking carefully about what preceded the Revolution. Furthermore, emphasis on the period prior to the Haitian Revolution places the focus on slavery and what enslaved people endured during this time. The setting and the time are important because while many Haitian novels are set during the Revolution, very few focus on the time period beforehand. As Edwidge Danticat explains in her introduction to the English translation of *Rosalie l'infâme*,

> ... when discussing Haitian history, we tend to linger more on the battles we've won, rather than the ones we lost, the ones where we lost our people, our humanity, ourselves ... few people know what it meant for these eventual victors, or their parents and grandparents, to have survived the specific route of the Middle Passage. (Danticat in Trouillot ii)

The diverse experiences of the enslaved women lay the groundwork of the course by providing a textured representation of Haitian womanhood. For example, in the novel we see the different ways that women responded to their enslavement through diverse acts of resistance. A discussion about the different strategies that these enslaved women deployed to survive life on the plantation is a necessary part of recognizing their subjectivity, as they had disparate responses to their experiences. Of particular focus will be the relationship between the protagonist Lisette and the generations of women before her as well as how gender impacted the experience of slavery. As one of these women tells the protagonist,

> You see Lisette, watching you grow up on this island is to open yourself to so much misfortune, to hold your stomach so firmly it takes the layers of pain and accepts them with less indignity. It's always keeping an eye

turned inwards so misfortune doesn't take us by storm. It's praying, hoping, cursing, and often being afraid to smile. (70)

The range of women, some who die and some who live, also gives students access to thinking about women's vulnerable positions on the plantation and how they devised ways to respond to it. This is the beginning of destabilizing the idea of Haitian women as capable of enduring all things, as the poto mitan suggests. At the same time, because the protagonist Lisette runs away to become a maroon, the novel demonstrates that even enslaved women cannot be reduced to the status of victims only, because they found ways to exercise their own forms of agency and resistance.

Dance on the Volcano by Marie Chauvet

In order to establish an immediate connection and counterpoint to the Trouillot novel, I then teach Marie Chauvet's novel *Dance on the Volcano*. This novel also serves as an introduction to the different roles women played during the Haitian Revolution, but it focuses much more on how these are again calibrated by color and class. This novel presents an unconventional heroine who is drastically different from the women in the documentary and in Trouillot's novel. The story about two sisters whose lives end up on very different paths further underscores the point of the diversity in women's lives, even in the same family. The protagonist, Minette, is a creole, or mixed-race, woman. The inclusion of this detail is important for a study of how racial hierarchies functioned in gendered ways in eighteenth-century Haiti.

Dance on the Volcano is also significant for how it incorporates a representation of theater in Haiti during the eighteenth and nineteenth centuries. The novel provides helpful exposure to how intertextuality occurs across disciplines, since Chauvet bases her plot on the book *Le Théâtre à Saint-Domingue* by Jean Fouchard, which was published two years prior to the original publication of *La Danse sur le volcan*. Students can read excerpts from Fouchard's history alongside the novel as a way to better understand how historical fiction is written. A consideration of nineteenth-century theater will also provide an opportunity for students to conduct their own theatrical readings and mini-performances. As a revolutionary historical novel that focuses on the lives of two *affranchi* women, *Dance on the Volcano* is the perfect text to read after *The Infamous Rosalie* not only chronologically but also thematically. Pairing the novels helps to create a more robust picture of the Haitian Revolution that imagines the events through the eyes of women characters. Furthermore, in its attention to how gender, class, and sexuality come together in the revolutionary context, this novel helps to foreground the importance of an intersectional approach to studying Haitian womanhood.[4] Another compelling element of the novel is its incorporation and use of Vodou, the religion practiced by the majority of Haitians, and which should be approached as an essential component of Haitian culture.

Kettly Mars, *Savage Seasons*

Savage Seasons by Kettly Mars is set during another historical period of great significance—that of the Duvalier dictatorship. Teaching this novel in a course about Haitian women also serves the purpose of introducing students to the Duvalier period (1957–1986) so that they can begin to understand how women were affected by, and responded to, the dictatorship. The novel focuses on the life of the protagonist Nirvah Leroy, whose husband Daniel has been jailed by the dictatorship for his suspected dissident activities. Nirvah's unconventional choices make her a fascinating point of departure for the question of right and wrong when faced with difficult choices in the context of the dictatorship. Nirvah Leroy's background is important as well because she comes from the middle class, a fact that will allow students again to consider the importance of the multiple locations of identity and how those impact individuals who are forced to live in terror (Charles 136). In order to provide more historical background about this novel, I would include several readings from Elizabeth Abbott's *Haiti: The Duvaliers and Their Legacy* as well. Kettly Mars's novel is especially instructive because of the author's embrace of an ambiguous ending, which calls upon students to ask hard questions about the role and function of narrative as a way to think about the dictatorship. The book explores Nirvah's actions in response to her husband's imprisonment, the effects of which also extend to her entire household. Like the other two novels taught in the course, *Savage Seasons* takes a sexualized and gendered approach to examining a specific historic period under the terror of Duvalier.

Film: *Woch Nan Soley*

Following *Savage Seasons* students will view the film *Woch Nan Soley* (2012), directed by Patricia Benoit, which is also about the Duvalier dictatorship although it is set in the 1980s, to explore the question of memory in relation to the regime. By delving into how the past is apparent in the present, *Woch*

Nan Soley serves as a reminder that history is never simply left behind. Like each of the works selected for this class, the film presents three different kinds of women who have been affected by Duvalier, each of whom not only has different experiences, but chooses to interact with those experiences differently. There are women like Vita, a rape survivor who experienced the terror of the regime in her body firsthand. The example of the two sisters, Yannick and Shelley, is especially helpful in demonstrating how in one family two women can have very different relationships to their Haitian identities. For Yannick, a professor and political activist, Haiti must live on in the diaspora, whereas for Shelley—who vividly recalls the execution of her father—the past must be left behind. *Woch Nan Soley* continues the project of reminding students that Haitian women must not be viewed as monolithic.

Claire of the Sea Light (2013) by Edwidge Danticat

The final work included on the syllabus offers multiple perspectives on Haitian women through the form of the short story cycle—a series of stories with related characters. Edwidge Danticat's book *Claire of the Sea Light* will introduce students to life in Haiti today as opposed to during a historical period. It is also helpful in showing the different class considerations of Haitian women. In this novel, we meet a host of different characters from the same town, Limye. There are rich women, middle-class women, and poor women in these stories. There are women with children and women who have never conceived, women who are highly visible in society and those who seem to be unseen. Throughout *Claire of the Sea Light*, students are introduced to multiple women from different class backgrounds and with a range of life experiences. By featuring a diverse set of characters from different age groups, the book highlights the idea that there is no one single story of Haitian womanhood.

Danticat is also the most well-known author publishing in English on the syllabus, so it will be helpful to provide students with a view of the scope and the impact of her work, especially on the topic of Haitian women. To do so, we will read two of her essays: the chapter on Marie Chauvet from *Create Dangerously: The Immigrant Artist at Work* and "We Are Ugly, but We Are Here" from *The Caribbean Writer*. These articles are also helpful in that they point to a distinct, more public way of engaging points of comparison and conjunction between Haitian Studies and Women's Studies and will allow students to think about the implications of this work outside of the classroom.

Conclusion: Getting around the Poto Mitan

A feminist approach to Haitian Studies reveals the ways in which fixed ideas about gender and gender inequality surface in creative expression and scholarship. Black feminist scholarship pays close attention to the articulation of race, class, gender, and sexuality, and how they intersect and inform identity in ways that are multiplicative. In the case of Haitian womanhood, a feminist approach is compelling because it allows us to consider the ways that race, gender, sexuality, language, and nationality form the core of women's experiences. By shifting the focus from only examining these negative, stereotypical, or dominant images of Haitian women to the idea of "reconstructing" Haitian womanhood inspired by texts created by Haitian women, I am purposefully echoing the work of Black feminist scholar Hazel Carby. In her book *Reconstructing Womanhood: The Emergence of the Afro-American Woman Novelist*, Carby argues that Black women novelists had to do the work of "reconstruction" because of the ways that their identities were constructed in opposition to Southern white womanhood. To reconstruct womanhood means to create and search for explorations of Black women that not only expose the negative images that ensnare them, but also posit new narratives that point to alternative directions. Throughout this chapter, and with the creation of this course, I have tried to construct such a narrative—first, considering the poto mitan as one of the most prevailing images of Haitian women, then presenting a series of readings that counter this image. Or, as the title of this essay reflects, getting around the poto mitan so as to not do away with the construction altogether, but rather to acknowledge that it is important and look for ways to teach Haitian womanhood beyond this single story.

Syllabus

Course Description

As the first independent Black Republic in the world, born from a historic revolution, Haiti occupies a prominent place in the African diaspora. The Kreyòl expression *Fanm se poto mitan* is well known throughout Haiti and the diaspora; it means that the woman is the pillar or pole in the middle of a room that holds it up. The term poto mitan translates literally as "post in the middle," a central pillar in the middle of a room around which the majority of the action of a Vodou ceremony unfolds. The title of poto mitan also suggests a number of character traits like strength, tenacity, and resilience with which Haitian women are often associated. In this class, "Reconstructing Haitian Womanhood," we will explore Haitian womanhood from a perspective that moves beyond the poto mitan model, or, rather, around it, which is to acknowledge its centrality but also account for its significant limitations.

One of the main objectives of this class is to utilize an interdisciplinary approach that draws on historical documents, political theories, poetry, novels, memoir, and film to obtain a critical perspective on the Haitian past, present, and future. Taken together, these novels, films, and essays help to create a more dynamic picture of Haitian womanhood that allows students to seriously interrogate rigid notions of what it means to be a Haitian woman.

Required Readings

Books

1. Marie Chauvet, *Dance on the Volcano* (*La Danse sur le volcan* 1957, 2016)
2. Evelyne Trouillot, *The Infamous Rosalie* (*Rosalie l'infâme* 2003, 2013)
3. Kettly Mars, *Savage Seasons* (*Saisons sauvages* 2010, 2015)
4. Edwidge Danticat, *Claire of the Sea Light* (2013)

Articles/Book Chapters

- Lenelle Moïse, "Quaking Conversation"
- Claudine Michel, "Unequal Distribution"
- Nadève Ménard, "The Myth of the Monolingual Haitian"
- Régine Jean-Charles, "The Myth of Dyaspora Exceptionalism"
- María José Rendón and Guerda Nicolas, "Deconstructing Portrayals of Haitian Women in the Media"
- Edwidge Danticat, *Create Dangerously: The Immigrant Artist at Work*
- Claudine Michel (ed.), *Brassage: An Anthology of Poetry by Haitian Women* [selections]
    - "To Haitian Womanhood" by Florence Bellandre-Robertson
    - "Workshop, 1987" by Myriam Chancy
- Beverly Bell, *Walking on Fire: Haitian Women's Stories of Survival and Resistance*
    - Chapter 4, "Resistance for Gender Justice," pp. 149–62
- Erica Caple James, *Democratic Insecurities: Violence, Trauma, and Intervention in Haiti*

- Marie-José N'Zengou-Tayo, "Fanm Se Poto Mitan: Haitian Women, the Pillar of Society"
- Myriam Chancy, *Framing Silence: Revolutionary Novels by Haitian Women*
- Marie-Denise Shelton, "Haitian Women's Fiction"
- Gina Ulysse, *Why Haiti Needs New Narratives*
- Jean Fouchard, *Le Théâtre à Saint-Domingue*
- Edwidge Danticat, "We Are Ugly, but We Are Here," *The Caribbean Writer*

Films

- *Woch nan soley*, dir. Patricia Benoit (2012)
- *Poto Mitan: Haitian Women, Pillars of the Global Economy* (2009), dir. René Bergan and Mark Schuller
- *Douvan jou leve*, dir. Gessica Généus (2018)

Music

- Emeline Michel
- Boukman Eksperyans
- Rutshelle Guillaume

Digital Resources

- Haiti: An Island Luminous
- Small Axe Archipelagos
- Chimamanda Ngozi Adichie, TED Talk: "The Danger of a Single Story"

Week 1

- Discussion, "How to Write About Haiti" [handout]
- "A Cage of Words," Dreyfuss, pp. 57–60

Week 2

- Lenelle Moïse, "Quaking Conversation"
- Chauvet, *Dance on the Volcano*
- N'Zengou-Tayo, "Fanm Se Poto Mitan: Haitian Women, the Pillar of Society"

Week 3

- Chauvet, *Dance on the Volcano*
- Trouillot, "An Unthinkable History: The Haitian Revolution as a Non-event"
- Fouchard, *Le Théâtre à Saint-Domingue*

Week 4

- Chauvet, *Dance on the Volcano*
- Rendón and Nicolas, "Deconstructing Portrayals of Haitian Women in the Media"

Week 5

- Trouillot, *The Infamous Rosalie*
- Bell, "Resistance for Gender Justice," pp. 149–62

Week 6

- Trouillot, *The Infamous Rosalie*
- James, *Democratic Insecurities: Violence, Trauma, and Intervention in Haiti*

Week 7

- Trouillot, *The Infamous Rosalie*
- Glover, "Revisiting Marie Vieux-Chauvet"

Week 8

- Mars, *Savage Seasons*
- Bell, Chapter 4, "Resistance for Gender Justice," pp. 149–62
- Poetry, "To Haitian Womanhood" by Florence Bellande-Robertson

Week 9

- Mars, *Savage Seasons*
- Ulysse, *Why Haiti Needs New Narratives*

Week 10

- Mars, *Savage Seasons*
- Ménard, "The Myth of the Monolingual Haitian"

Week 11

- Danticat, *Claire of the Sea Light*
- Chancy, *Framing Silence: Revolutionary Novels by Haitian Women*

Week 12

- Danticat, *Claire of the Sea Light*
- Ulysse, *Why Haiti Needs New Narratives*
- Laferrière, *The World Is Moving All Around Me*

Week 13

- Danticat, *Claire of the Sea Light*
- Ulysse, *Why Haiti Needs New Narratives*
- Michel, "Unequal Distribution"

Notes

1. The title of this course purposely invokes Black feminist scholar Hazel Carby's book *Reconstructing Womanhood: The Emergence of the Afro-American Woman Novelist*.

2. See Régine Michelle Jean-Charles, *Conflict Bodies: The Politics of Rape Representation in the Francophone Imaginary*.

3. I am referring here to the use of women's bodies to symbolize the land, for example in the story of Sor Rose offered by Timoléon Brutus in *L'home d'airain* (1946), or in Jacques Roumain's *Gouverneurs de la rosée*, in which the protagonist makes the analogy that a woman is like the land ("la terre est comme une femme"). For a longer discussion on the use of gendered ideology in Haitian literature, see also Myriam Chancy, *Framing Silence: Revolutionary Novels by Haitian Women*.

4. Following the chronological structure of the class, the next book I would like to teach is Anne Desroy's *Le Joug* (1934) or Virgile Valcin's *La Blanche négresse*, both of which are set during the US Occupation of Haiti (1915–1934); however, neither has been translated into English. For a French version of this class I would highly recommend including one of these.

Works Cited

Bell, Beverly. *Walking on Fire: Haitian Women's Stories of Survival and Resistance.* Cornell University Press, 2001.
Brutus, Timoléon. *L'home d'airain.* N. A. Théodore, 1946.
Carby, Hazel. *Reconstructing Womanhood: The Emergence of the Afro-American Woman Novelist.* Oxford University Press, 1987.
Chancy, Myriam. *Framing Silence: Revolutionary Novels by Haitian Women.* Rutgers University Press, 1997.
Chauvet, Marie. *Dance on the Volcano.* Translated by Kaiama Glover, Archipelago Books, 2017.
Danticat, Edwidge. "We Are Ugly, but We Are Here." *The Caribbean Writer* vol. 10, 1996. faculty.webster.edu/corbetre/haiti/literature/danticat-ugly.htm
———. *Create Dangerously: The Immigrant Artist at Work.* Vintage Books, 2010.
———. *Claire of the Sea Light.* Knopf, 2013.
Fouchard, Jean. *Le Théâtre à Saint-Domingue.* Impr. de l'État, 1955.
James, Erica Caple. *Democratic Insecurities: Violence, Trauma, and Intervention in Haiti.* University of California Press, 2010.
Jean-Charles, Régine Michelle. *Conflict Bodies: The Politics of Rape Representation in the Francophone Imaginary.* Ohio State University Press, 2014.
———. "The Myth of Diaspora Exceptionalism: Wyclef Jean's Performance of Jaspora." *American Quarterly,* vol. 66, no. 3, September 2014, pp. 835–852.
Mars, Kettly. *Savage Seasons.* Translated by Jeanine Herman, University of Nebraska Press, 2015.
Ménard, Nadève. "The Myth of the Monolingual Haitian: Linguistic Rights and Choices in the Haitian Literary Context." *Small Axe* vol. 18, no. 3(45), 2014, pp. 52–63.
Michel, Claudine, et al., editors. *Brassage: An Anthology of Poetry by Haitian Women.* Center for Research on Black Studies, 2005.
———. "Unequal Distribution." *Meridians,* vol. 11, no. 1, 2011, pp. 158–162.
Moïse, Lenelle. "Quaking Conversation," *Haiti Glass.* City Light Books, 2014, pp. 34.
N'Zengou-Tayo, Marie-José. "Fanm Se Poto Mitan: Haitian Women, the Pillar of Society." *Feminist Review,* vol. 59, no. 1, Summer 1998, pp. 118–143.
Rendón, María José, and Guerda Nicolas. "Deconstructing Portrayals of Haitian Women in the Media: A Thematic Analysis of Images in the Associated Press Photo Archive." *Psychology of Women Quarterly,* vol. 36, no. 2, June 2012, pp. 227–239.
Roumain, Jacques. *Masters of the Dew.* Translated by Mercer Cook and Langston Hughes, Heinemann, 1947.
Shelton, Marie-Denise. "Haitian Women's Fiction." *Callaloo,* vol. 15, no. 3, 1992, pp. 770–777.
Trouillot, Evelyne. *The Infamous Rosalie.* Translated by Marjorie Salvodon, University of Nebraska Press, 2013.
Ulysse, Gina. "Papa, Patriarchy, and Power: Snapshots of a Good Haitian Girl, Feminism, & Dyasporic Dreams." *The Journal of Haitian Studies,* vol. 12, no. 1, 2006, pp. 24–47.
———. *Why Haiti Needs New Narratives: A Post-Earthquake Chronicle.* Wesleyan University Press, 2015.

2

Teaching Haiti through the Work of Rodney Saint-Éloi, écrivain *engagé*

BONNIE THOMAS

The French term *engagement* is generally understood as referring to a political commitment or involvement. The works of many writers from the Caribbean could be described as *littérature engagée*, including those by such distinguished figures as Aimé Césaire (Martinique), who occupied the dual roles of poet and politician throughout his long life, and Edouard Glissant (also from Martinique), who consistently remarked upon the inextricability of poetry and politics. Haiti has been particularly associated with a poetic tradition of engaged writing. As celebrated Haitian author Dany Laferrière states in his memoir of the 2010 earthquake, *The World Is Moving Around Me*, "My confidence in poetry is unlimited. It alone can reconcile me with the horror of the world" (71–72). For the classroom teacher, the poetry and other writings of the Haitian écrivain *engagé* constitute rich material for informing students about the political and historical context of contemporary Haiti. Writer and publisher Rodney Saint-Éloi's work is particularly compelling for teaching these themes. Not only does he bear witness to key Haitian events such as the traumatic earthquake of 2010, but his literary "working through" of the catastrophe provides insights into the wider experience of Haitian exile. While his literary compatriots, such as Laferrière and Edwidge Danticat, are much celebrated and studied, Saint-Éloi offers a unique perspective as a more recent Haitian writer exiled in Francophone Canada, and a passionate literary activist through his work as an independent publisher. His writing is lyrical and accessible, and offers new insights into issues affecting past and present Haiti, as well as global issues.

As Saint-Éloi's writings are largely untranslated into English, this course would be most suitable for advanced-level French students at either the undergraduate or graduate level. (A sample syllabus appears at the end of this chapter.) However, there is much secondary literature in English surrounding the wider literary, intellectual, and historical context of Saint-Éloi's work that would both support this course and allow a committed instructor to transform it into one suitable for English-speaking students through their own translations. For the purposes of this chapter, though, we will consider Saint-Éloi's works in their original French with related secondary material in both French and English.

Exile, Home, and Belonging

Before examining Saint-Éloi's texts, it is essential first to introduce students to the context from which he writes, including his personal background, the tradition of the écrivain *engagé* in the Francophone Caribbean, and his particular situation as a writer and activist in both Haiti and Canada. Such themes could be usefully set out in a lecture or PowerPoint presentation that evokes the striking cultural and physical differences between his two principal places of residence and introduces issues surrounding home, exile, and belonging. Depending on the level of detail the instructor wishes to convey, these ideas could be explored through extracts from other Haitian writers such as Laferrière and Danticat before proceeding to a consideration of Saint-Éloi's own views. Extracts from relevant texts such as Laferrière's memoir of his first year after going into exile in Montreal in 1976—*Chronique de la dérive douce [A Drifting Year]*—and Danticat's *Create Dangerously: The Immigrant Artist at Work* would be informative here, and students could debate some of the differing responses to exile they contain. Of course, there is a huge amount of primary and secondary material on these themes and instructors could expand or contract as they wish, but the principal aim would be to set the scene for Saint-Éloi's own experience of exile, which he explores in his writing.

Rodney Saint-Éloi was born in 1963 in Cavaillon, Haiti, and is a distinguished poet and writer as well as the founder of the publishing houses Les Éditions Mémoire in Port-au-Prince (1991) and Mémoire d'encrier in Montreal, Canada (2003). Saint-Éloi distinguished himself intellectually from a young age, becoming a writer, journalist, teacher, and publisher in his native Haiti. As he states in his 2016 memoir *Passion Haïti*: "I had a name and a situation" (13).[1] However, Saint-Éloi also reveals the deeply conflicted feelings that accompany this status, and that culminate in the difficult decision he made to relocate his family to Montreal in 2001. The opening chapter of *Passion Haïti*, "Un goût de terre et de poème," gives students excellent insight into the contradictions that plague contemporary Haitian intellectuals such as Saint-Éloi. Saint-Éloi's inner turmoil pivots around the notion of how best to serve Haiti and its people as the gap between rich and poor continues to grow. Realizing the privileges he has gained as a result of his successful career, Saint-Éloi is equally cognizant of the fact that he may become part of the despised elite if he stays in his homeland: "I didn't want to join this barbarous and repugnant elite. I had pride in choosing exile" (15). At the same time, however, Saint-Éloi details the deep wrench that this move entails: "My body and soul hurt" (15). The issues Saint-Éloi details in this chapter give students a unique window into themes explored by many Haitian writers, past and present: those of exile and belonging, how to contribute meaningfully to society, and how to find a balance between collective and individual responsibility. Saint-Éloi's contribution offers the perspective of a Haitian intellectual who chooses to fight for Haiti from abroad, using *littérature engagée* as his sword.

Un écrivain *engagé*

In addition to Saint-Éloi's role as a writer, it is important for students to appreciate his position as an editor, which injects a wider political purpose into his literature. After arriving in Montreal in 2001, Saint-Éloi established Mémoire d'encrier, which draws together writers from Africa, the Caribbean, the Arabic-speaking world, Canada (with an increasing emphasis on Indigenous writers), and other diverse regions. According to its website, Mémoire d'encrier is a "place of crossroads where meetings, dialogues and exchanges weave themselves together in order for diverse voices to be visible and vibrant."[2] The language Saint-Éloi employs in this description is reminiscent of Edouard Glissant, the Martinican founder of the Antillanité [Caribbeanness] movement and author of such works as *Caribbean Discourse* and *Poetics of Relation*. A valuable line of inquiry for students, then, is to examine the parallels between Saint-Éloi and his Caribbean predecessor, which could be done in a secondary introductory lecture. A major contribution of Glissant's was to introduce the idea of diversity into notions that were previously dominated by the One or the Same. One of Glissant's early and most famous images to encapsulate this diversity is the rhizome, with its chaotic merging of connected roots. Borrowed from Gilles Deleuze and Félix Guattari's *Mille plateaux*, the rhizome underlines interconnection and exchange. In his 2009 publication *Philosophie de la Relation*, Glissant provides snapshots of several of his key concepts, including "La pensée archipélique" [archipelagic thinking], "La pensée de l'errance" ["wandering" thought], and "La pensée de la Relation" [relational thought], which could form the building blocks of the instructor's lecture. These pared-down presentations of Glissant's complex concepts could also be supplemented by some of the secondary material available on the subject, such as Thomas's article "Rodney Saint-Éloi: Writer and Publisher of the 'Whole-World.'" As Glissant is not the focus of the course, the main goal is to alert students to the wider intellectual significance of Saint-Éloi's work so they can have a deeper appreciation of how the latter's literature both springs from and develops his thought, taking its place in a longer tradition of politically engaged writing. What both authors emphasize, which is summarized in Saint-Éloi's introduction to Mémoire d'encrier's website, is that literature is "a platform where imaginations confront each other to learn and respect difference and cultural diversity."[3] A concrete example of such literary activism is Saint-Éloi's establishment of "Espace de la Diversité" in 2008 as part of the Salon du Livre du Québec, "a space in which to transmit the literatures of diversity, to promote the values of 'living-together' and to confront history, racism and inequalities."[4] "Espace de la Diversité" formed part of Mémoire d'encrier's mandate from its creation until 2015, after which it became an independent not-for-profit organization called the "Diversity District," focused on disseminating the work of authors of diverse origins, although retaining links with Mémoire d'encrier.

Teaching Haiti through the 2010 Earthquake

After establishing this important context for Saint-Éloi's literary activities, an examination of two of his recent texts about the horrific earthquake that devastated Haiti on January 12, 2010, gives students the opportunity to gain rich insights into issues affecting historic and present-day Haiti. Both published in 2010, *Refonder Haïti?* is a jointly edited collection in which Saint-Éloi and others explore questions relating to the earthquake and wider Haitian society, while *Haïti kenbe la!: 35 secondes et mon pays à reconstruire* is Saint-Éloi's eyewitness account of the event. Both demonstrate an insight into the politics and passions that characterize Haiti's tumultuous history: from the triumphant moment of gaining independence from France in 1804 to the complexity of Haitian political history following the Revolution, from its vulnerable environmental position to the unwavering optimism of its people. In *Refonder Haïti?*, Saint-Éloi and his fellow editors Pierre Buteau and Lyonel Trouillot approach the earthquake as a way to re-envisage Haiti's future from the diverse perspectives of 42 contributors. As they state in the introduction, leaders in Haiti and around the world have endlessly debated the idea of the "refondation" [refoundation] of Haiti since the earthquake.[5] However, the fundamental question remains: "Quoi refonder?" [Refound what?] (5). The authors muse on whether such reconstruction would involve simply recovering from the devastating physical effects of the earthquake or whether it is an opportunity to reappraise Haiti's past to create a more just society for its future. As they affirm, the "secret of the future, of any future, resides in its past" (6).

The structure of *Refonder Haïti?* is reminiscent of a collage, a characteristic of many works of Caribbean literature whose writers feel an acute sense of responsibility to speak on behalf of those who have been silenced. In the Haitian context, this collage-like approach has been linked to writers such as Edwidge Danticat as well as Saint-Éloi whose work consistently extends beyond their individual experiences to blend their voices with those of others. In *Refonder Haïti?* the authors employ distinctly Glissantian terms when describing the collage-like contributions that make up their volume, describing them as a "grouping of voices" that aim to "displace some certitudes and evaluate others." Moreover, they "are in dialogue with each other. The hope is that these voices accompany the 'living together' and desire for refoundation" (6). The political aim of this text can thus be linked back to Saint-Éloi's stated aims for his publishing house Mémoire d'encrier as well as to his wider commitment to literary *engagement*. The following discussion will focus on three of Saint-Éloi's own texts, which will be most illuminating for students when presented through close readings and guided questions from the instructor. An example of the format this could take can be found at the end of the chapter.

"Haïti: prolégomènes à la refondation"

Saint-Éloi's personal contribution to *Refonder Haïti?*, "Haïti: prolégomènes à la refondation," characteristically begins with a quote about poetry—"No people is smaller than its poem" (301)—by Palestinian poet and writer Mahmoud Darwish. The inclusion of a non-Haitian writer in a book about Haiti demonstrates the globality of contemporary Haitian writing. In this simple example, Saint-Éloi underlines his commitment to the notion that the future of humanity resides in the enriching possibilities of different cultures interacting positively with each other. For students, it is also a chance to see Saint-Éloi's form of literary *engagement* in action: that it is the imagination that unites people and not their race or creed. From this outward-looking prelude, Saint-Éloi's text in *Refonder Haïti?* meanders through time and space as he considers his relationship to his birth country while writing alongside a lake in the Laurentian mountains in Canada. Saint-Éloi acknowledges his status as an exile and how his experience of being "here and there in divided time" (301) conditions his approach to the question of Haiti's possible rebirth. Furthermore, he reveals his unyielding belief in the beauty and power of the written word: "[H]oping that [it] will open the path to beauty, to poetry and the freedom of living, thinking and existing . . . to refound [Haiti] it is necessary to find the right words since 'words never lie'" (301). From this pensive and poetic introduction, Saint-Éloi proceeds to order his essay with five subheadings: "in class," "international community," "leave?," "rebellion," and "imagine."[6] In addition to structuring his article, these titles can be fruitful when approaching Saint-Éloi's work more generally, and for this reason they provide an ideal entry point into his thought for students. Encouraging students to consider these aspects of his writings provides a framework for them to link the different aspects of his literary project, in particular how he conceives of his place in relation to Haiti and how he uses writing to act politically. While the form and function of his writings vary from pure poetry to reflective essay, Saint-Éloi revisits many of the same themes, all of which strive toward an understanding of Haiti and its people and how he might contribute to its future through the literary imagination. By examining "Haïti: prolégomènes à la refondation" first among Saint-Éloi's texts, students gain insight into the key concerns that motivate all aspects of his work.

In the section titled "in class," Saint-Éloi recalls his first experience of the social divisions that have plagued Haiti since its successful revolution for independence. At the age of 13, his friend Coby asks Saint-Éloi to join in his childhood games, but says that he must check with his grandmother first. When Saint-Éloi fails to give satisfactory answers to the questions, What is your father's name? What is your mother's name? What suburb do you live in?, the happy friendship is over. As he recalls, "With that I lived my first experience of exclusion and imbecility" (302). Saint-Éloi goes on to note the deep divisions within Haitian society, divisions exacerbated by the international community, which has continued a long history of systemic and extremely consequential forms of colonial and imperial intervention. Saint-Éloi captures the end result of such disastrous politics in his description of the attitude of the country's president, René Préval, after the earthquake: "He took up residence at the international airport to wait for international aid" (303). Such sociopolitical realities could be emphasized by the judicious use of secondary texts such as *Haiti After the Earthquake* (Paul Farmer), *The Big Truck That Went By: How the World Came to Save Haiti and Left Behind a Disaster* (Jonathan M. Katz), and *The Idea of Haiti: Rethinking Crisis and Development* (Millery Polyné), which give context and background to Saint-Éloi's descriptions. A comparison of the different perspectives presented by these authors also drives home to students the politically motivated nature of much Haitian writing.

In contrast to the destructive passivity of the country's leaders, Saint-Éloi details the fortitude of everyday Haitians, a quality that has attained an almost mythic status in much writing about Haiti. It would be useful to introduce a discussion of the trope of Haitian "resilience" here, reinforcing to students that what writers are offering are *representations* of Haitians rather than immutable truths. Author Gina Athena Ulysse has been particularly vocal in her criticism of such stereotypes, arguing that Haiti and its people have become limited by "singular narratives and clichés" (xxii). According to Saint-Éloi, though, the Haitian spirit remains extraordinary, and he records that in "the streets, early on 13 January, thanks to the immeasurable energy displayed by the people, the population was on its feet, without guide or orders, in the process of forging life, even under the rubble" (304). While Saint-Éloi dislikes the term "resilient"—which he sees as a Western construction, an idea he explores in *Haïti kenbe la!*—he nonetheless maintains his focus on the ability of Haitians to keep going no matter what, and he remains committed to his belief in Haiti's people. As we have seen in the opening chapter of *Passion Haïti*, the unbridgeable gap between the country's leaders and the rest of the population is ultimately what drives Saint-Éloi into exile, where he feels he may best support the Haitian people. By taking up residence in Montreal, Saint-Éloi fosters the reworking of Haiti's narratives through his own writing and by nurturing other writers through Mémoire d'encrier, contributing to what Martin Munro has described as "a golden age of Haitian writing" (*Exile* 206). The cosmopolitan space of Montreal has become a haven for many Haitian exiles and offers Saint-Éloi the safety to comment on his country of birth and to work through the personal and political dilemmas of exile. Most importantly, it gives him a direct link to the "outside world" that allows him to dramatize Haiti's plight and advocate for its future, a position he could never have achieved from within the country. His life's work becomes driven by his belief in the need to "re-establish the myth of the country. Re-establish one's truth" (306). The way Saint-Éloi achieves this goal in the global context of Montreal offers an additional avenue of inquiry for the interested student.

Haïti kenbe la!

Saint-Éloi's extended memoir of the earthquake, *Haïti kenbe la!: 35 secondes et mon pays à reconstruire*, is an excellent book with which to teach students about Haiti because of its portrayal of Saint-Éloi's key themes as well as those relating to Haitian literature more widely. It is a highly readable and poignant text that is particularly valuable for its collage-like style, melding the personal and collective. Having contextualized both Saint-Éloi as an author and the Haitian context more specifically, students should be well prepared to delve into this powerful book. The narrative begins with Saint-Éloi's description of his preparations to attend the Étonnants Voyageurs literary conference in Port-au-Prince.[7] In fact he had only landed in the country a short time before and was just preparing to eat at the Hotel Karibe with fellow writers and academics Dany Laferrière, Thomas Spear, and Michel le Bris when the earthquake struck. Saint-Éloi's resulting narrative serves a number of purposes: It is a deeply personal eyewitness account of the earthquake, it is a book of the testimonies of others who experienced the catastrophe in both direct and indirect ways, and it is a literary "working-through" of trauma.[8] Each facet of the book reinforces the notion that Saint-Éloi's objective in literature is to bear witness, bring about change, and foster optimism in a world that is frequently beyond comprehension. *Haïti kenbe la!* opens with two quotations that effectively sum up the main themes of this and many of his other works: "We are not in the habit of allowing our sadness to reduce us to silence," which he attributes to Edwidge Danticat, and the African proverb, "As long as the lion doesn't have his historian, hunting stories will always glorify the hunter." These two powerful citations underline the stoicism that stereotypically characterizes Haiti and the need for the collective and individual stories of its people to be told. The following discussion draws out some of the main themes of *Haïti kenbe la!*, in particular Saint-Éloi's concern to portray the resourceful nature of his people and the role such qualities play in contributing to his wider goal of cultural understanding. These attributes could be presented in a variety of ways to students—through close examination of key sections of the text, a progressive analysis of the memoir as a whole, or through a collage-like approach, with Saint-Éloi's reflections being placed alongside other memories of the earthquake such as Laferrière's in *The World Is Moving Around Me*.

Against the backdrop of the horrific earthquake, *Haïti kenbe la!* emerges as a spiritual journey as much as a physical one, with Saint-Éloi searching "under the rubble to unearth the smallest light to join, up high, a small star. The lucky star that is capable of changing life in Haiti" (266). The unwavering search for beauty and hope and, moreover, the belief that there are such things, is a defining characteristic of Saint-Éloi's life and work, as we have seen. This belief is linked to Saint-Éloi's commitment to allowing Haitian people's voices to be heard and not be lost under the rubble. As he recalls in the letter to his editor at the end of his narrative, "I wrote this book to say that life never trembles.

A people upstanding in search of the way by the light of candles. A people upstanding in search of water and bread, and burying their dead. Because the dead know how to cross gardens and knock on the windows of dreams to give the living hope" (266). The image of a people upstanding is reminiscent of Césaire's *Notebook of a Return to the Native Land*, in which he repeatedly uses the word "debout" [upstanding] to characterize the potential for Martinicans to resist colonial oppression. Like Césaire, Saint-Éloi consistently attributes strength to Haitian people, whom he portrays as remarkable in their ability to continue on despite adversity.

In addition to this optimism, *Haïti kenbe la!* focuses attention on the practical, non-sentimental nature of the Haitian people who simply get on with things. As Saint-Éloi recalls, his first question upon arriving in Port-au-Prince each time he visits Haiti is, "Comment va le pays?" ["How is the country?"] with the inevitable answer: "Ni pire, ni mieux" ["No better, no worse"] (26). "Un jour, ça marche, et un autre, ça ne marche pas" [One day things work and the next they don't] (27). Another facet of the Haitian acceptance that life contains both highs and lows can be summed up by the Creole proverb: "*Se lavi*. C'est la vie. La vie s'organise" [That's life. No matter what, life goes on] (46), which runs like a thread through *Haïti kenbe la!* As Saint-Éloi's cherished grandmother Tida reminds him, "The history of the country is a succession of earthquakes. Natural earthquakes. Human earthquakes" (20), which means that coping with adversity is a well-established pattern of Haitian life.

Bringing students to the understanding that History with a capital "H" remains a constant backdrop to the unfolding of personal and collective stories, with each interlacing with the other, can be successfully effected through an analysis of this work. To give a few examples that could be used to structure classroom discussions, Saint-Éloi underlines the historical and emotional significance of the Creole (or Kreyòl) language for the Haitian people as he reveals that his former lecturer, Pierre Vernet, perished in the earthquake, and the Faculty of Applied Linguistics was destroyed (155–158). His narrative pauses over the clash of colonial History and the myriad histories that make up the Haitian past (198–215), and he concludes with the wise words of Tida, who again reminds him of the need to face life with one's eyes open: "Tida had the wisdom to pepper her tales with lessons about life . . . it is true that the history of the country since Independence is a series of earthquakes followed by regular aftershocks" (215). Saint-Éloi expands on these themes in *Passion Haïti* and this narrative serves as a useful counterpoint to *Haïti kenbe la!*

Both texts underline the inextricable link between the individual and the collective voice, not only between writers and "everyday" Haitians, but also among writers themselves. Indeed, as an examination of any of his books highlights, Saint-Éloi has frequent recourse to inspirational quotations, which often frame and reinforce the power of his own words. Moreover, the presence of many of Haiti's well-known literary and cultural figures as "characters" in his narratives, as well as his in theirs, contributes to the impression that Saint-Éloi's work is larger than just telling a tale from an individual point of view.[9] Like his compatriot and friend Edwidge Danticat, who declares in *Create Dangerously* that she "merge[s] [her] own narratives with the oral and written narratives of others" (62), Saint-Éloi adds his voice to a chorus.[10] This commitment to collectivity is explicitly stated in the postface to *Haïti kenbe la!*, where he writes of plunging into a narrative space teeming with stories: "At the end I no longer know what comes from me and what comes from others. In order not to betray these stories I meld them into my existence. For it is these stories that bring people together" (266). This sense of collective responsibility is a fundamental part of Saint-Éloi's *engagement* and is essential to stress to students of his work.

Passion Haïti

Saint-Éloi expands on the political possibilities of writing in *Passion Haïti*. As he describes in the book, his exile to Montreal paradoxically serves both to cement his "Haitianness" and to give him the tools to contribute meaningfully to the country of his birth: "It is in Montreal that my Haitianness came to me. The question came to me here: How to participate in the construction of the country?" (18). Furthermore, he evokes literature as the way to create new, empowering narratives about Haiti: "Writer and publisher, I would like to erase borders and dream of the archipelago, draw lands together, relegate the ocean to the outside so that islands are no longer separated. In order to make a crowd and dream together about a *rise in humanity*, about a cry and a common destiny" (21). Saint-Éloi's evocation of an archipelago links back to Glissant's concept of Relation, which also emphasizes a sense of openness and connection to others.[11] From a linguistic point of view, Saint-Éloi also reiterates these themes in the way he conceives of the contrast between French and Creole:

> [I]f I write in French it is to remind myself of a childhood, a song, an image of the world and the beauty of a grandmother. All that came to me in Creole. The invention is to seal together, end to end, these two imaginaries and to exist in the end in these voices and these sonorities. Refuse monolingualism by seducing language and form in their fascinating diversity. ("Mes langues" 25)[12]

Writing in Saint-Éloi's hands becomes a means to weave together disparate elements in a way that does not deny difference, but that allows each individual component to occupy a necessary place in the whole.

It would be useful to reinforce the theoretical affinities that exist among Saint-Éloi, Glissant, and others here in order to remind students of the collective aspect of Haitian literature. By placing passages from Saint-Éloi and Glissant side by side, students can see the ways in which one influences and inspires the other, but also the ways in which each writer puts their own unique spin on interpreting the world. Glissant and Saint-Éloi share a particular bond, as they both believe passionately in the power of poetry. In an interview with Lise Gauvin, for example, Glissant explicitly links poetics and politics: "[P]oetry is up until now the only art which can really go behind appearances. I think that is the most important of its vocations" (29). As for Saint-Éloi, Glissant identifies the "imaginaire" [imagination] as paramount and charges the poet with the responsibility to find those "imaginations open to all sorts of futures of creolization" (*L'Imaginaire* 33). As a way to draw together the different strands of Saint-Éloi's *engagement*, it would be beneficial for students to listen to a recording of a 2011 literary evening he shared with Lise Gauvin in Montreal, entitled "Écrire, lire et habiter: Une manière d'habiter le monde" [Writing, reading and living: a way of inhabiting the world].[13] Saint-Éloi explicitly links his philosophy of writing to two theoretical concepts developed by Glissant. This literary soirée took place shortly after the famous Martinican's death, and Saint-Éloi discusses the ideas of Relation and "l'imaginaire de la totalité-monde" [the imagination of the whole-world], which each emphasize the interconnectedness of all aspects of life and the importance of appreciating the uniting properties of diversity.[14] With his favored image of the rhizome suggesting the notion of new buds sprouting from a network of interconnected roots and the archipelago embodying openness to the sea and other lands, Glissant emphasizes the bonds among peoples, cultures, histories, and memories. When examining Saint-Éloi's career to date, it is evident that he too makes connections everywhere: between History and histories, between Canada and Haiti, between Haitian writers who are friends and collaborators and often appear in each other's books, between writers and artists more generally, and among the different texts Saint-Éloi has written. Both Saint-Éloi and Glissant remain committed to the idea that "literature has as its mission to demolish borders in order to bring together people and continents" (*Passion* 20). This insertion of Saint-Éloi's work into a literary genealogy serves as a useful way to remind students of his individual contributions as a writer, but also of the necessity to consider his significance more widely.

Conclusion

Saint-Éloi's body of work can be summed up in the title of his most recent work: *Passion Haïti*. Through the medium of literature—both his own and that he nurtures through Mémoire d'encrier—he contributes to an increased understanding of the world. Informed by a deeply compassionate philosophy, Saint-Éloi's life and work provide an inspiring example of how the written word can change lives. Teaching about Haiti through the work of Saint-Éloi, then, unveils the values of optimism and strength in the face of adversity that frequently characterize the Haitian people. As he asserts in *Haïti kenbe la!*, "It is thus that I recognize my country in the constant creation of this life. Never lacking in a story. The challenge of living in destitution with eyes wide open on tomorrow" (26). Whether his texts are read in full or through extracts, whether in isolation or in conversation with each other, Saint-Éloi's work holds extraordinary riches for students. He deserves to be studied in diverse ways in the contemporary classroom.

Sample Syllabus

Course Description

This course aims to teach students about the Haitian writer and publisher Rodney Saint-Éloi, whose significant body of work is largely unknown in scholarship. Born in Haiti in 1963 and going into exile in Montreal, Canada, in 2001, Saint-Éloi gives a unique perspective on Haiti's past, present, and future through his dual roles as writer and publisher. His work is passionate, lyrical, and accessible, and offers new insights into issues affecting Haiti and the wider world. This course will seek to introduce students to Saint-Éloi's writing and literary activism and set him alongside other, better-known Haitian writers of his generation.

Course Level

As most of Saint-Éloi's writings are not translated into English, this course is most suitable for advanced-level undergraduate or graduate students in French.

Course Readings

(English translations have been listed where they exist)

Week 1: Introduction and Context (Home, Exile, and Belonging)

- Extracts from *Chronique de la dérive douce* [*A Drifting Year*] (Dany Laferrière)
- Extracts from *Create Dangerously* (Edwidge Danticat)
- "Rodney Saint-Éloi: Cinq questions pour île.en.île"

Week 2: L'écrivain engagé (Saint-Éloi and Glissant)

- "La pensée archipélique," "La pensée de l'errance," and "La pensée de la Relation" from *Philosophie de la Relation* (Edouard Glissant)
- "Rodney Saint-Éloi: Writer and Publisher of the 'Whole World'" (Bonnie Thomas)

Week 3: The Haitian Earthquake of 2010

- "Introduction" and "Haïti: prolégomènes à la refondation" (Rodney Saint-Éloi, *Refonder Haïti?*)

Supplementary Readings

- *Haiti After the Earthquake* (Paul Farmer)
- *The Big Truck That Went By: How the World Came to Save Haiti and Left Behind a Disaster* (Jonathan M. Katz)
- *The Idea of Haiti: Rethinking Crisis and Development* (Millery Polyné)
- *Why Haiti Needs New Narratives: A Post-Quake Chronicle* (Gina Athena Ulysse)

Week 4: Writing the Haitian Earthquake

- Extracts from *Haiti Rising* (Martin Munro, ed.)
- "Writing the 'Haitian Soul': Post-earthquake Poetry" (Martin Munro, *Writing on the Fault Line*)

Week 5: Haïti kenbe la! (Rodney Saint-Éloi)

- Chapters 1–3 (pp. 9–102)

Week 6

- Chapters 4–6 (pp. 103–170)

Week 7

- Chapters 7–9 (pp. 171–232)

Week 8
- Chapters 10–12 & postface (pp. 233–267)

Week 9: Passion Haïti (Rodney Saint-Éloi)
- Chapters 1–4 (pp. 9–62)

Week 10
- Chapters 5–8 (pp. 63–85)

Week 11
- Chapters 9–12 (pp. 86–124)

Week 12
- Chapters 13–16 (pp. 125–163)

Week 13
- Chapters 17–20 (pp. 164–195)

Week 14
- Chapters 21–22 (pp. 196–206)

Week 15: Bringing It All Together
- "Écrire, lire et habiter: Une manière d'habiter le monde" (Interview with Lise Gauvin)

Sample Lesson Plan

Week 3

"Introduction" and "Haïti: prolégomènes à la refondation" (Rodney Saint-Éloi, *Refonder Haïti?*)

Aims: To introduce students to Saint-Éloi's thought through his contribution to the edited collection *Refonder Haïti?*, and to identify the main themes that structure his life and work.

Lead-in: Students discuss in pairs their own recollection of the 2010 earthquake or any words/images they relate to it through prior readings or lessons. Brainstorm on the board and have a brief discussion with the whole class.

"Introduction": Students to discuss the following questions in pairs and then compare as a class.

1. What are the main issues the editors identify as important for Haiti in the wake of the earthquake? Do you agree/disagree with their conclusions?
2. Explain the difference between the words "refonder," "reconstruire," and "renouveler." Can they be used interchangeably? Why/why not?
3. What are the advantages/disadvantages of presenting a text with short and varied contributions from diverse authors? How do the editors present this "regroupement de voix"?
4. Explain the phrase, "Le secret de l'avenir, de tout avenir réside dans son passé." Do you agree/disagree? Explain.

"Haïti: Prolégomènes à la refondation": As a class

1. Explore the significance of the quotation by Mahmoud Darwish.
2. Identify the main themes of Saint-Éloi's introduction. What does exile mean to him? What are some of the contradictions he describes? What is his understanding of the concept of "la parole"?
3. Divide students into five groups and assign each group one of Saint-Éloi's subtitles: "en classe," "communauté internationale," "partir?," "la rébellion," and "imaginer." Each group will discuss the important points and then present to the rest of the class.

Concluding discussion: As a class discussion or a written reflection

1. What themes emerge as the most important for Saint-Éloi?
2. What is your personal opinion of his article?

Notes

1. Unless otherwise indicated, all translations are my own.
2. See memoiredencrier.com/memoire-dencrier/. Accessed 14 April 2017. The page devoted to Rodney Saint-Éloi on the île.en.île website is also a rich source of material for the classroom teacher. See ile-en-ile.org/saint-éloi/.
3. See memoiredencrier.com/memoire-dencrier/. Accessed 14 April 2017.
4. See memoiredencrier.com/memoire-dencrier/. Accessed 14 April 2017.
5. While the term "reconstruction" is commonly used to refer to the period after the earthquake, Saint-Éloi affirms in personal correspondence with the author that he purposely chose the term "refondation" rather than "reconstruction." For Saint-Éloi, "refonder" takes into account nation, class, and culture, and the idea of starting again in a way that "reconstruire" does not. It is about probing the past, taking account of the present, and envisaging the future. It is a more subtle and human term than "reconstruct," thereby remaining consistent with Saint-Éloi's personal philosophy.

6. In the original, these appear as "en classe," "communauté internationale," "partir?," "la rébellion," and "imaginer."

7. Established by Michel le Bris in 1990, the Festival des Étonnants Voyageurs began as a way to challenge the primacy of France's literary culture and the opposition of "French" and "Francophone" literature, proposing instead that such writing just happens to be in French. Further information can be found at www.etonnants-voyageurs.com as well as in Le Bris and Jean Rouaud's edited volume *Pour une littérature-monde*.

8. For further detail on these issues see, for example, Martin Munro, *Writing on the Fault Line: Haitian Literature and the Earthquake of 2010*, pp. 42–51; Kasia Mika, "Histories of the Past, Histories for the Future: Representing the Past and Writing for the Future in Rodney Saint-Éloi's *Haïti kenbe la!*," *Journal of Haitian Studies*; and Bonnie Thomas, "Narrating Trauma: Distance and Proximity in the Haitian Earthquake of 2010."

9. To give just a few simple examples, Saint-Éloi and Laferrière feature in each other's memoirs of the 2010 earthquake, *Haïti kenbe la!* and *Tout bouge autour de moi [The World Is Moving Around Me]*, as do other well-known writers such as Frankétienne and Edwidge Danticat, who recalls her guided tour through one of Haiti's centuries in her travelogue *After the Dance*. Saint-Éloi refers to the former in *Passion Haïti* on pp. 125–128, and the latter on p. 154.

10. Edwidge Danticat, *Create Dangerously: The Immigrant Artist at Work*, p. 62.

11. See, for example, Glissant's chapter on "la pensée archipélique, la pensée de l'essai" in Edouard Glissant, *Philosophie de la relation: poésie en étendue*, pp. 45–53.

12. "Mes langues à moi sont toutes mortes," *Relations*, mai-juin 2015, p. 25.

13. radiospirale.org/capsule/rencontre-avec-rodney-saint-Éloi

14. For further details on these issues and how five contemporary Francophone writers explore these ideas in their personal narratives, see Bonnie Thomas, *Connecting Histories: Francophone Caribbean Writers Interrogating Their Past*.

Works Cited

Buteau, Pierre, Rodney Saint-Éloi, and Lyonel Trouillot, editors. *Refonder Haïti?* Mémoire d'encrier, 2010.

Césaire, Aimé. *Cahier d'un retour au pays natal*. 1939. Présence Africaine, 1983.

———. *Notebook of a Return to the Native Land*. Translated by Clayton Eshleman and Annette Smith, Wesleyan University Press, 2001.

Danticat, Edwidge. *Create Dangerously: The Immigrant Artist at Work*. Vintage Books, 2011.

Deleuze, Gilles, and Félix Guattari. *Mille plateaux*. Minuit, 1980.

———. *A Thousand Plateaus*. Translated by Brian Massumi, University of Minnesota Press, 1987.

Farmer, Paul. *Haiti After the Earthquake*. Public Affairs, 2011.

Glissant, Edouard. *Caribbean Discourse*. Translated by Michael Dash, University of Virginia Press, 1989.

———. *Le Discours antillais*. Gallimard, 1990.

———. *Poetics of Relation*. Translated by Betsy Wing, University of Michigan Press, 1997.

———. *Poétique de la Relation*. Gallimard, 1997.

———. *Philosophie de la relation: poésie en étendue*. Gallimard, 2009.

———. *L'Imaginaire des langues: entretiens avec Lise Gauvin (1991–2009)*. Gallimard, 2010.

Katz, Jonathan M. *The Big Truck That Went By: How the World Came to Save Haiti and Left Behind a Disaster.* Palgrave Macmillan, 2014.

Laferrière, Dany. *Chronique de la dérive douce.* Grasset, 2012.

———. *A Drifting Year.* Translated by David Homel, Douglas & McIntyre, 1997.

———. *Tout bouge autour de moi.* Grasset, 2011.

———. *The World Is Moving Around Me: A Memoir of the Haiti Earthquake.* Translated by David Homel, Arsenal Pulp Press, 2013.

Le Bris, Michel, and Jean Rouaud, editors. *Pour une littérature-monde.* Gallimard, 2007.

Mika, Kasia. "Histories of the Past, Histories for the Future: Representing the Past and Writing for the Future in Rodney Saint-Éloi's *Haïti kenbe la!*" *Journal of Haitian Studies*, vol. 20, no. 2, 2014, pp. 4–19.

Munro, Martin. *Exile and Post-1946 Haitian Literature: Alexis, Depestre, Ollivier, Laferrière, Danticat.* Liverpool University Press, 2007.

———, editor. *Haiti Rising: Haitian History, Culture and the Earthquake of 2010.* University of the West Indies Press, 2010.

———. *Writing on the Fault Line: Haitian Literature and the Earthquake of 2010.* Liverpool University Press, 2014.

———. "Gina Athena Ulysse: *Why Haiti Needs New Narratives.*" *New West Indian Guide*, vol. 91, 2017, pp. 341–342.

Polyné, Millery, editor. *The Idea of Haiti: Rethinking Crisis and Development.* University of Minnesota Press, 2013.

Saint-Éloi, Rodney. "Cinq questions pour île.en.île." ile-en-ile.org/rodney-saint-éloi-5-questions-pour-ile-en-ile.

———. "Ecrire, lire et habiter: Une manière d'habiter le monde." radiospirale.org/capsule/rencontre-avec-rodney-saint-Éloi.

———. *Haïti, kenbe la!: 35 secondes et mon pays à reconstruire.* Michel Lafon, 2010.

———. "Haïti: prolégomènes à la refondation." *Refonder Haïti?* Edited by Pierre Buteau, Rodney Saint-Éloi, and Lyonel Trouillot, Mémoire d'encrier, 2010, pp. 301–307.

———. "Mes langues à moi sont toutes mortes." *Relations*, mai-juin 2015, pp. 23–26.

———. *Passion Haïti.* Septentrion, 2016.

Thomas, Bonnie. "Narrating Trauma: Distance and Proximity in the Haitian Earthquake of 2010." *Australian Journal of French Studies*, vol. 53, nos. 1/2, 2016, pp. 70–81.

———. *Connecting Histories: Francophone Caribbean Writers Interrogating Their Past.* University of Mississippi Press, 2017.

———. "Rodney Saint-Éloi: Writer and Publisher of the 'Whole World.'" *Small Axe*, 57, 2018, pp. 28–36.

Ulysse, Gina Athena. *Why Haiti Needs New Narratives: A Post-Quake Chronicle.* Wesleyan University Press, 2015.

3

Teaching Haitian Theater

Franck Fouché's *Bouqui au Paradis*

JOUBERT SATYRE

When it comes to teaching Haitian literature in foreign universities, the Haitian novel is almost exclusively the genre taught, while other genres, such as poetry and theater, are set aside. This simplification merely follows the general tendency in the contemporary teaching of literature, where the novel has been the main genre deemed worthy of interest. If, as Roland Barthes declared, "literature is what gets taught" (64), one of the consequences of this monopoly is a disinterest in other literary genres, such as poetry and theater, that precede the novel.[1] And yet, since the teaching of Haitian literature is first and foremost a way of revealing to the student that which is specifically Haitian, theater should be added to literary forms of study.

For the sake of mimesis, Haitian theater has always been interested in all aspects of Haitian society in order to unveil its foundations. While staging the Haitian world, plays offer a journey of discovery into Haitian imagination and culture. Through their undertones, plays invite the active and creative participation of the reader, who must then make explicit what is implied. That is what some of the exercises proposed at the end of this chapter exemplify. The goal of these exercises is to help students build their own representation of Haiti through *Bouqui au Paradis* and understand how this theatrical text works.

The chapter consists of three parts. The first provides a brief overview of Haiti's theatrical tradition.[2] The second analyzes the renewal of theater, notably thanks to the creative and theoretical work of the dramatists Félix Morisseau-Leroy (1912–1998) and Franck Fouché (1915–1978). The final part examines

Bouqui au Paradis and offers suggestions for teaching it. Because the play, originally written in Kreyòl (Haitian Creole) under the title *Bouki nan paradi* (1960), has not yet been translated into English, it will be appropriate for use in French-language courses.[3]

Dramatic Genres: Historical Drama and Comedy of Manners

Haitian theater was born after the proclamation of independence in 1804. For more than a century (1804–1915), a period that Robert Cornevin refers to as "theater in the time of the bayonets" (43), historical drama and the comedy of manners or of characters shared the theatrical scene, influenced by a conception of the dramatic arts founded on French classicism, largely indebted to Aristotle's *Poetics*.[4] Indeed, seventeenth-century scholars drew from this work to theorize the two dominant dramatic genres: tragedy, the noble genre par excellence, and comedy, the rules of which were less stringent. Historical drama would thus be a Haitian adaptation of French-style tragedy, while the comedy of manners or of characters would be derived from French-style comedy. It is because of this lineage that Théodore Beaubrun, called Languichatte, was known as the "Haitian Molière."[5]

The generic duality of the theater scene in Haiti resulted in another division in terms of thematic and linguistic matters. Dramatic works drew from Haitian national history and were written almost exclusively in French, whereas comedic works depicted local customs and made extensive use of Kreyòl. The demise of the historical drama by the second half of the twentieth century coincides with the appearance of new theatrical forms written exclusively in Kreyòl.

Cornevin reminds us of the double objective of early Haitian dramatists—to provide the population with a civic education while looking for sponsors and protectors: "For these precursors, theater was the only way to make themselves known and to spread the word of great national causes to a public that was nine-tenths illiterate. Alas, it was also a way to win the favor of the rulers of the day" (63). Haitian theater continued with this double theme for at least three generations of writers, according to the periodization of Berrou/Pompilus: namely, from the start of Haitian Romanticism (1836–1870) to the Generation of the Ronde (1898–1930). Among the important dramatic authors of these three periods, we should mention Henry Chauvet (1863–1928), whose play *The Kacik's Daughter* is, according to Robert Cornevin, one of the first great works of Haitian theater.

Theater Under the US Occupation (1915–1934)

During the US Occupation, Haitian theater was a call to resistance. Dramatists brought the past back to life, depicting heroic figures in order to revive the patriotic flame. Thus, Dominique Hippolyte (1889–1967), considered one of the most important dramatic authors of the first half of the twentieth century, drew from the revolt against the French anti-revolutionary campaign known as the Leclerc expedition (1801–1803) to depict Haitian leader Jean-Jacques Dessalines in *The Torrent,* which was a historical drama alluding to the situation in the country at that time. In *The Convict,* he criticizes the politicians who played into the hands of the occupiers.

Indigénisme: The Formulation of a Haitian Theatrical Aesthetic

Haitian theater knew no great aesthetic upheavals from independence until *Indigénisme,* a movement initiated by Jean Price-Mars with his book *Thus Spoke the Uncle* in which he harshly criticized the cultural "bovarysme" of the Haitian elite while pleading for an acknowledgement of Haitian culture's African heritage, which manifests in part in the practice of Vodou and in the Kreyòl language. It is thanks to this defense of popular culture that Haitian theater went through a renewal. But the dramatists who gave the theater its second wind also drew ideas from Marxism, which had a decisive influence on Haitian intellectuals in the second half of the twentieth century. The plays that emerged from these reflections broke with a vision of theater as bourgeois entertainment, and amounted to a revolutionary project. The target audience for these dramatists were the local laborers, the proletariat, in an attempt to make them aware of their oppression.

Two dramatic authors, Félix Morisseau-Leroy (1912–1998) and Franck Fouché (1915–1978), greatly contributed to the regeneration of Haitian theater, thanks to their use of Kreyòl as a language of expression and their dramatization of elements of Vodou and of folklore, as praised by Jean Price-Mars.[6] For these engaged dramatists, popular culture, including the people's language of expression, was an important focal point. Accordingly, the Kreyòl language would be used exclusively whenever they wanted to speak to a monolingual audience. In his *For a Creole Theater*, Morisseau-Leroy emphasized the need to use Kreyòl, for the sake of believability:

> It is in the theater... that Creole has been used most successfully, because even the Haitian dramatist with the greatest affection for complex lan-

guage was forced to admit that sometimes characters speak "the language of their condition." The maids, the boys, the peasants will speak Creole in the plays by the most authentic representatives of Haitian literature in the French language. (qtd. in Cornevin 202)

Putting his own theories into practice, Morisseau-Leroy adapted Sophocles's *Antigone* into Kreyòl in 1953, transplanting the plot to a rural Haitian context. This adaptation allowed him to enrich his own theatrical practice, while staging a universal symbol of resistance. Moreover, Morisseau-Leroy saw many similarities between ancient Greece and the rural world of Haiti. He then founded the Théâtre d'Haïti at Morne Hercule and recruited actors from among the local working people. His dramaturgic practice can be connected to agit-prop theater, Teatro Campesino, or guerrilla theater, as analyzed by Augusto Boal in *Theater of the Oppressed*.[7]

Fouché's Ethnodrama

Like Morisseau-Leroy, Franck Fouché began his theatrical career with the Kreyòl translation/adaptation of a Greek tragedy, Sophocles's *Oedipus Rex*, but he turned from Greek myths to the Haitian myths present in Vodou. His reflections on the dramatic potential of Vodou resulted in one of the most complete treatises on Haitian theater, entitled *Vodou et théâtre: Pour un théâtre populaire* (which translates to *Vodou and Theater: For a Popular Theater*). Fouché developed his ideas starting from two complementary notions: *ethnodrama*, defined by the psychiatrist Louis Mars as a phenomenon connected to both drama and religion, and *pretheater*, which André Schaeffner defines as all spectacular practices containing theatrical elements. In Fouché's view, "Vodou would be defined as the matrix of a future theater, the framework capable of one day producing a theater" (22). The exploration of Vodou would enable the creation of a new theatrical language and the awareness of the spectator, because this theater, "while referring...to the social conflicts that it portrays, would simultaneously be an open stage for the collective awakening" (42). The theatrical elements of Vodou are costumes, dance, sacred chants, the peristyle, the equivalent of the Greek theatron, and the possession crisis. Furthermore, Fouché compares the actor to the possessed person being mounted by the *lwas*. Nevertheless, far from wanting to demonstrate an adherence to Vodou, Franck Fouché proposes a critical staging of that religion. Thereby, he shares Jacques Roumain's ambivalence regarding Vodou: it is a key part of Haitian culture, but as ideology in the Althusserian sense—as internalized rules and norms—he considers it to function also as a mode of alienation.

With Fouché, theater looks back to its religious sources. According to most researchers, including Nietzsche, Greek tragedy was derived from the rites observed in honor of Dionysus. Furthermore, modern theorists like Brook and Grotowski have called for a return to ritual in theater. The originality of Fouché's approach is to have proposed Vodou as a springboard for the transformation of Haitian theater. Inspired by Vodou, founded on the popular carnival, his theater is a total spectacle, a baroque blend of dances and chants that employs various semiotic systems.[8]

Bouqui au Paradis (1967)

This play was originally written in Kreyòl, as *Bouki nan paradi*, before being translated into French by Jacqueline Fouché, in collaboration with the author.[9] Both versions depict the duo from Haitian folklore: Bouqui, the fool, and Malice, the trickster. Bouqui symbolizes the naive peasant who is easily duped. In his article entitled "Folklore in the Theatre of Franck Fouché," Carrol F. Coates reminds us that the material of both versions is drawn from popular culture:

> In the two plays, Fouché draws inspiration from legends involving Bouki and Malis. The Haitian legends about Bouki and Malis, which originated in West African and Bantu folk tales of "Lièvre," relate how the clever hare repeatedly dupes his slow-witted companion, the hyena. Fouché had available the ethnographic work of Price-Mars and of Suzanne Comhaire-Sylvain, although the latter's compilation of tales, *Le roman de Bouqui*, was published over a decade after the composition of *Bouki nan paradi*. (256–257)

Structure

In terms of structure, *Bouqui au Paradis* breaks with traditional theater. Instead of traditional denominations like *act* or *scene*, Fouché divides his play into four *lies*, the last two of which are subdivided into *tableaux*, and one *truth*, which also contains two *tableaux*.[10] The word *tableau* refers to a theater in which the dramatic progression is of secondary importance. Rather than unraveling in a logical manner, the action resembles a succession of snapshots, hence the impression of discontinuity given by this play. Patrice Pavis notes that

> the appearance of the tableau is linked to that of the epic elements in the drama: the dramatist does not focus on a crisis, he breaks down dura-

> tion, offers fragments of a discontinuous time. He is not interested in slow development, but in disruptions of action. . . . [I]nstead of dramatic movement, he opts for the photographic capturing of a scene. (345)

Malice encounters Bouqui near "a great dwelling" (101) and convinces him that they are at the gates of Paradise.[11] Bouqui erupts with joy at the idea of being able to satisfy his legendary gluttony. Maître-Terre, who embodies the people who steal peasant lands, arrives and Malice passes him off as General Saint Peter. Then the action takes place in Bouqui's courtyard, where Malice announces to Bouqui that Papa Bondieu wants to offer him Saint Peter's job, because the latter is eyeing Saint Peter's position. While both are on their way to Paradise, Malice asks his "compère" to go and wash himself in a blue spring, in order to appear acceptable in front of Papa Bondieu. When Bouqui returns, Malice, who is posing as Papa Bondieu, tells him that they have arrived in Paradise. Bouqui will indeed have Saint Peter's job, but he must be patient. After coming up with a plan with Dilara, the "hougan," to steal Bouqui's money, Malice meets Bouqui and asks him how his job is going. The fool "compère" replies that Papa Bondieu has promised it to him. But Malice tells him to stop waiting and to dismiss Saint Peter with Dilara's help. The hougan supposedly bewitches Saint Peter and is paid handsomely by Bouqui, who leaves. Malice strikes Dilara to steal the money from him. The first tableau of the "first truth" shows Malice attempting to reassure Maître-Terre, who is furious because a "juif bourré" was then was left in his pathway.[12] The denouement is approaching. In the second tableau, the play takes on a collective dimension: anonymous voices of men and women comment on the action, like the choruses of ancient theater. Mrs. Bouqui is abused. Far from being his usual passive self, Bouqui strikes Maître-Terre and Malice. He is quite proud of this act, which liberates him from the world of illusion in which he had been trapped.

The instructor may point out the link between these terms (*lie, truth*) and theater as a play on masks and faces, truth and falsehood. Indeed, the four lies form the nucleus of the action and correspond to the strategies Malice uses to fool Bouqui, whereas the "first truth" resolves the drama. The play thus follows a movement that goes from illusion toward the discovery of truth, from ignorance to knowledge. At the end of the play, the roles of Bouqui and Malice are reversed: Bouqui has become an active character. The fact that he alone occupies the whole stage attests to his new status. Henceforth, Malice is absent from the stage; he therefore no longer exists in a dramaturgical sense. Nevertheless, the dramatist hardly touches on Bouqui's awareness process. This absence of causality falls within the dramaturgy of discontinuity, one of the characteristics of modern theater.[13]

Dramaturgical Processes

Dramatic Irony

The main process that forms the basis for the comedic effects in *Bouqui in Paradise* is dramatic irony, which creates a sort of second level of theater, a theater within theater.[14] Pavis reminds us of the link between dramatic irony and the double communication of theater: "Dramatic irony is often linked to the *dramatic situation*. It is felt by the spectators when they perceive elements of the plot that remain hidden from the character and which prevent him from acting knowingly" (180). By doing so, the dramatist confers a certain superiority on the spectators, who are then able to laugh at the character, who does not know what is going on around him.

In Haitian culture, the roles of Bouqui and Malice are codified: the former is constantly duped by his crafty "compère."[15] In this sense, Malice's name suits him well, as it connotes duplicity. All of his actions and his words convey some theatricality insofar as they do not correspond to reality. It is thus fitting that Fouché employs the word *lie* to designate the events preceding the denouement. He portrays Malice as an actor playing the role that tradition has given to him: creating a world of illusion to fool Bouqui. This manipulation also shows, as an indirect result, the power of words to alienate those lacking a critical mind. Malice's first lie spawns the others right up until Bouqui's revolt. Malice initiates his chimeric universe in the first stage direction, where he "shows Bouqui a dead tree with rags hanging from its branches" (102). The fool indeed sees "dead tree and some rags on it" (102) and says so. But Malice retorts that it is a flag. Bouqui acquiesces. Thus, the cunning "compère's" phantasmagoric world takes shape. The dead tree bearing the rags becomes the great doorway displaying the flag of Paradise. The illusions come one after the other according to an irrefutable logic: a dog who "is little more than skin and bones" (102) is, according to Malice, "a fattened pig" (102). The illusionist counts on the gluttony of his "compère" to create a nonexistent land flowing with milk and honey, a Cockaigne Country: "Here, every piece of earth is a sweet potato plantation; the thickets are mango trees; all cacti bear fruit" (102–103). At the idea that he will have a feast, Bouqui erupts with joy: "We're going to pig out! We're going to stuff our faces! After that, I can die of indigestion. No more misery for me!" (103). Then he starts to dance while singing a traditional Haitian song that thanks Bondieu for putting an end to misery by sending rain. It is worth noting the coherence of this universe, which functions as a sustained metaphor. Paradise serves as a matrix for the other lies that Bouqui swallows right up until the "first truth." He interprets everything in reference to that blessed place. Also, he takes the raspy song of a band of vagabonds for a celestial hymn: "These angels and these saints sing like nightingales" (104).

The other lies, such as Bondieu's decision to dismiss Saint Peter and to give his job to Bouqui and the necessity for the latter to eliminate Saint Peter by magical means, flow from this matrix. All the tricks constitute dramatic ironies, which create an effect of overhang and confer upon the hall a "privileged position" (Prunier 22). The instructor could ask students to identify the different stages of this dramatic irony: its beginning, its exploitation by the playwright and its end. This last stage corresponds to the awareness of Bouqui.

Amplification of Stage Direction

The second process that contributes to the modernity of *Bouqui au Paradis* is the amplification of stage direction. Anne Ubersfeld has highlighted the importance of this trait in contemporary theater: "Contemporary performance often sees an inflation of written stage direction, the stage direction serving to construct a particular space that corresponds to a text and the author often encroaching upon the director, in order to write a serious autonomous text" (31). For his part, Michel Viegnes explains the proliferation of stage direction in modern theater: "First of all, these plays are written to be read as well as performed. Also, the avant-garde dramatic author is no longer content with his role as writer. He wants, in a sense, to partly assume the directing of his play" (37).

Nevertheless, unlike in traditional theater, where the initial stage directions give information on the setting of the dramatic action, the dramatis personae, their relationships, and sometimes the causes of their conflicts, those in *Bouqui au Paradis* are quite vague. Fouché is content to name the protagonists without indicating their roles or relationships. Other characters are indicated vaguely: a man, a second, a woman, a second.

The instructor can explain that this imprecision is justified by the fact that the Haitian spectator is well acquainted with the adventures of the Bouqui/Malice duo. The dramatist did not judge it necessary to give details regarding these characters. Likewise, for Maître-Terre and Le Baka, he counts on his cultural complicity with the Haitian spectator, as he does not say anything about their roles. For the Haitian spectator, Maître-Terre and Le Baka carry their dramaturgic programs within their names. Maître-Terre can only be a large landowner, ready to use any form of violence to dispossess the peasantry. Le Baka comes straight out of popular belief: this evil spirit, which might symbolically be associated with the forces of repression, will be a natural ally of Maître-Terre. Thus, the characters' roles will be distributed in accordance with the Bouqui/Malice duo.

The second initial stage direction—"The scene is not situated within time"—is somewhat baffling, as it seems to substitute time for space. While pointing out its unusual meaning, the instructor can insist on its function within the symbolism of the play, which thus takes on a universal value. The moral of *Bouqui au Paradis* applies to all of humanity, to all men and all women falling victim to deception.

The amplification of stage direction only begins after the initial instructions. After that, the expressive and kinetic stage directions seem to compete with the dramatic text.[16] Because of their strategic position, only the first and last stage directions will be considered in this study. They enable us to see the evolution of the character Bouqui. Here is the first:

> A great dwelling.... When the curtains rise, Uncle Bouqui, looking disoriented is walking along. He gives the impression that he is looking for something or someone. The character's attitude, his gestures clearly indicate that we are in the presence of an oaf. A moment later Malice appears. By his approach, we see that he is a clever devil, a cunning "compère." Noticing Bouqui, Malice acts surprised and clutches his sides to burst out laughing. (101)

This long descriptive stage direction highlights the opposition between the two main characters. It functions as a preamble for their action. Bouqui is presented as someone who has lost his way. He is "looking disoriented."

We should note that the adjective "égaré" used in the French text exists in Kreyòl as a noun, and is a synonym for *simpleton*. In contrast, Malice appears as "a clever devil," "a cunning 'compère,'" which is to say a trickster. Furthermore, he "acts surprised." This note highlights his manipulative side. He is an actor conscious of his game, prepared to carry out the role of illusionist that tradition has bestowed upon him. It is understandable that his interactions with Bouqui are characterized as *lies*.

The second stage direction is part of the denouement of the play, after Bouqui has discovered Malice's deceptions. The amplification of this extra-dramatic passage illustrates the dramatist's wish to make his voice heard, to intervene in the action, telling rather than showing. The novelistic thus competes with the dramatic:

> A few moments later, a noise erupts. We hear: Stop him, stop Malice! Don't let him escape.... Bouqui listens carefully to the footsteps hurrying in his direction. He looks surreptitiously and sees Malice, running like a maniac. He waits patiently for the "compère" to pass to give him a

good blow with a stick. Malice indeed passes by. Bouqui does as planned. Malice crumples under the force of the blow. . . . Bouqui is happy with himself for what he has done. He bursts out laughing in triumph. His chest swells up, satisfied. Suddenly, he notices the ladder leaning against the wall. He takes a few steps toward it and, gradually, he climbs it. . . . The ten characters who were singing at the end of the third lie come back onto stage to sing the following couplets.[17] (136)

This stage direction shows Bouqui's evolution. Whereas in the previous tableaux he had been a marionette in the hands of Malice, he alone now occupies the whole stage. Admittedly, he seems to miss the presence of his "compère," but he quickly becomes aware of his new state and accepts his solitude, and thus his liberty. The blows he deals to Malice are the fruit of an autonomous decision. Moreover, the ladder he climbs symbolizes his awakening. A figure of ascension, the ladder refers to Bouqui's exit from the darkness that had been keeping him prisoner. Liberated from Malice's condescending tutelage, Bouqui can finally stand up straight like a man. In this sense, the ladder is the symbol of a super humanity.

These stage directions fall within "what Bakhtin calls the novelization of the dramatic form" (Sarrazac 188), which is to say the integration of novelistic elements within theater, such as description and narration. Sarrazac also sees within the amplification of stage direction a form of *epicization*, a process that allows the dramatist to "introduce a break in the dramatic action as defined by Aristotle in his principles of unity, continuity or causality. Fiction thus transforms into reflection" (76). For Mélissa Simard, it is thanks to this proliferation of stage directions that Franck Fouché regenerated Haitian theater:

> By appealing to scenic indications in the hopes of inciting the performance-ritual, the movement of bodies and the theatrical rhythm, Fouché initiates a renewal of the dramatic art. Thus, he contributes to giving the actor's body the place that is returned to it in the advent of a theatrical ritual ensuring that this corporality is expressed in its universal dimension. (202)

The instructor can ask students to consider the functions of the stage directions. For example, are they narrative, explicative or descriptive?

Symbolism of the Play

The couplets sung by the chorus express the symbolism of the play (cf. note 16). Bouqui is the figure of the laborer duped by those who use lies and illusions to keep him in his place. But it is not inevitable. The marginalized can deflect the spell of the obscurantist forces in order to taste liberty, like the enslaved Haitians who broke their chains. Of course, in the logic of theater, which permits discontinuity, Fouché does not show the event that led Bouqui to become aware of his situation. Nevertheless, he transforms a folkloric tale into political theater in the service of the masses. The intervention of the chorus, which enlarges the dramatic action to the scale of the community, illustrates in its own way the political scope of the play. This choral aspect is another characteristic of epicization, a mark of the author's intervention in the dramatic space by means of "stories, suppression of dramatic tension, breakdown of illusion and speech of the narrator, mass scenes and intervention of the chorus" (Pavis 117). Along with politics practiced by buffoons, the dramatist also denounces Vodou when it is used as a manipulative force that allies with the powerful in order to dispossess the people. That is why Malice, the master illusionist, is not fooled when Dilara brags of his powers as a "hougan." He contests the science of the supposed magician in these terms: "What work, what money, what science? You think you're talking to a simpleton. Save your pitch for Uncle Bouqui. Me, I'm Malice! . . . Getting the simple-minded to take a stinking bath; playacting, preparing a filthy infusion made from leaves of the thickets, that's your science?" (125) As a professional illusionist, Malice knows how to unmask him. Paradoxically, here he is acting as spokesman for Fouché, who wrote in *Vodou et théâtre: Pour un théâtre populaire* that he drew from "national traditions [in order to] flush out their negative side and get rid of superstitions, and erroneous perceptions of reality" (93).

Conclusion

Bouqui au Paradis exemplifies the dramatic art of Franck Fouché. In terms of content, this play, inspired by folklore and popular traditions, offers a reflection on the sociopolitical situation in Haiti. The playwright definitively breaks with traditional theater to create a work of popular theater. In this context, Fouché's ambivalence regarding the Vodou religion is worth highlighting. As a vital part of Haitian culture, Vodou is an essential part of any artistic or literary production, but Fouché views it as contributing to alienation. That is why he does not hesitate to compare Vodou to a theatrical illusion through the character of Malice, who is himself a master of illusion. In terms of form, the main theatrical process is dramatic irony, the various tricks that Malice uses to cheat Bouqui and to lure him into doing what he wants him to do. Nevertheless, Bouqui frees himself from the foolish role conferred on him by tradition as he ends up rebelling against his abuser. This revolt is the central lesson of the play: the Haitian people, often duped by politicians because of their supposed ignorance, will one day put an end to their tricks.

Haitians generally love to discuss politics. This play is the quintessential representation of Haitian popular theater that reflects the mindset of politicians who make false promises to the people. Like those politicians, Malice promises Bouqui Paradise, but it is just an illusion. The play alludes to the fact that the political realm is very much about showing off. It reflects a life philosophy perhaps inspired by the history of marronage in Haitian culture that is known as "le mouricorisme," meaning "act like a dead person," from the verb "mourir," to die. This ideology can be positive, because it can represent a survival strategy for the have-nots as they encounter the violence and selfishness of the two percent who control the country. For all these reasons, *Bouqui in Paradise* can be an effective tool to enable students to have complex conversations about religion, class, language, illusion, and politics.

Course Outline

Introduction to Modern Haitian Theater: *Bouqui in Paradise* by Franck Fouché

Objective

The main objective of this course is to discover modern Haitian theater through the play entitled *Bouqui in Paradise* (1967) by Franck Fouché. Excerpts from the short story entitled *Dit de Bouqui et de Malice,* published in *Romancero aux étoiles* (1960) by Jacques Stephen Alexis, can be read to give another point of view on this myth.

Learning Outcomes

At the end of the course, students will be able to:

- analyze and explain both orally and in written form the main theatrical processes in *Bouqui in Paradise*
- describe the relation between the play and Haitian society
- Create their own version of the myth (in any genre)

Method of Presentation

Lectures, discussions, oral presentations.

Primary Texts (required)

Fouché, Franck. *Bouqui au Paradis*. Translated from Creole to French by Jacqueline Fouché, Montréal, Éditions de Sainte-Marie, 1967.
Alexis, Jacques Stephen. "Dit de Bouqui et de Malice." *Romancero aux étoiles*, Paris, Gallimard, 1960, p. 17–43.

Essays and Related Studies

Coates F., Carrol. "Folklore in the Theatre of Franck Fouché," *Theatre Research International*, vol. 21, no. 3, Autumn 1996, pp. 256–261.
Comhaire-Sylvain, Suzanne. *Le roman de Bouqui*. Leméac, 1978.
Fouché, Franck. *Vodou et théâtre: Pour un théâtre populaire*. Mémoire d'Encrier, (1976) 2008.
Pavis, Patrice. *Dictionnaire du théâtre*. Dunod, 1997.
Price-Mars, Jean. *Ainsi parla l'Oncle*. Mémoire d'encrier, (1928) 2009.
Prunier, Michel. *L'analyse du texte de théâtre*. Nathan, 2003.
Sarrazac, J.-P. *Lexique du drame moderne et contemporain*. Les Éditions Circé, 2005.
Simard, Mélissa. "Le théâtre populaire selon Franck Fouché: éclatement dramaturgique et résistance." *Journal of Haitian Studies*, Special Issue on Vodou and Créolité, vol. 18, no. 2, Fall 2012, pp. 196–211.

Projects and Questions for Discussion

1) Ask students to create a comparison between Bouqui and Malice and other folktales in the Caribbean, the United States (especially the US South), and West Africa. To prepare students to do this project, instructors should provide some historical and cultural background in regard to the play. Instructors should explore with students the significance of the fact that the play was written in Kreyòl in the context of the Indigenist movement initiated by Jean Price-Mars. This movement was highly critical of the Haitian elite, who denied their African roots and wanted to claim French culture. Price-Mars was instead promoting local culture, especially Vodou, the Kreyòl language, oral traditions, folktales, and proverbs. The play is born of and inspired by Haitian oral traditions, especially the adventures of Bouqui and Malice, two characters that have their roots in the hyena and hare in West African folktales. The African origin of these folktales is evident in the fact that the pair are found by other names in other Caribbean folktales. For instance, according to Maximilien Laroche,

Maryse Condé believes that characters from Caribbean folktales, Lapin (Rabbit) and Zamba, as well as Jean Esprit (literally translated as smart or witty Jean) and Jean Sot (literally translated as stupid Jean), are reminiscent of Malice and Bouqui (1968). Students can also be asked to find examples of the uses of Haitian folklore in the play.

2) With your group (or partner), analyze several characters based on their defining traits. For example, the character Bouqui is defined by his naivety. In general, why do you think focusing on character traits is so important for playwrights? Does theater offer a form of performance that explores human traits differently from other media (novels, cinema)?

3) With your group (or partner), map out Bouqui's evolution in the play. Where do you see key moments in his character development?

4) Stage directions are usually narrative, descriptive, and explicative. Using several scenes, discuss which stage direction is the most useful for the development of the scene. Provide reasons for your answers.

5) Instructors can ask students to give concrete examples of how this play can be read as a political satire in the context of Haiti, both in the period in which the play was written—under the Duvalier dictatorship—and today.

6) Dramatic irony means that there is complicity between the dramatist and the spectator. Where do you see instances of dramatic irony in the play? The dramatic irony that Fouché used is often ambiguous. What do you think are the reasons for this?

7) The very foundation of theater is the relationship between illusion and "reality." How can Vodou and politics, two central themes in the play, be interpreted as playing on this dichotomy? In order to explore how illusion works here, instructors can ask students to examine who is fooled by whom in the play. How is the illusion of Paradise represented in the play? Provide concrete examples that show that Malice is a master of illusion (see, for example, the various lies he tells Bouqui). The play also highlights the complicity between the playwright and the spectator. The latter is able to laugh at Bouqui since he sees all of Malice's schemes. Why is this dramatic irony ambiguous?

8) How does Malice use language to overpower Bouqui in the play? In general, how can language be used in society to outsmart people?

9) Analyze the various lies in the play. What functions do they serve?

10) How is religion represented in the play? How is the practice of Vodou shown to be connected to theatrical performance? Does the play suggest or point to tensions between Vodou and Christianity? Is the portrayal of Vodou positive or negative, or a mix of the two? Find places in the text where Malice challenges the powers of Dilara, the "hougan."

11) Ask students to analyze the happy ending of the play, when Bouqui becomes aware that he has changed from someone who has on a blindfold of sorts to someone who can see fully.

12) Analyze the character of Bouqui. How can we describe Bouqui? Can you think of some examples of another character you have encountered in popular culture that resembles Bouqui? Elaborate on Bouqui's evolution in the play from beginning to end. Does he learn anything?

13) What can we make of Malice's character? On the one hand, he is the master trickster and master of illusion, but on the other, he denounces the "hougan" character, who is also a liar and a trickster. What makes Malice a master of illusion?

14) What have you learned about Haitian folklore from reading *Bouqui au Paradis*?

15) What does this play teach us about human nature? Are there certain "moral codes" that we learn through the characters? Define these.

Notes

1. Even in Haiti, the teaching of Haitian literature does not escape the exclusivity of the novel. Theater continues to be neglected by those who define education policies.

2. This overview is necessarily incomplete, given the richness of Haitian theater. In his work published in 1973, Robert Cornevin counted 233 plays written by 80 authors. Fifty years later, the number of plays is at least 400.

3. According to a preliminary note, the French translation was by Jacqueline Fouché in collaboration with the author. The text that I have used appeared in a collection entitled *L'Haïtien*, published in Montréal in 1968 by Éditions de Sainte-Marie.

4. Although Aristotle played a leading role in the formation of classicism, particularly in the realm of the dramatic arts, it is known that some rules of tragedy, for example the unity of time and place, have been wrongly attributed to him.

5. Théodore Beaubrun (1918–1998), called Languichatte, was an author, an actor, and a director.

6. It is worth mentioning that Vodou as a literary theme was not new to this period, nor was Creole as a language of literary expression. *Mimola*, the first Haitian novel dealing with Vodou, was published in 1906 by Antoine Innocent (1873–1960); *Cric Crac*, a Creole adaptation of the fables of La Fontaine by Georges Sylvain (1866–1925), dates from 1901.

7. Inspired by Che Guevara and by Happening techniques, the guerrilla theater enacts spontaneous performances in public places in order to draw attention to social and political problems.

8. In the continuity of this avant-garde theater, Franketienne must be mentioned as perhaps the only great Haitian dramatist still alive today. He can be considered the heir to Morisseau-Leroy and Fouché because of the importance of Creole, the myths of Vodou, and the sociopolitical critiques in his work.

9. The version used in this article was published in a collective work entitled *L'Haïtien* (Les Éditions de Sainte-Marie, 1968). The other texts are: *Portrait de l'Haïtien*, written by Maximilien Laroche, and *Sang de bêtes, Ventre d'hommes, suite poétique* by Charles Tardieu-Dehoux.
10. The denouement of the play is called "Première vérité" (First Truth) but there are no others.
11. All English translations of *Bouqui au Paradis* in this chapter are by Matthew Robertshaw.
12. A marionette that is struck during Carnival.
13. J.-P. Sarrazac speaks of the "crisis of the fable" (78) and "death of the beautiful animal" (31) to describe this dramaturgy of discontinuity.
14. In the case of this play, it is not the *theater within theater*, which consists of setting one play within another, but rather a sort of generalized theatricalness. Thus, the spectator is well aware from the first tableau that there is interplay between appearance and reality in the fictional universe of the play.
15. Anne Ubersfeld uses the expression "role actoriel" (actor role) (*Lire le théâtre* 131).
16. Expressive stage direction "specifies the effect that the author hopes the text will produce" (Prunier 16), while kinesic stage direction gives information regarding the movement of characters on stage.
17. Here are the couplets: Uncle Bouqui, oh, where are you climbing so high / The "nègre's" heaven is on earth / Look. You will enter the entrails of life on foot / Now your forehead wants to kiss the sun / [. . .] The general "coumbite" has already begun / No longer will a Bouqui let himself be fooled by Malice / the fragile fan of clutched fingers / on the palm of a hand places a fist on life (136–137).

Works Cited

Barthes, Roland. "Réflexions sur un manuel." *L'enseignement de la littérature*. A. De Boeck-Duculot, 1981, pp. 64–71.
Berrou, Raphaël, and Pradel Pompilus. *Histoire de la littérature haïtienne*. Éditions Caraïbes, vols. 1 and 2, 1975; vol. 3, 1977.
Boal, Augusto. *Théâtre de l'opprimé*. La Découverte, 1996.
Coates, Carrol F. "Folklore in the Theatre of Franck Fouché." *Theatre Research International*, vol. 21, no. 3, 1996, pp. 256–261.
Cornevin, Robert. *Le théâtre haïtien: des origines à nos jours*. Leméac, 1973.
Fouché, Franck. *Bouqui au Paradis*. Les Éditions de Sainte-Marie, 1967.
———. *Vodou et théâtre: pour un théâtre populaire*. Mémoire d'Encrier, (1976) 2008.
Hyppolite, Dominique. *Le Forçat*. Jouve, 1933.
———. *Le Torrent*. Presses Nationales, 1967.
Laroche, Maximilien. *L'Haïtien*. Les Éditions de Sainte-Marie, 1968.
———. *Juan Bobo, Jan Sot, Ti Jan et Bad John: figures littéraires de la Caraïbe*. Grelca, 1991.
Pavis, Patrice. *Dictionnaire du théâtre*. Dunod, 1997.
Price-Mars, Jean. *Ainsi parla l'Oncle*. Mémoire d'encrier, (1928) 2009.
Prunier, Michel. *L'analyse du texte de théâtre*. Nathan, 2003.
Romane, Jean-Jacques. *La mort de Christophe*. N.p., 1818.
Sarrazac, J.-P. *Lexique du drame moderne et contemporain*. Les Éditions Circé, 2005.

Simard, Mélissa. "Le théâtre populaire selon Franck Fouché: éclatement dramaturgique et résistance haïtienne." *The Journal of Haitian Studies*, vol. 18, no. 2, 2012, pp. 194–209.
Ubersfeld, Anne. *Lire le théâtre*. Éditions Sociales, 1978.
———. *Les termes clés de l'analyse du théâtre*. Seuil, 1996.
Viegnes, Michel. *Le théâtre: problématiques essentielles*. Hatier, 1995.

4

Engaging Haiti through Art and Religion

CÉCILE ACCILIEN

> I cannot imagine a Vodou temple without its cultural drums, its sacred arts and crafts collection that beautifies it for the ancestral lwas. By the same token, I cannot envision a cathedral without its embodiment of the architectural and artistic beauty and sculptures of saints produced by artists. Through my artistic viewpoint, each Haitian Vodou temple is a micro-museum that incubates the fragments of Haitian collective memory.

These words, spoken by the Haitian artist Ulrick Jean-Pierre, set the scene for my discussion of Haitian art and religious traditions. So closely linked are art and religion—particularly Vodou—in Haitian society and culture that we cannot think about one without considering the other. And when we study these two major pillars of Haitian culture together, we can better understand the richness and complexity of Haiti itself.

In the European context, visual art and religion are often studied together; in studies of Haitian culture and society, however, art and religion are less often combined (and this is true in the popular mindset, as well as in teaching and scholarship)—owing, I think, in part to racist and imperialist attitudes toward Vodou. Vodou is typically viewed outside Haiti as something terrifying and ultimately unknowable, while Haitian visual art is seen as unthreatening, an unlikely source of revolution. I push back against both of these popular misconceptions—art as tame, and Vodou as frightening—as I propose ways to teach Haitian art and religion together. The two are, indeed, tightly intertwined, as we will see, and considering the relationships between them can generate creative and transformative avenues through which students gain more profound understandings of Haitian society and culture.

The arts are a feature of everyday life in Haiti, and Haitian artists and writers remain among the most prolific in the Caribbean, despite the nation's low literacy rate and an economy that limits the ability of Haitians in Haiti to buy art. In Haiti, many people are artists, but they may not identify themselves as such. Art is everywhere, and it transcends economic and social class. And Haitian artists often do not separate their work from the nation's past and present. For art historian Michel-Philippe Lerebours, Jacques Stephen Alexis's notion of *réalisme merveilleux* is the best way to characterize the unique vision that binds Haitian artists:

> Magic realism ... is all of Haitian art that, without losing touch with reality, bathes in dreams. It is all of Haitian art that constructs a fantastical world from the banalities of everyday life. The dream is certainly not always a happy dream; but even the rough, purulent and painful nightmare is still a part of the dream. (qtd. in Célius 286–87)

Perhaps it is partly because Haiti has such a long, complex, tumultuous history that the nation's artists and writers feel constantly compelled to tell its stories. And often these stories are directly linked to Vodou practices.[1] Haiti's very foundation as an independent nation is connected to the Vodou religion, for it was during the 1791 Ceremony of Bois Caïman that enslaved Haitians made a pact to fight for their freedom. There is a common saying that Haiti is 90 percent Christian and 100 percent Vodou. Whether the claim is true or not is irrelevant. The point is that it shows the importance of Vodou in Haitian culture. A friend who was an artist and a *manbo*, or Vodou priestess, once told me, "Vodou is art and spirit is art."[2] Vodou, as both religious and aesthetic practice, is filled with colors, rituals, and symbols. An *ounfò*, or Vodou temple, contains various items that serve specific ritual and aesthetic purposes, and are also works of art in and of themselves. For example, the chambers is a space that contains altars with ritual objects, among them gourds, drums, *asons*,[3] banners, beaded flags, and *vèvè* drawings. The vèvè are iconic symbols drawn on the floor by a manbo or hougan (a Vodou priest) with ashes, cornmeal, or flour prior to a Vodou ceremony to invite the *lwas* or spirits to come down to earth.

As these descriptions suggest, art is found everywhere in Haiti, from temples and museums to the grafitti in the streets and on the tap-taps or public buses, which are elaborately decorated with proverbs depicting people's beliefs and hopes. Haitian artists, whether they are painters, photographers, or decorative artists, function in Haiti as guardians of memory. They are inspired by the landscape, water, vegetation, soil—the very topography of the land—and religion, which constitutes a crucial part of everyday reality.

Works of art are intricate cultural signifiers, and art is therefore a crucial tool for teaching about the complexity of Haiti. By engaging with Haiti's long tradition of art, which has spanned multiple genres, students become visually immersed in Haiti's history and current realities. As they examine this work, they can consider questions such as, What are the intersections among art, social class, history, economy, and religion? Is art being used as a vehicle to promote religious ideologies and/or economic, social, and environmental equity and sustainability? If so, in what contexts? What are some of the challenges in trying to effect social change through art? What are some of the ways in which the work of a visual artist can challenge or uphold religious beliefs and transmit collective knowledge differently from that of a writer?

For the benefit of teachers who are interested in developing students' engagement with Haitian culture and society using the visual impact of art coupled with an awareness of the significance of Vodou—but who may be unfamiliar with the basics of Vodou and/or the Haitian artistic tradition—I will offer a synopsis of the Vodou religion and its role as a cornerstone of Haitian culture. I will then provide an overview of Haitian painting, focusing specifically on its relationship with religion and the influence of religion on artists' practices, processes, and thematic choices. While I acknowledge the importance of sculpture, photography, decorative arts, and architecture, for the sake of space I will not discuss them here. However, I encourage instructors to go beyond the frame of this essay to investigate the wide variety of Haitian artistic production, much of which is likely to inspire students' interest. I touch on Haitian art as tourist art, and then discuss the work of some contemporary Haitian artists who refuse the dynamics contained in a simplified, globalized tourist art, investigating the role that Vodou plays in their work. Throughout, I suggest approaches to teaching this material, and conclude with a lesson plan and extensive resources that instructors anywhere can use to introduce their students to Haitian art.

Vodou as Religion and as Culture: A Short History

Religion is an important, if historically contested, feature of daily life for a great number of people in Haiti, and it forms a central part of Haitian artists' aesthetic, vision, inspiration, and influence. Christianity and Vodou have a long history of coexistence in Haiti, but unlike Christianity, Vodou has faced significant national and international condemnation, and as a religion, discrimination comparable to that practiced against Haiti as a whole. The "anti-superstition" campaign known as "rejeté" (or "rejected"), which took place in the 1940s during the government of Elie Lescot, was supported by the United

States government and by Catholic churches. It brutally destroyed a countless number of Vodou temples, and several symbolically central trees associated with Vodou ceremonies were chopped down. The rejeté also resulted in the theft of lands of Vodou practitioners and many other abuses. The goal of this campaign against Vodou—the roots of which dated back to the earliest days of the slave trade—was to make Catholicism the sole religion of Haiti.

"Vodou" is a Fon word from Benin (formerly Dahomey) meaning spirit or sacred object. In Vodou we find a complex rapport between the natural and supernatural world, the living and the dead. Vodou offers ways of explaining unexplainable events, and reliance on the gods makes it possible to establish and maintain order, avoiding chaos. In this sense Vodou is no different from other religions. But an element that sets Vodou apart is the fact that it does not put forth a governing authority, a single centralized figurehead such as the pope in the Catholic Church. Instead we find multiple religious communities led by a manbo or hougan. The manbo or hougan has a variety of tasks, including performing ceremonies, healing, reading dreams, and initiating new members. Lwas are the backbone of the Vodou religion, and during a ceremony, a *sèvitè*, or devotee, participates in a *sèvis lwa* (service to the spirit).

The Vodou religion is based on Bondye (God) as the supreme being. Other Vodou spiritual beings fall into three categories. The lwas or spirits govern the major forces of the universe and play an important role in everyday life; they interact with human beings, and during a ceremony they can mount or "possess" a person to whom they may give a specific message about an aspect of their lives, or about their family members or friends. Second are the *marasa* (sometimes spelled marassa), or twins, a set of forces that exist in contradiction—for example, good and bad, rich and poor, happy and unhappy. They are children who died young and became lwas. It is believed by many that people who are born twins have certain special powers. Finally, there are *lèmò*, the dead, the souls of family members who have died but have not yet been reclaimed by the family. It is important to honor and care for them through specific rituals and ceremonies.

In Vodou, the lwas or spirits that a devotee serves are divided into three families: Rada, Petro, and Gede, each associated with their own sites and colors. The lwas have distinct personalities and duties. The Rada lwas originate in Africa; these spirits were honored by the Africans brought in chains to the New World. They are associated with the color white. The Petro lwas originate in Haiti and are generally associated with the color red. The Gede lwas are associated with the color black and are believed to transport dead souls.

Since enslaved people were not allowed to practice their own religions, it is not surprising that they chose to perform reverence for the Catholic saints while remaining faithful to their own gods. In the Vodou religion there are many Catholic counterparts to the lwas, such as the different Èzilis representing the various Virgin Marys, Saint Patrick as Damballah, Saint Peter as Legba, and Saint James as Ogun. Vodou is thus a mix of religions, rituals, and symbols from various cultures. For example, Legba, whose Catholic counterparts are Saint Peter, Saint Lazarus, and Saint Anthony, is the guardian of the gate. He must be present during all ceremonies because his role is to allow communication between the spirits and the devotees. A Vodou ceremony generally begins with an invocation to Atigba Lebon, whose primary role is to open the gates that separate people and spirits. He is the intermediary between the lwas and humans.

Lasirèn, also known as Èzili in the waters, is a beautiful, charming woman, a seductress who can bring wealth and luck. Her Catholic counterparts are Mary, star of the sea, and Saint Martha. She is the goddess of the sea, which she rules with Agwe, her husband. We can understand why she is so important in Haitian culture when we remember that modern-day Haiti is part of an island; before the division of the island into Haiti and the Dominican Republic, Haiti was completely surrounded by water. Water is important on so many levels. The enslaved had to endure the Middle Passage across the Atlantic to the New World. With the crushing economic and political hardships that Haiti has been facing for centuries, Haitians must often cross waters to find opportunities *lòt bò dlo* (on the other side of the water). So Lasirèn and Agwe are constantly there and Haitian people call out to them for protection at sea.

Azaka, also called Papa Zaka or Kouzen Zaka, is the god of agriculture and harvest. His Catholic counterparts are Saint Isidor and Saint Andrew. Bawon Samdi is in charge of the kingdom of the Barons, or the spirits of the dead. He is portrayed wearing a black suit and black hat and holding a skull. He is associated with Saint Andrew and Saint Expedite. Danbala and Ayida Wedo are the male and female lwas of happiness and health. Dambala's Catholic counterpart is Saint Patrick. Ayida's counterpart is Our Lady of the Immaculate Conception and her colors are white and blue.

As readers may have gathered from the above descriptions, Vodou in the Haitian context is an entire way of life. The practice of Vodou is reflected in people's daily activities. One of Vodou's most important principles is to live in harmony with oneself, with others, and with one's surroundings. One of its greatest strengths is its capacity to adapt to its environment. Like the enslaved Africans transported to the New World who maintained their own version of Vodou to survive the inhuman brutality of colonialism, today many Haitians both in Haiti and abroad maintain their connections to Vodou in order to survive in a hostile postcolonial world. As Leslie Desmangles eloquently puts it in *Faces of the Gods: Vodou and Roman Catholicism in Haiti*, Vodou "uplifts the spirits of the downtrodden who experience life's misfortunes, instills in its devotees a need for solace and self-examination, and relates the profane world of humans to that of incommensurable mythological divine entities called lwas who govern the cosmos" (2–3).

The visual landscapes of the Haitian past and present are inflected by Vodou symbology. Haiti's very birth as a nation is linked to the Vodou religion, and the color red that is found in all the various Haitian flags is specifically associated with Ogun, the warrior god. This powerful spirit presides over iron, fire, hunting, politics, and war. It is natural for Haitian artists to be inspired by this fundamental aspect of Haitian culture as they bring awareness to the people, and illuminate the complexities of their nation and culture beyond the stereotype of "the poorest country in the Western Hemisphere." Instructors interested in teaching about Haiti should always keep in mind the need to problematize that reductive image, and emphasize the diversity of Haitian culture—something that visual art is uniquely equipped to help us do in the classroom.

Haitian Painting: A Brief Overview

As the previous paragraph suggests, the infrastructure of Haitian art is profoundly linked at once to history, religion, and cross-cultural encounters. The history of Haitian painting has been influenced by the nation's African, European, and Native American roots. The island of Saint-Domingue (present-day Haiti and the Dominican Republic) was a wealthy colony, and French artists spent time in its major cities. Many free people of color were also known in art circles on the island, and some were commissioned to paint portraits of plantation owners. Some enslaved people were also given permission by their owners to paint, since any money they earned as artists benefited the masters.

In 1944, Dewitt Peters, an American artist who went to Haiti to teach English instead of fighting in World War II, opened the Centre d'Art in Port-au-Prince. Its main goal was to train Haitian artists formally and put them in contact with other artists in the Western Hemisphere. In consequence, some critics have viewed Peters as the founder of Haitian art. But long before Peters, Haitian artists were creating work influenced by local culture as well as by their interactions with artists from France and the United States. The governments of several Haitian heads of state, including Henri Christophe, Alexandre Pétion, Jean-Pierre Boyer, and Emperor Faustin Soulouque, had supported the arts. For example, King Henri Christophe invited both local and foreign artists to his court and commissioned them to paint pictures that glorified the Revolution. Emperor Soulouque founded an academy of the arts.

Some of the most renowned Haitian painters were influenced by the indigenist movement, which emerged in 1927 and 1928 in reaction to the American Occupation of Haiti (1915–1934). One of its main goals was to value and reaffirm Haitian cultural identity through returning to Haitian roots as found in popular culture, language, and folkways, including in their reflections of African heritage. Work by the renowned artist Philomé Obin from the early part of the twentieth century, influenced by both the indigenist and negritude movements, depicts historical scenes from daily life. Meanwhile, artists from the period of the American Occupation considered themselves the founders of Haitian art and the inventors of the notion of Haitianity. Thus the idea of an Indigenous modernism predated Peters's Centre d'Art.

Peters did, however, have an influence on the direction taken by Haitian art in the mid-twentieth century. Upon his arrival in Haiti, he was fascinated by the talent he saw in the work of artists who had never received formal training. With Selden Rodman, an American poet, critic, and co-director of the Centre d'Art, Peters encouraged "naïve" painting and rejected the influence of European modernism. This training model is typical for modernist artists in many cultures outside the West, and represents the very contradiction of modernism. As the Centre d'Art became the nexus of what came to be called "primitive" or naïve art in the world outside Haiti, it globalized a particular image of Haitian art. In the Haitian context, the term "naïve art" or "primitive art" usually describes a blend of African and European cultural imagery, Catholic iconography, and Vodou symbols used to depict Haitian realities. Many of the artists characterized as naïve or primitive are associated with a particular town or region, and their work depicts the landscape of that place. This art is filled with raw, vivid colors, and it does not respect Euro-American notions of traditional aesthetics—by which I mean that it does not necessarily conform to what is typically expected of Haitian naïve art as it was characterized by an outsider like Dewitt Peters. Rather, this art represents pan-cultural and historical elements as well as the artists' individual philosophies and worldviews.

The artists of the naïve period include André Pierre and Hector Hyppolite, who were both hougan, as well as Rigaud Benoît, Wilson Bigaud, and Castera Bazile. Vodou played a key role in the work of these artists. In a mural they created together in the Cathedral of Sainte Trinité in Port-au-Prince, for example, they Haitianized traditional Christian religious iconography such as the Ascension of Christ, adding Black faces as well as drums. A useful exercise is to show students an image of this mural and then ask them to describe it carefully, focusing on the ways in which it depicts traditional religious iconography. I then ask them to consider specifically how the artists transformed this iconography to make it "Haitian."

From this first movement of naïve or primitive painting came a second wave of artists, including Sénèque Obin (Philomé Obin's brother), Gérard Valcin, Gesner Armand, and Préfète Duffaut. Philomé Obin created the School of Cap-Haïtien, and Duffaut the School of Jacmel. These painters also had opportunities to interact with artists abroad and were influenced by international styles. In the 1950s, artists such as Dieudonné Cédor and Lucien Price founded the Foyer des Arts Plastiques, an academy of painting that promoted both formalist approaches and specific techniques.

During the 1940s, Dewitt Peters, Selden Rodman, and André Breton became the main "authorities" on naive or primitive art in Haiti by encouraging some to apply more formal techniques in their art and by making Haitian artists more visible on the international scene. In 1948, Rodman published *Renaissance in Haiti*, the first English-language book on Haitian art. He also was closely involved in the creation of the mural paintings at the Cathedral of Sainte Trinité.[4] Dewitt Peters, co-founder of the Centre d'Art, ran a studio where artists like the well-known painter Hector Hyppolite worked. In 1944, André Breton traveled to Haiti with Cuban painter Wifredo Lam, where he encountered Hyppolite's work. Breton was fascinated by it, and indeed found a close link between Vodou and surrealism. He bought some of Hyppolite's paintings and even wrote about him in his book *Surrealism and Painting*. This exposure helped bring Haitian art to a wider audience. Haitian art became polarized: Philomé Obin was associated with popular realism, and Hector Hyppolite with Vodou painting. Breton famously declared, "La peinture haïtienne boira le sang du phénix et, des épaulettes de Dessalines, ventilera le Monde" [Haitian painting will drink the Phoenix's blood and Dessalines's epaulettes will give life to the world] (qtd. in Celius 127), a line that became a leitmotif of this style.[5] For Breton, Haitian painting became both the link between Haiti and the outside world and a way to represent Haiti's complex history.

But too often the visibility these three men provided to Haitian art has been misinterpreted, even by Haitian art critics, and they are characterized as "discovering" the hidden talent of Haitian artists. This is an arrogant and colonial perspective that is clearly refuted by a glance at the historical record. For example, in the early part of the nineteenth century, the Lycée Pétion, named after President Alexandre Pétion, taught art classes. Henri Christophe, who ruled the north of Haiti, founded an art academy during that period. Thus while Peters, Rodman, and Breton were indeed very involved in the system of artistic training and patronage in Haiti, they did not discover Haitian art, just as Christopher Columbus did not discover America.

Perhaps inevitably, Haitian art became politicized. It has been used by critics and dealers to enrich themselves and their galleries. The dialectic of "primitive craft" versus "modernist art" is not, or should not be, as important as many have suggested. Both movements are part of Haiti's rich artistic heritage. Yet what many critics often fail to mention is how Haitians and non-Haitians alike have used this distinction as a way to line their own pockets and to market Haitian art to non-Haitians.

When I teach about Haitian art, I help students to get a sense of the complexity and variety of art in Haitian culture by asking them to research museums that have collections of Haitian art. To enable students to become more fully immersed in the history of this art, I also ask them to do some research in the anthropology collection of the Yale Peabody Museum of Natural History and obtain information about Haitian paintings that are believed to have been acquired by the Smithsonian in 1885, after the World's Industrial & Cotton Exposition was held in New Orleans in 1884. These paintings represent various Haitian leaders, including an image of Toussaint Louverture from the 1870s painted by artist Louis Rigaud. Students consider questions such as: What surprised you when you viewed nineteenth-century Haitian art? What images most struck you, and why? Among other things, via this assignment, students can clearly see that Haitian art was not "discovered" by a white American in the twentieth century. To contextualize this assignment, "Behind the Surface: Nineteenth-century Haitian Paintings Provide Link to Past," by Mark Stricker, is a useful resource for students, as is the "Retrospective of 200 Years of Haitian Art at the Grand Palais Nationale in Paris." Both are available online.[6]

I also divide students into groups and assign each group a specific museum. Some virtual museums include the Selden Rodman Gallery of Popular Arts at Ramapo College in New Jersey, the Yale University Art Gallery in New Haven, the Milwaukee Art Museum in Wisconsin, the Waterloo Center for the Arts in Iowa, and the University of Kansas Spencer Museum of Art's Mary Lou Vansant Hughes collection. (See the end of this chapter for a comprehensive list.) These museums contain a number of works by Haitian artists such as Hector Hyppolite, Levoy Exil, Philomé Obin, Senèque Obin, Castera Bazile, Rigaud Benoît, Jacques-Richard Chéry, Mireille Delice, Laurent Casimir, and André Pierre. Among the questions I ask students to consider as they explore these collections are the following: In what context was the art acquired by the museum? What type of art is depicted in the collection? What are the display strategies?

What are some themes of Haitian culture that are represented in the paintings? Are there any women artists? What are some of the stories that the works tell? How and where are religion and spirituality represented?

As I have noted, Haitian artists living both inside and outside of Haiti have been inspired by religion in general and by Vodou in particular. Art objects, including paintings and sculptures, are found in ounfò. Sometimes, the lwa requests that a specific artist paint the peristyle or temple; at other times, the artist is commissioned by the hougan or manbo, or hougan or manbo themselves may produce the art for their peristyle.

For artists, among them Hector Hyppolite and André Pierre, who are also hougan and manbo, the representations of Vodou found in their work are inspired by dreams and the lwas. Others are inspired by the sounds of the drums from the mountains near and far. Rose-Marie Desruisseau, one of the leading Haitian women artists whose paintings have been exhibited internationally, focused heavily on Vodou. In her work we see the necessity for constant harmony between the lwas and human beings, the spirit and material worlds, and the natural and the supernatural.

Hërsza Barjon is a self-taught contemporary artist whose career began with painting decorative fabrics, patchworks, and crafts. Inspired by different art forms, her work is very personal, and at the same time deeply enmeshed with the Vodou religion. Her paintings depict the specific characteristics and types of power associated with each lwa. Looking at Barjon's colorful and mesmerizing series of 109 paintings entitled "Divine Haiti: Portraits of the Lwa," you can almost feel the spirits calling you, and feel that they can see through you. Barjon states that she was possessed by the lwas to do this series. Her passion is immediately evident in her work. She is a medium through which the lwas send their messages for humans. In her own words, she is a "missionée," someone whose role is to record the Haitian cultural patrimony. She states,

> I chose the name "The Descent of the Lwa" for the collection to indicate the beginning, the return to the source, to Africa, to the ancestral deities that accompany us in our terrestrial journey, the return to the primeval Haiti—Haiti/Bohio/Quisqueya—to the Haiti of the Indian, to the Haiti of our ancestors. I was guided and inspired by Déita's book *La Légende des Loas* that presents our Vodou pantheon and its lwas. I was not brought up in Vodou but I am profoundly mystical. My art demands that I go search for my roots and that I become spiritually engaged. (22)

Vodou as spirit and Vodou as art are the essence of Barjon's work. When I teach about modern Haitian art, I ask students to choose one of the Haitian lwas

Figure 4.1. Malcolm X is Ogoun X, the warrior god, the fighter. Vladimir Cybil Charlier, *Ogou X*. 2017. Digital print on archival paper. 24 × 36 inches, edition of 3. Collection of the artist.

and describe how it is depicted in her paintings. I ask them to consider why this lwa is important in Haitian culture, as well as whether there is a Catholic counterpart in one of the saints, and if so, which one.

Like Barjon, Vladimir Cybil Charlier, a Haitian American artist living in New York, is inspired by Vodou to create art that invites viewers to rethink and understand Vodou in a globalized framework by taking historical figures and cultural icons and superimposing them on specific Vodou lwas. For example,

Figure 4.2. The Irish saint Brigid of Kildare and Mary Magdalene, merged with Rosa Parks to create an image of the Vodou lwa Grann Brigitte. Vladimir Cybil Charlier, *Grande (Grann) Parks*. 2017. Digital print on archival paper. 24 × 36 inches, edition of 3. Collection of the artist.

Malcom X is Ogoun X, the warrior god, the fighter. He represents the force of politics and can be very violent.

Miles Davis, one of the most important jazz musicians of the twentieth century, represents Bawon Samdi, the head of the Gede family, who is filled with sagacity and humor. Charlier depicts Bawon Samdi's wife, Grann Brigitte, a lwa who cares for the dead and preserves their memory, and whose corresponding figures are the Irish saint Brigid of Kildare and Mary Magdalene, as merged with Rosa Parks. Charlier thus draws out the profound power that Parks exerted within the civil rights movement, which incorporated past and present, living and dead.

During a ceremony for the lwa, the Gede lwa is the last one to descend and is considered the life of the party. The Gede lwa also dances a sexual, sensual dance known as banda. In an interview, Charlier notes:

> I think that my work is influenced by Vodou insofar as Vodou imagery permeates Haitian visual culture and that my work is a rethinking of many of these images from a Haitian American perspective. The "Pantheon" series conflates Haitian Vodou gods disguised as Catholic saints with American heroes and pop figures. The beads and sequins that I use in my work are also an allusion to the beading of Vodou flags, but also, on the other hand, derive from a feminist tradition of art making and to "women's work." (Charlier interview)

Like Charlier, Colette "Kokko" Brésilla is a contemporary Haitian American artist whose work connects Vodou to the world. She is deeply influenced by Haitian artists such as Jean Michel Basquiat, Dieudonné Cédor, and Ti Ga. She is unapologetic about the role of religion in her work. She says that having grown up with a strict theologian father, she was aware of the power of religion from an early age. Her painting "Marassa Séparé" represents two Èzili: Èzili Dantò and Èzili Freda. In Vodou, the marasa (or marassa) are often represented by children, and protect children. They are very powerful because they consist of two forces that come together.

Cross-cultural connections are at the heart of Vodou, and Brésilla's work invites viewers to consider ways in which they may be connected across different landscapes of culture and spiritual practice. She plays with cross-cultural tropes, and has been influenced by Japanese imagery and history, as her painting of a geisha smoking a pipe, among other pieces, clearly shows. Her abstract work "Koneksion" contains the essence of her approach.

Another contemporary Haitian American artist whose work is deeply influenced by Vodou is Ulrick Jean-Pierre. Known for his imposing historical paintings depicting monumental landmarks in Haiti's history, Jean-Pierre's early work is very much influenced by Vodou as well as by various other historical and cultural themes. As a boy, he was fascinated by elements of Vodou, including a Vodou temple near his home and the sound of the drums he heard emanating from it, as well as the rara bands that paraded through the streets. Like many other Haitian artists, he grew up living a syncretism of Catholicism, Vodou, and Protestantism. "As a young artist," he says,

Figure 4.3. Painting of "Marassa Separé," who represent two Èzili: Èzili Dantò and Èzili Freda. Colette Brésilla, *Marassa Separé*. 2006. Acrylic, wax, and pencil on canvas. 29 × 27 inches. Collection of Société Oshun. Colette B. Studio.

it was an exciting challenge to be able to capture the dignity of a manbo or hougan, the drummers' movement during a Vodou ceremony and drawing a vèvè live. Witnessing Gede and Zaka ceremonies as a teenager definitely influenced my work. . . . For me, art and religion complement one another. I cannot imagine a Vodou temple without its cultural drums, its sacred arts and crafts collection that beautifies it for the ancestral lwas. By the same token, I cannot envision a cathedral without its embodiment of the architectural and artistic beauty and sculptures of saints produced

Figure 4.4. This piece of abstract art by Colette Brésilla contains the essence of her approach. Colette Brésilla, *Koneksion*. 2006. Acrylic and wax. 38 × 32 inches. Collection of Cécile Accilien. Colette B. Studio.

by artists. Through my artistic viewpoint, each Haitian Vodou temple is a micro-museum that incubates the fragments of Haitian collective memory. I left Haiti physically but never spiritually, mentally, or psychologically. (Jean-Pierre interview)

Jean-Pierre's paintings include *Crucified Liberty*, in which he took the common theme of crucifixion so privileged by various Haitian artists and put it in a modern context. The painting depicts a boat with people from all walks of life (they are literally "in the same boat"). The figure of the woman at its center could be Native American or African. The painting plays on the image of the Statue of Liberty, as well as the fact that Haitians and Haiti itself are crucified and exploited by fellow Haitians, Americans, and others. Instead of Christ on the cross, we see a woman who resembles Èzili. Her children are around her feet but she is unable to feed them. The painting's other symbols include a snake, money, and a Bible. The interplay between Vodou and Christianity is evident. One possible interpretation of this painting is that Haitians are crucified by religion, forced to choose between Vodou and Christianity.

André Pierre, probably one of the most important hougan painters of the twentieth century, has said,

> I paint to show the entire world what the Vodou religion is. Because three fourths of the terrestrial globe thinks that the Vodou religion is diabolical. I paint to show them that Vodou is not diabolical. The Vodou religion is purely Catholic, apostolic but not Roman. It is not directed uniquely by God. Since all people are liars, no one is a Catholic. Only God and his spirits are Catholic. The spirits of Vodou are the limbs of God. God is the body and the spirits are the limbs. (qtd. in Constantino xx)

Vodou continues to be at once demonized and exoticized by many outside of Haiti. At the same time, in many circles, Haitian art remains little more than an object of curiosity in the form of a souvenir from an island trip. *Crucified Liberty* may be the only work by Haitian artists that students and instructors have encountered, if they have encountered Haitian art at all.

In their book *Tourist Art*, Gabrielle Civil and Vladimir Cybil Charlier challenge the uses of Haitian art in tourism, commercialization, and the global market:

> Tourist art is always selling time. wood carvings, figurines, postcards of sans souci. in santo domingo, viejo san juan, nassau, brooklyn, miami, detroit, in holes in the wall. tourist art by Haitians doesn't need Haitians at all.[7]

Figure 4.5. This painting by Ulrick Jean-Pierre plays on the image of the Statue of Liberty, as well as the fact that Haitians and Haiti itself are crucified and exploited by fellow Haitians, Americans, and others. Ulrick Jean-Pierre, *Crucified Liberty*. 1996–1997. Oil on canvas. 48 × 60 inches. Collection of the artist.

This view highlights the disconnect between the larger fascination with Haiti and its culture and the contempt or disregard for that culture. Tourists traveling to the Dominican Republic, San Juan, Martinique, and Guadeloupe, for example, buy "exotic" art made in Haiti by Haitians but marketed within these other Caribbean tourist industries as simply "Caribbean folk art." Consumers do not have to think about the context out of which this art emerged, nor be directly or consciously associated with "those people" from the "poorest country in the Western Hemisphere." Furthermore, labeling the art "Caribbean" suggests that it is "authentically" from whatever island one is visiting, thereby erasing its cultural specificity. It is useful to invite students to consider images or artifacts of this kind of art and to ask them to think about how and why "Haiti" becomes globalized in this way, and the effects that this circulation of anonymous (Haitian) artwork as a commodity may have.

Many artists believe that part of their mission and artistic vision is to challenge such simplistic and easily consumable representations, and they focus on depicting Haiti's history and contemporary realities as a way of contributing to public awareness of the nation's multi-faceted culture, both within and outside Haiti. Tourist audiences can also influence the artists' perceptions of their public. For example, in a painting titled *Grand'mère me disait que la riv. massacre était en sang*, circa 1975, Ernst Prophète depicts the 1937 Parsley Massacre, when Dominican dictator Rafael Trujillo ordered the killing of thousands of Haitians living in the Dominican Republic. It is safe to say that tourists to the Dominican Republic will not be offered tourist art that depicts this event, which has largely been erased from that nation's history. In Haiti, however, as one of the most significant events in the first half of the twentieth century, the Parsley Massacre would be seen as an appropriate subject even for generally values-neutral tourist art.

In order to help students see and think about new developments in Haitian art, thus reinforcing their awareness of the dynamic unfolding complexity of Haitian culture, I ask them to choose one of the following contemporary artists whose work is available online—Josué Azor, Sergine André, Tessa Mars, Florine Demosthène, Zeek Mathias, Edouard Duval-Carrié, or Karim Bléus—and write a short biography and two paragraphs about their work. Among the questions students consider are: Does the artist have an artistic philosophy? What medium do they use? Where were they trained? Do you find aspects of Haitian history in these images? If so, what purpose or purposes do they seem to serve, what messages do they seem to convey? Do you find elements of spirituality or religion in these images? If so, what seems to be their role in the image?

The syncretism of cultures from Africa, Europe, and America is apparent in the work of many Haitian artists; it is not surprising that Haitian artists are inspired by religion, because Vodou and its sometimes uneasy connections with Christianity, especially Catholicism, are inescapable elements of Haitian visual and cultural landscapes. And as they depict Haiti's religious culture, artists depict the disparities and contradictions that exist in Haiti between rich and poor, Christians and non-Christians, and past and present. Artists also use religion, especially Vodou, as a means of preserving Haiti's history and culture, for Vodou played a crucial role in Haiti's emergence as an independent nation. Haitian artists consistently dramatize ways in which the spiritual, the creative, and the practical are interconnected. While religion and art, both crucial elements of Haitian society, can be taught on their own, combining them allows for a deeper understanding of Haitian life. It also allows students and instructors to consider the reasons why they are not taught together more often—a process that goes to the heart of perceptions of Haitian culture both within and outside Haiti. The sample lesson plan below and the accompanying list of resources will help to bring the richness of Haitian art and spiritual imagery within reach of instructors and students, no matter where they are located.

Lesson Plan and Resources for Teaching about Haitian Art and Religion

I recommend that instructors find a current or recent exhibit (whether virtual or physical) about Haitian art, such as the one at the Grand Palais Galeries Nationales in France entitled "Haïti: deux siècles de création artistiques," held in November 2014. Students should think about the main themes of the exhibit. When I do this assignment, I give them the names of at least four artists who were represented and ask them to find information about those artists, including where they reside, their training, and their artistic philosophies. Students imagine that they are art critics and write short essays about how the exhibit represents or represented religious/spiritual aspects of Haitian culture. If at all possible, depending upon the instructor's location, it is ideal to take the students to a local museum that has a Haitian art collection. If not, the virtual museums that I mention at the end of the chapter will work as well.

Students should choose a work of art (painting, ironwork, print, sculpture, etc.) from either a physical or virtual museum and write a two-page reflection paper that considers the following questions:

1. What drew you to that piece? In other words, what made you choose that particular work of art?
2. Research the context in which the work of art was created. Under what circumstances did the artist produce this work? Under what circumstances was the work bought or acquired? Who is the current owner of the work? Where is the artist now?
3. How does the work of art relate to issues of religion and/or spirituality in Haiti, specifically Vodou, that we have discussed in class?
4. What are some of the stories of belief, faith, and spiritual practice in Haiti that the work seems to convey? Where do you "read" these stories in the image? For example, what symbols or iconography do you find there?

Guidelines for writing are as follows: In the first paragraph, provide the name of the artist (if known), title (if applicable), the date the artwork was created (or date range), the medium or media (color print, woodcut, sculpture, bronze, glass beads, etc.), and the region of Haiti where the artist is from (if known).

Start with a short formal analysis of the object. Devote a few sentences to a paragraph that describes (rather than interprets) what it is that you see. Examine the work and notice its details, its surface textures, its subject matter, its colors, and so on. This close examination will in turn help you to better interpret, analyze, and contextualize it. Next, use some of the themes/key concepts discussed in class as you talk about that work of art. As you write, consider how the symbols, myths, spiritual imagery, and/or history that you find in this work are in dialogue.

Virtual Museums

1. Figge Art Museum, Davenport, Iowa
2. Huntington Museum of Art: Winslow Anderson Collection of Haitian Art, Huntington, West Virginia, www.hmoa.org/flipbooks/HaitianArt/files/inc/2112261667.pdf
3. Nova Southeastern University Art Museum, Fort Lauderdale, Florida
4. University of Kansas Spencer Museum of Art, Lawrence, Kansas
5. Milwaukee Art Museum, Milwaukee, Wisconsin
6. National Gallery of Art, Washington, D.C.
7. Waterloo Center for the Arts (Dubuque Museum of Art), Waterloo, Iowa

Selected Exhibits on Haitian Art and Culture

1. Pomona College – "The Crossing/La Traversée: Art in Haiti and the US"
2. Haitian Heritage Museum – "Digital Media of the Caribbean"
3. Mindwarehouse Connect – "From Haiti with Love"
4. The Field Museum – "Vodou: Sacred Powers of Haiti"
5. Northern Illinois University – "Reconstructing Haiti: Current Conditions, Lessons Learned" and the Future Speaker Series
6. "The Ties That Bind: Haiti, the United States and the Work of Ulrick Jean-Pierre in Comparative Perspectives" (This virtual exhibit is available as part of a website I created with Cassandra Messick Braun entitled "Encountering Haiti and the University of Kansas" [encounteringhaiti.ku.edu], and includes a section specifically on Vodou.)
7. Exposition de Tessa Mars, "Île modèle, Manman Zile, Island Template" Centre d'art, Maison Dufort, Port-au-Prince, Haïti, www.youtube.com/watch?v=JrzWoxtBfO4&t=106s; www.naimaunlimited.com/biblio/tessa-mars-ile-modele-manman-zile-island template/?fbclid=IwAR1jnpcqIMVkJ9aaC2QEjwJrSaGE5DDFk2e5MBmpxue-uLTSlqTuLhPH1QM
8. Zeek Mathias, "A Reflection of Me," Solo Exhibit: muce305.org/2947-2/

Selected Haitian Art Galleries in the United States (Physical and Virtual)

Galerie Lakaye: Los Angeles, California
Galerie Makondo: Pittsburgh, Pennsylvania
HaitianArt.Com: Boca Raton, Florida
Indigo Arts Gallery: Philadelphia, Pennsylvania
MedaliaArt.com: East Setauket, New York
Myriam Nader Art Gallery: Haverstraw, New York

Suggested Readings

Accilien, Cécile, Elmide Méléance, and Jessica Adams, editors. *Revolutionary Freedoms: A History of Survival, Strength and Imagination in Haiti*. Caribbean Studies Press, 2006.

Armand, Margaret Mitchell. *Healing in the Homeland: Haitian Vodou Traditions*. Lexington Books, 2013.

Bloncourt, Gérald, and Marie-José Nadal-Gardère. *La peinture haïtienne*. Editions Nathan, 1986.

Brown, Karen McCarthy. *The Vèvè of Haitian Vodou: A Structural Analysis of Visual Imagery*. University Microfilms, 1975.

———. *Mama Lola: A Vodou Priest in Brooklyn*. University of California Press, 1991.

———. "Voodoo." *Encyclopaedia of Religion*, Vol. 15, ed. Mircea Eliade, 296–301. Simon and Schuster/Macmillan, 1995.

Célius, Carlos. *Langage plastique et énonciation identitaire: L'invention de l'art haïtien*. Les Presses de L'Université Laval, 2007.

Civil, Gabrielle, and Vladimir Cybil Charlier. *Tourist Art*. Charleston, SC, print on demand, 2012.

Chalom, Léon. *Religion in the Art of Haiti*. Exhibition at Seton Hall University, March 17-April 10, 1968. Exhibition catalogue published by Seton Hall University.

Christensen, Eleanor Ingalls. *The Art of Haiti*. A.S. Barnes & Co., 1975.

Constantino, Donald J., editor. *Sacred Arts of Haitian Vodou*. UCLA Museum of Cultural History, 1995.

Dayan, Joan. *Haiti, History and the Gods*. University of California Press, 1995.

Deita. *La légende des Loas du Vodou haïtien*, 3rd edition. L'imprimeur II, 2004.

Desmangles, Leslie. *Faces of the Gods: Vodou and Roman Catholicism in Haiti*. University of North Carolina Press, 1997.

Franciscus, John Allen. *Haiti: Voodoo Kingdom to Modern Riviera*. The Franciscus Family Foundation, Inc., 1980.

Hewitt, John H. "Shopping for Haitian Art." *Black Enterprise Magazine*, vol. 7, no. 9, 1977, pp. 31–34.

Hurbon, Laennec. *Vodou: Search for the Spirit*. Harry N. Abrams, 1995.

Laguerre, Michel. *Voodoo and Politics in Haiti*. St. Martin's Press, 1989.

Largey, Michael. *Vodou Nation*. University of Chicago Press, 2006.

Lerebours, Michel-Philippe. "The Indigenist Revolt: Haitian Art, 1927–1944." *Callaloo*, vol. 15, no. 3, 1992, pp. 711–725.

———. *Haïti et ses peintres de 1804 à 1980. Souffrances et espoirs d'un peuple*. 2 vols. Imprimeur II, 1989.

M'Bow, Babacar, and Claudine Michel, curators and editors. *The Descent of the Lwa: Journey Through Haitian Mythology. The Works of Hërsza Barjon*. Exhibition catalogue. Broward County Florida Library and KOSANBA: The Congress of Santa Barbara, 2004.

Métraux, Alfred. *Voodoo in Haiti*. Translated by Hugo Charteris, Schocken Books, 1972.

Murphy, Joseph. *Working the Spirit: Ceremonies of the African Diaspora*. Beacon Press, 1994.

Murrell, Nathaniel Samuel. *Afro-Caribbean Religions: An Introduction to Their Historical, Cultural, and Sacred Traditions*. Temple University Press, 2010.

Rigaud, Milo. *Secrets of Voodoo*. Arco Publishing, 1969.

———. *Vèvè: Diagrammes Rituels du Vaudou*. New York: French and European Publications, 1974.

Robinson, Theresa Jontyle. *A History of the Haitian Popular Art Movement, 1944 to 1972*. PhD dissertation, University of Maryland, 1983.

Rodman, Selden. *Renaissance in Haiti: Popular Painters in the Black Republic*. Pelligrini & Cudahy, 1948.

———. *The Miracle of Haitian Art*. Doubleday & Co., Inc., 1974.

———. *Where Art Is Joy: Haitian Art, the First Forty Years*. Ruggles de Latour, Inc., 1988.

Stebich, Ute. *Haitian Art*. New York: The Brooklyn Museum Catalogue. Catalogue exhibition, 1978.

———. *A Haitian Celebration: Art and Culture*. Milwaukee Art Museum, companion to an exhibit held at the Milwaukee Art Museum April 24–August 16, 1992, Milwaukee, WI.

Thompson, Robert Ferris. *The Flash of the Spirit*. Random House, 1983.

Wilcken, Lois. *The Drums of Vodou: Lois Wilcken Featuring Frisner Augustin*. White Cliffs Media, 1992.

Williams, Sheldon. *Voodoo and the Art of Haiti*. Morland Lee, Ltd., 1969.

Acknowledgments

I wish to thank Jessica Adams and Jessica Gerschultz for their feedback on this chapter. I also would like to thank Colette Brésilla, Vladimir Cybil Charlier, and Ulrick Jean-Pierre for taking the time to answer my questions about how religion influences their work and for allowing me to reproduce images of their work in the book. All quotes from these three artists are drawn from personal interviews and conversations that took place between January and April 2013.

Notes

1. I use the term Vodou to differentiate this religion from the many stereotypes and pejoratives contained in spellings such as "voodoo," "hoodoo," and "vodu." Unless it is a direct

quote, I use the most common Haitian spelling when referring to the lwas or other Haitian divine figures.

2. My conversation took place in 2014 with the late *manbo* Dr. Margaret Mitchell Armand. As an artist and a Vodou practitioner, Armand discussed how and why many artists are influenced by Vodou, including how Vodou itself is a space filled with creative energy, from the music that is played during a ceremony to the specific colors that are used to the *vèvè* drawings.

3. An ason has been described as a liturgical tcha-tcha; in the Vodou religion it is used like a rattle to invoke the spirits during a ceremony.

4. For more on Haitian art in the 1940s, see Marta Dansie and Abigail Lapin Dardashti's "Notes from the Archive: MoMA and the Internationalization of Haitian Painting, 1942–1948," 3 January 2018 post.at.moma.org/content_items/1078-notes-from-the-archive-moma-and-the-internationalization-of-haitian-painting-1942-1948. Accessed 28 July 2019.

5. Unless otherwise noted, all translations are mine.

6. See news.yale.edu/2012/11/05/behind-surface-19th-century-haitian-paintings-provide-link-past; arcthemagazine.com/arc/2014/09/retrospective-of-200-years-of-haitian-art-at-the-grand-palais-galerie-nationale-in-paris/

7. All the names of the places mentioned in this quote use lower case. Perhaps it is a way for the authors to emphasize the superficial manner in which Haitian art is perceived by tourists visiting those places. The authors are also deconstructing language and subverting the status quo. By using lower case they are trivializing the places where Haitian tourist art can be found in the same ways as the buyers of that art primarily view Haitian art in a trite manner.

Works Cited

Barjon, Hërsza. *Divine Haiti: Portraits of the Lwa*. Broward County Library Catalogue Exhibition, 2004.

Célius, Carlos. *Langage plastique et* énonciation *identitaire: L'invention de l'art haïtien*. Les Presses de L'Université Laval, 2007.

Civil, Gabrielle, and Vladimir Cybil Charlier. *Tourist Art*. Charleston, SC, print on demand, 2012.

Constantino, Donald J., editor. *Sacred Arts of Haitian Vodou*. UCLA Museum of Cultural History, 1995.

Desmangles, Leslie. *Faces of the Gods: Vodou and Roman Catholicism in Haiti*. University of North Carolina Press, 1997.

5

Creating Interdisciplinary Knowledge about Haiti's Creole Language

DON E. WALICEK

> *Men anpil, chay pa lou.*
> Many hands make the load lighter.
>
> —Haitian Proverb

Learning about Haiti's Creole language, which is called *Kreyòl* or *Kreyòl Ayisyen* by its speakers, is never only about language.[1] It is the exploration of an intimate dimension of a people's past, one that speaks to their trans-Atlantic origins and tracks their quest for solidarity, independence, knowledge, and new freedom. It is also an invitation to contemplate our own cognitive processes, how we understand and negotiate meaning, the relationship between oral and written language, links between differences of language and race, the dynamics of language change, and the basic human desire to communicate. As suggested in this chapter, knowledge about language is inflected by ideologies and history, as well as multi-layered dynamics that shape the relationships among individuals, groups, races, and nations. This is the case for laypeople as well as linguists. Recent developments in the field of creolistics—new insights, shifts in theories, and growing interest in language rights and policies—signal that change is on the horizon, in Haiti and other parts of the Caribbean as well as in linguistics and academia more generally.[2] The call here is for teaching to nurture enlightened, participatory witnessing, a pedagogy for knowledge creation through interdisciplinarity and critical reflection that instills strong analytical skills and optimism about the future in learners.

Providing a forward-looking profile of Kreyòl, the discussion below suggests that information about various long-standing challenges, all of which emerged as the result of the colonization of the Caribbean, should be incorporated into classroom teaching about Haiti. The framework that linguist Michel DeGraff calls "postcolonial creolistics" is presented as an effective platform for overcoming these challenges and for demonstrating that interdisciplinary approaches to language, social life, and science have much to contribute to the development of an effective pedagogy. The challenges that are discussed include: (i) obstacles to the expansion of *Kreyòl*'s use as a medium of instruction in Haiti's educational system, (ii) Eurocentric assumptions that sustain negative language myths and misunderstandings of language structure and language history, and (iii) issues related to effective language planning and the protection of speaker's language rights. These are linked to details about the cultivation of interdisciplinary perspectives, seminal work in creolistics by Mervyn Alleyne, and an important agreement signed by numerous countries in 2011, the Charter on Language Policy and Language Rights in the Creole-Speaking Caribbean, respectively.

Kreyòl is a thriving and vibrant language as well as a powerful symbol of the Haitian people's national identity.[3] It is spoken as the mother tongue of approximately 95 percent of the country's population, which amounts to more than 10 million people. An official orthography for the language, which was established by the National Pedagogical Institute, was formally recognized in 1979. A presidential decree from the same year authorized the use of Kreyòl in the country's schools, both as a language of instruction and as a subject. Haiti's current constitution, which was promulgated in 1987, recognizes the juridical equality of the country's two languages. It observes that Kreyòl is the language shared by the entire population and recognizes its status as a symbol of national unity. As proclaimed in its fifth article: "*Sèl lang ki simante tout Ayisyen nèt ansanm, se kreyòl la. Kreyòl ak Franse se lang o syèl Repiblik Ayiti*" ["All Haitians are united by a common language: Creole. Creole and French are the official languages of the Republic"] (1987 Constitution, ch.1, art. 5)]. French, however, remains the language of the elite, and long-standing language myths and highly questionable practices suggesting that French is superior to Kreyòl work together to maintain a social and economic order that disenfranchises the majority of the population.

In Haiti today, language use varies according to domain. The country's Creole language is widely used in radio and television programming. According to numerous reports, its use on local TV and the state television broadcaster *Télévision Nationale d'Haïti* (TNH) is on the rise. It is the language of public communication and religious life. The country's most widely spoken language is also the main language of Haitian music. Artists sing in Kreyòl in newer genres such as *rap kreyòl*, which began in the 1980s, as well as in more traditional genres such as *compas* and *rara*. Kreyòl has much more limited use in other domains, including newspapers, literature, the legal system, and government.

Student learning is severely undermined by stigmas associated with Kreyòl, as well as by an educational system that still teaches students in French even though French and Kreyòl are not mutually intelligible. This means that a significant number of people do not have the opportunity to become fully literate in their native language.[4] Linguists have signaled the many problems this causes for young people and society as a whole. The applied linguist Dennis Craig, for example, documents consistently sub-par performance by Creole language–dominant students who enter an educational system and are taught as if they are native speakers of standard European languages. He finds that these youth face serious challenges in learning, and that their educational development is more vulnerable than that of their counterparts who speak the European language of their territory (e.g., standard varieties of French and English) as a first language. Linguist Michel DeGraff describes the situation in Haiti as a "national tragedy" that repeats itself generation after generation (quoted in Dizikes). As discussed below, DeGraff has conceptualized a theoretical framework called "postcolonial creolistics" and a large-scale project that assists in responding to Haiti's predicament. Postcolonial creolistics nurtures changes in societies where Creole languages are spoken at the same time it contributes to new insights that can positively impact the production of scientific knowledge about Kreyòl and other Creole languages.

What Is Postcolonial Creolistics?

Postcolonial creolistics, explains DeGraff, asks important questions about languages that laypeople and linguists alike have traditionally misunderstood. In particular, this work "questions the scientific and methodological considerations [underlying] our knowledge and lack of knowledge about Creole languages" ("Against Creole Exceptionalism" 404). DeGraff holds that this framework can improve the quality of life for speakers of Kreyòl and other Creole languages in at least two ways: (i) through progress in our current knowledge about the history and structures of Creole languages; and (ii) through application of our improved knowledge to new and truly progressive paradigms in research, in education reform, and language policy.

Postcolonial creolistics, which builds on the legacy of applied linguistics, welcomes solutions to practical as well as theoretical problems. An example of a practical problem is lack of access to educational materials and classroom experiences in which the mother tongue of the student is the language of instruction. This is an issue in Haiti and other Caribbean societies, including, for example, Jamaica, Guadeloupe, and St. Lucia. Another practical problem is the systematic violation of the linguistic rights of the people who speak Creole languages. Theoretical problems concern the assumptions, models, and theories that have been used to analyze the grammatical structures of Creole languages and their histories. DeGraff and others hold that Creoles have long been allotted an "exceptional" status in linguistics. This means that they have been understood not in terms of theories of general linguistics, which are developed for all human languages, but in terms of models and theories that set them apart as a "special" group. Examples that are provided below show how the analysis of specific grammatical structures can be used to identify West African grammatical features in Kreyòl and simultaneously challenge Eurocentric assumptions that have contributed to the language's stigmatization.

Postcolonial creolistics is already bearing fruit. As explained by DeGraff and Stump, in July 2015, the Haitian Creole Academy and the Haitian government's Ministry of National Education signed an agreement to expand the use of Kreyòl as a medium of instruction through all levels of the education system. An agreement between the Ministry and the academy, this achievement is linked to the MIT Initiative, a project led by DeGraff that develops pedagogical materials in Kreyòl for mathematics, physics, biology, biochemistry, and chemistry. These state-of-the-art materials are referred to as resous pou edikasyon san baryè, or "resources for education without barriers," within the initiative (128–129). The project also involves the translation of innovative educational technologies that have been developed primarily at MIT from English into Kreyòl. Access to these materials has the potential to transform the country's educational system and to benefit the youth who study in it.

As interpreted here, postcolonial creolistics embraces interdisciplinary approaches to linguistics and questions about language in society that are relevant to teaching students in the university context. The assumption is that students can learn about language and linguistics at the same time as they are exposed to scholarship in which linguists wrestle with processes of critical reflection and the reformulation of questions that drive investigation, study, and dialogue. They can learn about debates related to phenomena such as language ideologies, grammatical structure, and the linguistic legacies of the Atlantic slave trade. These debates show that interdisciplinary collaboration is an effective means of analyzing and addressing complex social problems.

Interdisciplinary Perspectives and Kreyòl

The interdisciplinary perspective on Kreyòl described in this chapter can be thought of as an unfolding path, one on which students break new ground as they explore assumptions, topics, and conceptual resources that are likely to be out of reach from a strictly disciplinary perspective. This approach is especially useful for designing a course or unit on language for students with a limited background in linguistics. It could also be used for a writing course on Haiti taken by students from a diversity of majors. Students in such a course would strive not only to become better writers, but also to accumulate knowledge about Haiti in the process of becoming more adept at constructing interdisciplinary arguments and explanations.

Repko offers a review of material on instruction and learning that concludes that interdisciplinarity cultivates cognitive abilities in four areas:

(i)   formulation and application of perspective-taking techniques
(ii) development of structural knowledge about problems appropriate for interdisciplinary inquiry
(iii) integration of conflicting insights from multiple disciplines
(iv) production of a cognitive advancement or new understanding based on interdisciplinarity. (172)

Fostering the development of these cognitive abilities guides us toward productive tensions, the fruitful transgression of boundaries, and the creative navigation of information.

In the first meeting of my undergraduate course titled Interdisciplinary Approaches to Haiti's Past and Present, which I have offered at the University of Puerto Rico's Río Piedras Campus, we usually talk about how standard disciplinary approaches to knowledge formation have shaped highly specialized academic norms and led to divisions and breaches of communication that sometimes make it difficult to access holistic understandings of complex phenomena. Students have described how disciplines are reflected in the organization of our university (in its colleges, programs, majors, and budget) and in their degree requirements. This is followed up with my description of interdisciplinarity, one that focuses on the insights that it offers as a pedagogical framework for studying Haiti. As I lead a discussion on interdisciplinarity, I use Haiti's Creole language as an example of a topic for a hypothetical research project. I point out that language is a topic of research to multiple disciplines (e.g., linguistics, anthropology, literature, psychology, law, biology, and history) and provide a brief account of how specialists in each are likely to see language in general and "Kreyòl" in particular. Students formulate and turn in a question about Haiti's Creole language from the perspective of their respective majors, one that they will address in a writing assignment later in the course.

Reading the two-page essay "A Cage of Words" by Joel Dreyfuss is the last activity for the first class. Sitting in a circle, each person reads a paragraph. Dreyfuss offers a provocative discussion of "the Phrase," the seven words that are so often repeated when Haiti is mentioned in the news or official contexts: "The Poorest Nation in the Western Hemisphere." While students usually point out that the phrase is less of a standard trope in Spanish-speaking Puerto Rico than in the US, they are impressed by the glimpses of Haiti's rich culture and history that Dreyfuss offers. The essay challenges them and serves as a platform from which they can envision what's ahead, how studying Haiti and unpacking dominant discourse will lead them to rethink their understandings of themselves and their world. Fostering critical awareness, Dreyfuss assists us in breaking the chain of false connections that defines "Haiti" as poverty, fear, and violence. It calls upon them to think of language not just in terms of course assignments and representations of Kreyòl, but also in terms of stereotypes and dominant ideologies that obscure new understanding.

In our second meeting, students developed a list of concrete actions that researchers, writers, scientists, and others can rely on to make their work interdisciplinary. Their ideas:

- Pose direct questions about a topic to someone in another discipline and then use that response to improve questions, methods, and/or interpretation.
- Cooperate with people from different disciplines in research teams.
- Participate in conferences and professional meetings outside main area of expertise.
- Read outside your discipline or field.
- Involve non-academic people and perspectives close to the problem
- Be creative.

When I asked how we should approach interdisciplinarity with our final projects, students proposed that each member of the class should be responsible for integrating at least one academic article from a discipline other than ones clearly linked to topic. Once the search for articles and other resources was underway, students offered additional suggestions. One noted the importance of reading work in other languages, mentioning that "truly interdisciplinary courses, even English courses like ours, shouldn't ask bilingual students to pretend that they're monolingual in a foreign language."

My students repeatedly questioned why they knew so little about Haiti and basically nothing about its language or the political significance of its history. They saw the Haitian Revolution as an event of global significance but found it hard to believe that they had never been taught anything about it, not in school, in the media, or in popular culture. Some seemed to feel that it had been withheld from them. In similar fashion, they questioned why they had not been taught more about language. One of the first questions I asked them about Kreyòl was what languages they thought contributed to its formation. They enthusiastically offered an initial flurry of responses, but only after a couple of minutes of guessing and significant "hints" did someone finally mention an African language.

Several students sought out connections between Puerto Rico and Haiti. In one class, a student presented on connections between Haitian and Puerto Rican intellectuals in the nineteenth century, in particular the years that Ramón Emeterio Betances lived in Jacmel and his work as a translator of literature about Toussaint L'Ouverture. We also discussed the US government's detention of 800 Haitian asylum seekers in Fort Allen, a former military base in Puerto Rico, in the early 1980s. Our discussion focused on issues of language (the Haitians' access to interpreters and how the press linked language to questions about the credibility of their asylum claims) and expressions of solidarity on the part of local artists, performers, writers, and others. We talked about the tendency to decontextualize Puerto Rico from its Caribbean context and pondered how to restore popular memory of significant events and texts that link Puerto Rico and Haiti. These are some of the topics that students explored in their final papers.

Later in the course, as we began to make connections across readings, we observed that Haitian authors contributed a great deal to our discussions. They shared local knowledge and personal experiences in ways that "spoke" to students. Several engaging authors (e.g., Gage Averill, Myriam Chancy, Nikòl Payen, Assotto Saint, Michel-Rolph Trouillot) made it much easier for them to write and think from an interdisciplinary perspective. When we developed the evaluation rubric for the final project, students proposed that they should be required to incorporate relevant work by Haitian authors, given that it directly contributed to the overall goal of learning through interdisciplinarity.

Students also learned about the late Trinidadian linguist Mervyn Alleyne, who rejected negative views of Kreyòl and other languages that emerged in the context of slavery and the colonization of the Americas. Alleyne argued adamantly against two ideas: (i) the notion that these languages are the products of pidgins and (ii) the proposal that they are new autonomous systems cut off from their African heritage. In his words, "the emergence of so-called 'creole' languages should be seen within the framework of language and cultural change"; he argued for the parallel treatment of language forms and other cultural phenomena, while avoiding the treatment of elements of African language and culture as isolated and unusual 'survivals' or as 'borrowings' (*Comparative Afro-American* 16). These positions allowed students to see how the analysis of grammatical structure and language history relates to issues of history, politics, and debates about ideology.

We interpreted Alleyne's call for interdisciplinarity as one that is relevant to contemporary debates about Creole language origins and the contributions that relatively small fields like creolistics can make to large disciplines such as linguistics. After we reviewed some recent debates about Creole language formation, students planned a project in which a large, interdisciplinary team consisting of experts from linguistics, history, social anthropology, and archaeology would contribute to knowledge formation about Kreyòl among academics and the public at large. We discussed interdisciplinarity as useful for addressing misconceptions and myths about Haiti's language, people, and history, as well as its contemporary problems and our own, but we concluded that dismantling myths requires constructing new narratives that can replace them. Students turned to materials from our readings to construct narratives about language origins that could be shared with readers with no background in linguistics and others that would be directed at linguists. They found these hard to write. In the first instance, they observed that the debates are removed from the history and experiences of common people. In the second, they felt that many of the useful suggestions made by Alleyne and others decades earlier had not been addressed. They asked why scholars would overlook or ignore the contributions of others and not seek to establish common ground.

For a mid-term essay, students were required to consider a problem from two perspectives (e.g., history and linguistics, literary studies and law, education and sociolinguistics). This assignment proved to be a tall order, but it yielded positive results. Students used the "Idea Map" included at the end of this chapter as a planning document. They were instructed to formulate three interrelated arguments supporting a main thesis statement, combining reasons, data, or methodology from the two disciplines that they chose. Aligning the contents with the various parts of the map proved challenging for some students. I encouraged them to think about a general topic first, and to then move on to the main data and examples early on so that much of the paper, including its thesis statement, could be constructed around them. This helped them to avoid the problem of having a "good" thesis and discussion without the necessary data and examples.

This interdisciplinary pedagogical approach to language leads to interesting questions about social history, culture, and science. One of the important topics to emerge was how to confront the "coloniality" still present in academic paradigms and society at large, including in ideas about language.

Confronting Coloniality

The gradual but positive shifts in official government policies toward Kreyòl mentioned above are especially significant when we recall that the Caribbean's Creole languages are impacted both by the legacy of colonialism and aspects of neocolonialism. This duality of forces, which influences popular beliefs about language, culture, and identity, maintains strong and broad influence in the region's political and legal systems as well as in intellectual, philosophical, artistic, and aesthetic norms. While these forces are sometimes resisted and critiqued, they remain active. We can see their effects in some of the canonical works and abstract concepts on our syllabi, in the assumption that "good science" is logical and apolitical, and in knowledge that consistently marginalizes non-Western perspectives.

Colonialism and aspects of neocolonialism have ancient connections to how people interpret structures of language. Alleyne charges that the stigmatization and barriers that Creole languages and their speakers face in Haiti and other countries are sustained by language ideologies that are strikingly loyal to the tenets of the Greco-Roman tradition. These, he argues, were constitutive of colonialism in the Caribbean region and endure today:

> As a general rule, Caribbean languages continue to be seen as not belonging to the African tradition; they are judged by the general population against the Graeco-Roman norms of language structure, according to which, for example, inflections are the essential part of the language structure; they are thought to have "no grammar." ("Language and Identity" 4)

Acceptance of the norms that Alleyne refers to—including a sort of reverence for grammatical structures that feature inflection, which is discussed below—separates Haiti and other Caribbean speech communities from an essential part of their histories: the linguistic and cultural traditions of West Africa. The acceptance of external norms cultivates additional iterations of separation that influence how people in and outside the Caribbean—government officials, the elite, policy-makers, teachers, students, and linguists—are socialized to imagine what's important and normal with respect to language. Multiple manifestations of separation populate a larger episteme that marginalizes those who have been (and are) colonized—not only on the basis of the language that they speak, but also through processes that subject them to political, economic, social, and intellectual dependency.

As already pointed out, Alleyne is critical of dominant approaches to understanding Afro-Caribbean societies and languages. One of the problems that he sees with these approaches is the assumption of a strict disciplinary perspective that tends to divorce linguistic change from cultural change. He argued that adaptation to new circumstances and the retention of West African linguistic features were coexistent, complementary processes rather than an "either-or situation," and he saw these processes as ongoing. Thus, his scholarship encourages a holistic approach to Afro-Caribbean languages that positions them in terms of their relevant historical sources (i.e., West African languages and cultures in contact with European languages and cultures in a diverse set of contexts). He is known in linguistics for his interest in the "substrate features" of Creole languages, which in the Caribbean include sounds, syntactic patterns, words, meanings, and other structures of African origin. Alleyne argued that these are not primitive "holdovers" but elements of a rich heritage that emerged as natural pragmatic responses to lived experience.

The separation of Haiti and Afro-Caribbean life from Africa, like linguistic ideologies that perpetuate illiteracy or what Alleyne called Greco-Roman norms, are manifestations of coloniality, a stubborn legacy that Maldonado Torres describes as "long-standing patterns of power that emerged as a result of colonialism, but that define culture, labor, intersubjective relations, and knowledge production well beyond the strict limits of colonial administrations" ("Coloniality" 243). In Haiti, elements of the episteme structured by coloniality survived one of the boldest and most radical events in the history of the colonial world, the Haitian Revolution. The Revolution resulted in the abolition of slavery, national independence, and the defeat of Napoleon's army, but it did not manage to eradicate the idea that the language and culture of Haiti should be conceptualized in terms dictated by an expansive Western ethos. Maldonado points to an effective response to this predicament when he describes "the decolonial turn." It "posits the primacy of ethics as an antidote to problems with Western conceptions of freedom, autonomy, and equality; as well as the necessity of politics to forge a world where ethical relations become the norm rather than the exception" (*Against War* 7). Critiques of these powerful Western concepts often overlook highly problematic assumptions about language, in particular Creole languages. Considering these critiques alongside DeGraff's framework of postcolonial creolistics and the reality that generations after generations have been denied access to primary education in their mother tongue is essential to identifying the changes that are needed to realize the goal of establishing ethical relations as the norm.

The impact of the Greco-Roman tradition mentioned by Alleyne is also manifest in ideas about specific phenomena at the level of language structure. In fact, some of the dominant language ideologies that influence how Creole languages are viewed today can be traced back to the use of Latin as a universal standard for assessing and writing the grammars of other languages. Ironically, Latin's emergence as a model for grammar can be linked to the Romans' interest in Greek grammar and their belief that their language was inferior to that of the Greeks. The Romans modified their native language so that it conformed to patterns in Greek, which they considered highly prestigious and authoritative (see Joseph 68–72).

Negative ideas about Creole languages, Indigenous languages, and the languages of Africa that have prevailed historically have been used to justify conquest, bondage, and multiple forms of discrimination (e.g., racial, linguistic, economic) in the Caribbean and other regions of the world. In *Colonial Linguistics*, the linguistic anthropologist Joseph Errington shows that discourses about the languages spoken by colonized peoples were central, rather than marginal, to projects of European exploitation and imperialism. He explains that knowledge about language presented the colonized as biologically inferior, childlike, feminine, and incapable of self-government from the sixteenth century onward. Part of the intellectual inheritance of these ideas is the frequently encountered expectation that a "complete" language should exhibit inflection (the change of a word's form to express a particular grammatical function or an attribute such as tense, number or gender) and the belief that languages without inflection are deviant or underdeveloped. French, the source of most of Kreyòl's lexicon, has inflection, and within Western epistemology it is often imagined as the epitome of civilization in linguistic terms. Given French's link to Latin, the fact that it contributed to the formation of Kreyòl, and its global prestige, some of the differences that distinguish the two languages have led to assertions that Kreyòl is corrupt or deviant.

As hinted at above, the notion that inflection is a sign of civilization or an advanced culture shaped the history of linguistics in Europe. For example, the influential nineteenth-century linguist and philosopher Wilhelm von Humboldt (1791–1835) argued that Latin, Greek, and Sanskrit formed a category of "first rank languages" given that inflection was seen as "a living principle of development and increase" (86). "Isolating languages" (languages like Mandarin), seen as consisting of single elements, were said to have "no grammatical structure." Humboldt's views of inflection and his typological ranking of the world's languages have been rejected by contemporary linguists, but similar ideas linger in negative views of Creole languages that persist today.

Revisiting the language ideologies of linguists from an interdisciplinary perspective assists in identifying how coloniality acts to sustain negative myths about Creole languages and their speakers. It also reveals that these myths are more pervasive than many realize. The influential American linguist and Yale College faculty member William Dwight Whitney is often remembered for his contributions to uniformitarianism, including the principle that asserts that because all modern humans share the same cognitive functions and mental capacities, language change always responds to the same forces, across parameters of space and time. William Labov, a "founding father" of modern sociolinguistics, for example, draws attention to Whitney's importance, describing him as "the major proponent of uniformitarianism in linguistics" and a direct influence on the Neogrammarians (21); however, he does not address Whitney's arguments about groups that he and other linguists considered savage and uncivilized.

Whitney did indeed popularize the idea that language change among different communities of speakers is motivated by identical forces of the same kind across parameters of space and time. However, he argued *against* the idea that the forces were the same across all societies and languages. More specifically, he described some groups of people as exempt from "normal" linguistic processes. They include speakers of Creoles, contact varieties, and "patois," among others. Suggesting why their languages were not to be understood in terms of uniformitarianism, Whitney asserted—in language that today is recognized as racist and offensive—that they had been removed from opportunities to "rise out of savagery" due to "reasons of environment" that exposed them to processes (he refers pejoratively to contact, rapid change, corruption) that earned them an exceptional status and kept them close to humanity's "original state" (58).[5] While Whitney contemplates a broad theory of uniformitarianism, he insists that using analogies and conclusions drawn from the study of "cultivated nations and tongues" such as English, French, and other "civilized languages" to understand "barbarous races and uncivilized periods of human history" (a category that includes Kreyòl, other Creoles, many African languages, and Indigenous languages) is "the height of folly" (376).

It is difficult to pinpoint what future scientists will consider the blind spots of contemporary linguistics to be. Hopefully it will be possible to differentiate the true insights from the serious problems, as we can with the work of Whitney. Looking forward, it seems safe to say that some of our blind spots are likely to relate to ongoing debates in creolistics and the problem of coloniality.[6] These concern issues of history, language change, and arguments about whether a set of structural features is common to Creoles globally. Examples of ideas that are controversial in creolistics today:

- The processes of change leading to the emergence of Creoles is distinct from "normal" processes.
- Creoles derived from pidgins.
- All Creoles share a common set of structural features.
- The structures of Kreyòl and other Creole languages are simple.
- Kreyòl and other Caribbean Creoles are the result of Africans' failed attempts to acquire French.

In light of the above, I suggest that classroom learning about language in Haiti should include rethinking myths and stereotypical views perpetuated by coloniality as well as their persistence in popular beliefs and standard linguistic frameworks. It is important to have several topics that students can pursue as they learn about Haitian culture, and by extension Kreyòl. Information about specific grammatical phenomena can be useful. Grammatical gender, pluralization, and tense, for example, are topics that can be discussed to show how Kreyòl functions. The section below includes examples of these features that can be used to inspire meaningful conversation and reinforce the development of knowledge and new perspectives along the lines identified by Repko.

Grammatical Gender

The Haitian language has many structural characteristics that distinguish it from French. For example, it does not mark nouns for grammatical gender. This means that neither adjectives nor articles have forms that are inflected according to the gender of the noun that they modify. However, Kreyòl, like other contact languages that emerged in former French colonies in the Caribbean, does have natural gender, which refers to forms associated with the traditional biological distinction between females and males. It is expressed with the suffixes -è and -èz, which mark the feminine and masculine forms respectively.

Citing the example of *wangatè* and *wangatèz* (man/woman who believes in and or makes magical fetishes) from DeGraff ("Origins"), Neumann-Holzschuh mentions that the root of this word pair is from Bantu (the language Kikongo) in etymological terms, while the suffix is French. This fusion, which reminds us that it is incorrect to state that the language "doesn't have gender or inflection," is suggestive of the hybrid nature of Creole languages.

Natural gender is important for understanding the internal mechanics of specific lexical items and how linguists use features to theorize processes of change across languages. In a general description of grammatical gender, Dahl associates the absence of grammatical gender in any given language with newness or a relatively "early" position in the evolutionary cycle of a given language (112). At the same time, the presence of grammatical gender is typically associated with maturity and complexity. If we situate Kreyòl within this hierarchy of ideas, the language seems "simple" and "less evolved" than a language like French. However, Dahl also expresses interest in reconsidering traditional taxonomies. Data from Kreyòl and other languages that are sometimes represented as "young" could prove useful for the development of a novel approach to understanding gender cross-linguistically.

Pluralization

How does pluralization work in Kreyòl? It works differently than it does in European languages and may be misunderstood by some students. Examples 1 and 2 show that the monosyllabic marker *yo* can be used to make nouns plural.

Example 1:
klas mwen
class + 1st person possessive adjective
my class
klas mwen yo
class + 1st person possessive adjective + plural marker
my classes

Example 2:
liv la enteresan
book + definite article + interesting
the book is interesting
liv yo enteresan
book + plural marker + interesting
the books are interesting

These examples can be used to identify various characteristics of the language. Example 1 also presents information about syntax, showing that when a possessive adjective is present, it is post-posed, meaning it comes after the noun it modifies. This is of course different from English, in which the possessive pronoun is pre-posed. The second phrase, *klas mwen yo*, shows that the plural marker follows the possessive adjective.

In Example 2, the first phrase includes a definite article. It comes after the noun and before the adjective describing the noun, once again distinct from the pattern in English. In the second phrase, *yo* functions as a plural marker. It is positioned between the noun and the adjective. In addition, the phrases in Example 2 show that the copula (i.e. the verb *to be*) is understood but not stated and that the definite article is not used when the noun is plural. This phenomenon is sometimes called copula deletion. If students compare examples 1 and 2 above, then they should be able to correctly translate the sentences (i) *My class is interesting* and (ii) *My classes are interesting* into Haitian.

Examples 1 and 2 show some fundamental properties of Haitian, but they by no means provide an overview of pluralization in the language. Students should be reminded that the marker *yo* is not the only way of marking plurals in Haitian, just as *-s* is not the only way of marking plurals in English, French, or Spanish. Lefebvre shows that the West African language Fongbe also uses plural markers, and she identifies syntactic patterns that it shares with Kreyòl (noun + definite article + plural marker) (241). This is especially significant given that some enslaved Africans in Haiti were Fongbe speakers.

Tense

Tense is another topic that arises in discussions of inflection. Tense is the grammaticalized expression of location in time (Comrie viii). One way that Kreyòl marks tense is the use of preverbal markers. These monosyllabic words are also found in the languages of West Africa, which is of course the homeland of many of the ancestors of contemporary speakers of Kreyòl.

Te is one of several preverbal markers that are used to express tense in Haitian. Examples 3 and 4 provide sentences that use the preverbal marker *te* to form the past tense. Example 3 shows a case of vowel deletion. This straightforward phenomenon, which is fairly common in the world's languages, involves the deletion of the vowel in *te* because it immediately precedes a vowel that begins the word that follows, *etidye*.

Example 3:
mwen etidye
1st person pronoun + study
I study
mwen t etidye
1st person pronoun + past marker + study
I studied

Example 4:
mwen travay
1st person pronoun + work
I work
mwen te travay
1st person pronoun + past marker + work
I worked

One of the fascinating characteristics of Kreyòl's grammar is that its grammaticalized expression of time is based on a relative tense system, like many West African languages. Relative tense systems establish time through the use of a reference point that is communicated through discourse. This means that speakers can easily shift into the present-tense grammatical forms once they have established that they are talking about the past. The tense systems of French and other European languages, including English, are absolute tense systems. They rely on the moment of speaking as the reference point that distinguishes past from present.

This section has dealt with just a few features, but additional grammatical structures could also be discussed to show that critiques of Eurocentrism and commonalities that link DeGraff's description of postcolonial creolistics and "the decolonial turn" are important to linguistics and interdisciplinary teaching about Haiti and its linguistic landscape. These discussions could consider issues of terminology, questions of exoticism, literary movements involving Creole languages, the analysis of descriptions of Kreyòl found on the Internet, and questions about how to responsibly define "normal" processes of language change in cross-linguistic terms. Many theories of change assume that the situations of language contact that preceded the emergence of Creoles were abnormal.

Standardizing Kreyòl

Popular myths about Kreyòl and other Creole languages sometimes represent them as highly variable or unstable. These ideas detract from their overall prestige and can lead to the misconception that they cannot serve as a standard language or not be standardized. In Haiti, concerns about linguistic variation within the country raise questions about how society can function with a standard variety of Kreyòl. Dejean points out that the country's dialects are mutually intelligible. He rejects the idea that a single dialect should serve as the standard variety for the entire nation, suggesting that the imposition of a monolithic norm is not necessarily the best approach to language planning. In fact, he holds that establishing a standard this way could lead to serious problems. Dejean expresses concern that other one-dialect approaches could lead the majority of the population, a group that embraces Kreyòl as part of their identity, to become "artificially insecure in their language behavior" (88). Insecurity, he argues, could undermine teaching, learning, and language attitudes that are needed to make planning efforts successful.

What are the dialects of Kreyòl that account for some of the language's linguistic variation? Its dialects, like those of other languages, are associated with specific geographical areas and general circumstances and understandings of belonging and sociolinguistic identity that tend to cluster within them. Valdman identifies three regional dialects, each of which coordinates with a geographic space: (i) the North (generally the Cap-Haïtien area), (ii) the South (Jérémie and Les Cayes), and (iii) the Center (the capital and the Ouest department) (286–289). Bollee and Nembach reviewed data in more recent studies to see whether these have shifted. They found that these same general boundaries, which enforce a contrast between the Center and the peripheries, persist in the twenty-first century.

Some scholars have advocated for "internal standardization," a concept that is attuned with Haiti's realities and the sociolinguistic challenges it faces. Alleyne defines it as the official recognition of "emerging *de facto* norms" which are uncodified norms already accepted by a given community ("Problems" 89). He considers this approach ideal because the norms in question are already in use, familiar to the people, and stable given that they have organized communication in unofficial domains for more than 150 years. The idea is that having a small number of regional standards, probably three in this case, would not detract from the goal of a functional and effective system at the national level. This recommendation departs from the norms of European nation-states and one-size-fits-all policies, which have historically operated under a monolingual ideology.

Situating language planning and policy involving Kreyòl in terms of the Charter on Language Policy and Language Rights in the Creole-Speaking Caribbean, which was signed in Jamaica in 2011, is also useful in the classroom. The Charter, which is easy to access online, draws attention to ways in which interdisciplinary approaches to language involving history, public policy, communication studies, and the law can contribute to its goals. It points to general aims that students are likely to consider important and interesting, which are associated with notions such as linguistic rights, public pedagogy, and the principle of linguistic non-discrimination. At the same time, the Charter reminds students that government policies and popular attitudes vary considerably within the Caribbean region.

The Charter reminds readers that the Creole languages of the Caribbean are discrete and distinct from their European lexifiers, as well as multidialectal (Kreyòl and French are related but separate languages). Thus, Kreyòl is not a variety or a dialect of French, nor is it dependent upon French. Instead, it is an autonomous language with its own dialects.

International law informed the creation of the Charter. When the delegates at the conference where it was signed debated language policy and linguistic rights, they also discussed ideas that are found in various legal instruments to which numerous countries in the region were already signatories. These instruments contain clauses that can be used to eradicate linguistic discrimination and related problems, but they had rarely been used to advance language policies focusing on the rights of speakers of Creole languages. Among these instruments are: the Charter of the United Nations, the Universal Declaration of Human Rights, the International Covenant on Civil and Political Rights, and the American Convention on Human Rights (Brown-Blake and Devonish 5).[7]

The Charter's fifth article is an endorsement of the principle of linguistic non-discrimination and equality of language communities. This principle stipulates that the rights of all language communities are equal, independent of the political or legal status of the language in question. In other words, the members of all language communities have equal rights, whether the language in question is a Creole language, a European language, or any other language; official or unrecognized; standard or non-standard; written, spoken, or signed; native or immigrant; spoken by many or spoken by just a few. "Language community" as used in the document refers to any group established historically in a particular territorial space with members who use a common language as a natural means of communication and cultural cohesion. Haiti, as pointed out above, has multiple language communities, and individuals who are bilingual or bidialectal may belong to more than one.

Haiti is not among the Charter's current signatories, but the document includes provisions that can be used to boost educational achievement in the country as well as in other settings. For example, it recognizes early education in the mother tongue as important for language acquisition and overall cognitive development among youth, indicating that it "should be continued as long as practical" (see articles 24.5 and 24.6, respectively) (Brown-Blake and Devonish 12). This provision is compatible with recent studies in educational linguistics and neuroscience that underscore the importance of opportunities for youth to develop fluency in all of the languages of their repertoire. Like research done in Haiti, it suggests that the use of Kreyòl in schools and other formal settings is important not only for literacy, but also because it nurtures healthy levels of self-esteem, confidence, and trust.[8]

The Charter situates Haiti in regional context, pointing to issues that need to be addressed in various Caribbean settings. It recognizes the right to be multilingual and approaches language planning in a way that allows Creoles and other languages to coexist harmoniously. More to the point, it establishes that the teaching of Kreyòl or any other Creole language will not interfere with the teaching of standard European languages such as French, English, or Spanish. In terms of policy recommendations, it does not suggest that the teaching of European languages should cease.

Final Remarks

Exposing students to the richness of Haiti's Creole language and the scientific validity of arguments that can help to dismantle problematic myths about it is key to fostering interdisciplinary perspectives and developing new narratives about the country and its people. Language is so ubiquitous that it is sometimes left out of discussions of history, politics, and society, but as suggested above, it is a central aspect of the human experience, and the failure to discuss it can lead to the exacerbation of serious problems and the inability to communicate effectively. Beginning in the nineteenth century, a handful of individuals (native speakers of Creoles, linguists, writers, missionaries, grammarians) questioned assertions that enslaved people of African ancestry and their descendants spoke "gibberish" or simplistic pidgins, rather than full, complete, natural languages.[9] Their interventions assisted others in rejecting the notion that Creole languages are inferior or somehow removed from the plane of modern communication. Such examples signal that raising awareness about how language and linguistics take on meaning in the world is important in education and the arts, in efforts to promote democracy, in development initiatives prioritizing economic profit, and in struggles against poverty, coloniality, and other problems. The aforementioned interventions are also important to the language sciences. As is still the situation today, rejecting the dominant ideology was not always easy for those who pushed to empower the marginalized and imagine new ways of seeing and shaping society, knowledge, and scientific understanding. Their works suggest that they sometimes found it hard to transcend dominant myths and stereotypes. However, like many of the examples of critical reflection shared above, they assist us in navigating a crossroads of sorts and will ultimately nurture more humanistic views of language and society that we can pass on to our students.

Lesson Plan, Further Reading and Videos, and Idea Map

"Creating Interdisciplinary Knowledge about Haiti's Creole Language"

Lesson Plan

Freire in Haiti

Paulo Freire stands out as a provocative and foundational voice in the tradition of critical pedagogy, and his message is relatively unique, given its strong focus on language. He underscores that the question of which language should be used as a medium of instruction in the classroom is suffused with the history of power, pointing out that the particular assumptions and decisions related to the matter reflect the power relations prevalent in a given society and its vision of the future. Language policy is a site of contestation, where dominance and resistance clash as powerfully as along the many other fault lines of our riven world. It will come as no surprise, then that Freire's thought can extend our understanding of the dynamics that situate Kreyòl in the Republic of Haiti and in the Haitian diaspora. In the video clip identified below, Freire paints a concise picture of the core issues.

> Paulo Freire: On Language and Power
> https://www.youtube.com/watch?v=DTwY2nGONs8

Key concepts: dominant syntax, cultivated speech, rights, tolerance, empowerment, democracy

Key passages from the video for discussion

1. "Who says that this accent or that this way of thinking is the cultivated one? If there is one which is cultivated, it is because there is another which is not."

2. "[I]n being a democratic and tolerant teacher, it is necessary to explain, to make clear to the kids or the adults that their way of speaking is as beautiful as our way of speaking. . . . [T]hey have the right to speak like this."
3. "They need to learn the so-called dominant syntax for different reasons: the more the oppressed, the poor people, grasp the dominant syntax, the more they can articulate their voices and their speech in the struggle against injustice."

Discussion questions

1. What language(s) are associated with "cultivated speech" in Haiti? What factors account for this association?
2. What are examples of actions that can be linked to efforts to nurture the idea that Kreyòl should not be stigmatized?
3. How might a democratic and tolerant teacher, while conveying the dominant syntax, prevent the reproduction of its dominance in their pupils' understanding of language?

Further Reading and Videos

HAITIAN CANADIANS. *LINGUA*, 102701. HTTPS://DOI.ORG/10.1016/J.LINGUA.2019.06.002

Diasporic Haitian speakers are interviewed in order to obtain data on their phonological diversity and understand its role in diaspora formation. The Haitians' realizations of the examined phonological variables aligned with those of different non-Haitian speaker groups in Toronto, as well as with Haitian Creole realizations. These alignments depended on whether they were Haitian-born native speakers of a non-English language or born in Canada to Haitian parents while speaking English as their main language. Alignment with Black English speakers was observed, as well as variation according to individual aspirations of belonging. All informants spoke Haitian Creole and French with different degrees of fluency.

HODGSON, K. PAYS-LÀ CHAVIRÉ: REVOLUTIONARY POLITICS IN NINETEENTH-CENTURY HAITIAN CREOLE POPULAR MUSIC. *SMALL AXE: A CARIBBEAN JOURNAL OF CRITICISM*, VOL. 20, NO. 1 (49), PP. 18–36. DOI.ORG/10.1215/07990537-3481510

Archived Haitian Creole songs transcribed by a nineteenth-century French diplomat who became fluent in the language are analyzed closely in this article. It centers Creole-language popular music's role in Haitian politics, with an eye toward the methodological challenges faced by the archeological effort with which Hodgson proposes to enrich extant historical work on Haitian Creole music and its role in the nineteenth century. This "archaeological" approach to the reconstruction of the history of the Creole language text foregrounds the fragmented and decontextualized nature of written Creole in the nineteenth century. It notes the significance of a series of complex and interlinked issues relating to oral transmission, forgetting, individual and collective memory, and shifts in recording and transcription.

ZÉPHIR, F. CHALLENGES AND OPPORTUNITIES FOR HAITIAN CREOLE IN THE EDUCATIONAL SYSTEM OF POST-EARTHQUAKE HAITI. *INTERNATIONAL JOURNAL OF THE SOCIOLOGY OF LANGUAGE*, NO. 233, 2015, PP. 119–130. DOI.ORG/10.1515/ IJSL-2014-0055.

Zéphir describes Haitian Creole's marginalization in the education system relative to French despite the former being the most widespread language in the country. The author narrates how its marginalization in education reflects a wider subordination in a social hierarchy rooted in the stratification of French colonial rule, and highlights how the resultant language ideologies and power relations persevere against efforts to establish Haitian Creole as the medium of instruction in the country's schools. In addition, the article highlights positive developments and discusses various challenges related to the standardization process itself (e.g., how to create a shared orthography).

JANSEN, S. (2015). ETHNIC DIFFERENCE AND LANGUAGE IDEOLOGIES IN POPULAR DOMINICAN LITERATURE: THE CASE OF HAITIANIZED SPEECH. *INTERNATIONAL JOURNAL OF THE SOCIOLOGY OF LANGUAGE*, NO. 233, 2015, PP. 73–96. DOI.ORG/10.1515/IJSL-2014-0053

Jansen traces the construction of the Haitian as an "other" in Dominican culture through analysis of the language ideology processes found in the work of one of the Dominican Republic's most influential popular poets. The author focuses on semiotic processes that foreground how linguistic features perceived (correctly or not) to be Haitian are exaggerated and deployed in the poems to discursively construct the "Dominican" and the "Haitian," while drawing a sharp line between them. The prevalence of these constructs in contemporary culture is highlighted as evidence of the historical legacy of language ideologies in literature.

HAITIAN CREOLE—THE WORLD'S MOST WIDELY SPOKEN CREOLE LANGUAGE
HTTPS://WWW.YOUTUBE.COM/WATCH?V=8IUQCYIDEPE

A video providing a brief overview of the language's demographics, history, and features, with several examples comparing sentences in French and Haitian Creole. The host studied linguistics and is based in Canada.

HAITIAN VOICES: HAITIAN CREOLE
HTTPS://WWW.YOUTUBE.COM/WATCH?V=NQMYVWILFAA

Haitian Voices highlights topics relevant to South Florida's Haitian communities. In this broadcast, Haitian-American media and language professionals talk about the importance of Haitian Creole in their lives, as well as about the language itself and its use throughout the Haitian diaspora.

COOL FACTS ABOUT HAITIAN CREOLE
HTTPS://BILINGUA.IO/COOL-FACTS-ABOUT-HAITIAN-CREOLE

Bilingua is a website focusing on language exchange for language learners. It offers short language profiles in which brief descriptions of a language's history and statistics are provided, along with examples of salient structural features.

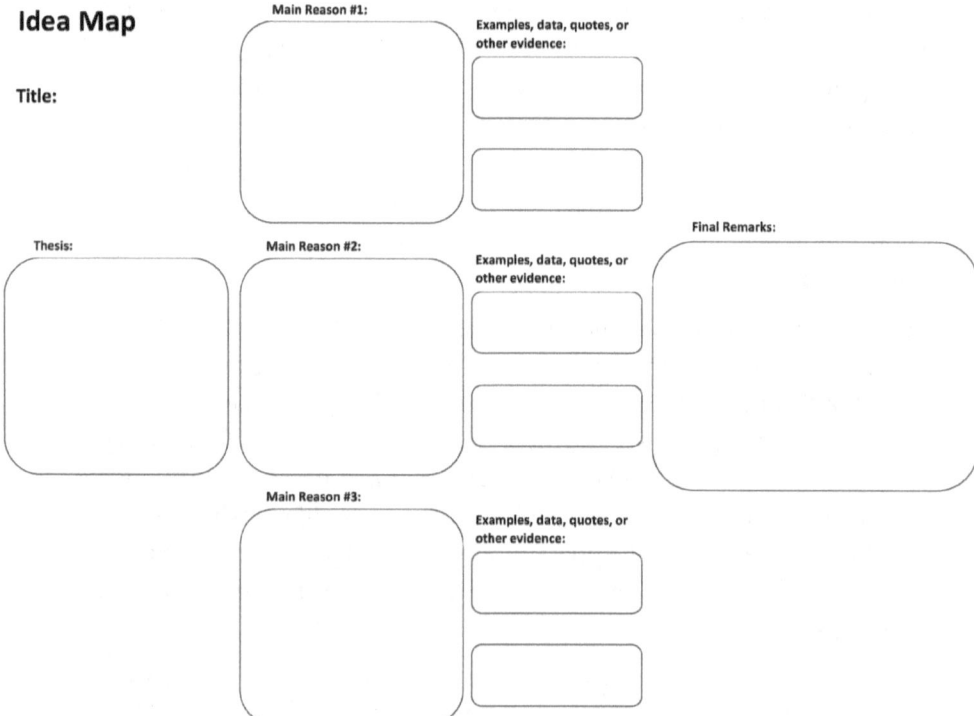

Figure 5.1. Idea map to be used as a planning document for essay writing. Developed by Don E. Walicek.

Notes

1. Please note that Kreyòl has multiple names. Linguists also call it Haitian and Haitian Creole.
2. Creolistics is also known as pidgin and creole studies.
3. In this chapter, Creole languages are defined as a category of languages that were formed in a specific set of sociohistorical conditions. In the Caribbean, they emerged in the context of language contact, the restructuring of grammars, sociocultural change, the Atlantic slave trade, and the region's colonization by various European powers.
4. UNESCO data from Haiti for 2016 show that the literacy rate among people between the ages of 15 and 24 is approximately 83 percent. Available data do not compare literacy rates in Haitian and French.
5. For a description of "Creole exceptionalism" and an argument against it, see DeGraff (2003).
6. For a useful summary of ideas debated in creolistics, see Bakker (2017).
7. The Universal Declaration of Linguistic Rights was used to establish broad precepts as a base from which policies and laws related to language could emanate; it was established in the 1990s by sociolinguists, NGOs, the International PEN Club, and members of UNESCO.
8. UNESCO has encouraged formal instruction in the mother tongue of youth since 1953.
9. Among those whose who challenged negative views of Creole languages in the nineteenth century are Auguste de Saint-Quentin, Thomas Russell, Hugo Schuchardt, and J. J. Thomas.

Works Cited

Alleyne, Mervyn. *Comparative Afro-American: An Historical-Comparative Study*. Karoma, 1980.
———. "Problems of Standardization of Creole Languages." *Language and the Social Construction of Identity in Creole Situations*, edited by Marcyliena Morgan and Mervyn Alleyne, Center for Afro-American Studies at UCLA, 1994, pp. 8–17.
———. "Language and Identity in the Caribbean: Symbols and Prerogatives." *Segundo Simposio de Caribe 2000: Hablar, Nombrar, Pertenecer*, edited by Lowell Fiet and Janette Becerra, 1998, pp. 37–48.
Bakker, Peter. "Key Concepts in the History of Creole Studies." *Creole Studies—Phylogenetic Approaches*, edited by Peter Bakker et al., John Benjamins, 2017, pp. 5–33.
Bollée, Annegret, and Pamela Nembach. "Diatopic Variation in Haitian Creole." *History, Society, and Variation: In Honor of Albert Valdman*, edited by J. Clancy Clements, Thomas A. Kingler et al., John Benjamins, 2006, pp. 225–233.
Brown-Blake, Celia, and Hubert Devonish. "Planning for Language Rights in the Caribbean: The Birth of the Charter on Language Policy and Language Rights in the Creole-speaking Caribbean." *Sargasso, Language Rights and Language Policy in the Caribbean*, edited by Celia Brown-Blake and Don E. Walicek, 2013, pp. 3–22.
"The Charter on Language Policy and Language Rights in the Creole-Speaking Caribbean," The International Centre for Caribbean Language Research Working Group, January 14, 2011, http://caribbeanlanguagepolicy.weebly.com. Accessed August 1, 2020.

Comrie, Bernard. *Tense*. Cambridge UP, 1985.
"Constitution of the Republic of Haiti of 1987," Base de Données Politiques des Ameriques, updated July 9, 2011. https://pdba.georgetown.edu/Constitutions/Haiti/haiti1987.html. Accessed July 25, 2020.
Craig, Dennis. *Teaching Language and Literacy to Caribbean Students; From Vernacular to Standard English*. Ian Randle, 2006.
Dahl, Östen. *The Growth and Maintenance of Linguistic Complexity*. John Benjamins, 2004.
DeGraff, Michel. "On the Origins of Creoles: A Cartesian Critique of Neo-Darwinian Linguistics. *Linguistic Typology*, vol. 5, no. 2, 2001, pp. 213–230.
———. "Against Creole Exceptionalism." *Language*, vol. 79, no. 2, 2003, pp. 391–410.
DeGraff, Michel, and Stump, Glenda S. "Kreyòl, Pedagogy and Technology for Opening Up Quality Education in Haiti: Changes in Teachers' Metalinguistic Attitudes as First Steps in a Paradigm Shift." *Language: Journal of the Linguistic Society of America*, vol. 94, no. 2, 2018, pp. 127–157.
Dejean, Yves. "Identifying the Standards for Haitian Creole." *Sargasso: Language Rights and Language Policy in the Caribbean*, edited by Celia Brown-Blake and Don E. Walicek, 2013, pp. 83–95.
Dizikes, Peter. "3 Questions: Michel DeGraff on Haiti's New Policy for Teaching in Kreyòl." *MIT News* July 20, 2015 http://news.mit.edu/2015/3-questions-michel-degraff-haiti-teaching-kreyol-0720. Accessed August 1, 2020.
Dreyfuss, Joel. "A Cage of Words." *The Butterfly's Way; Voices from the Haitian Dyaspora in the United States*, edited by Edwidge Danticat, Soho, 2001, pp. 57–59.
Errington, Joseph. *Linguistics in a Colonial World: A Story of Language, Meaning, and Power*. Blackwell, 2008.
Joseph, John E. *Eloquence and Power: The Rise of Standards and Standard Languages*. Basil Blackwell, 1987.
Labov, William. *Principles of Linguistic Change; Volume 2: Social Factors*. Blackwell, 2001.
Lefebvre, Claire. *Issues in the Study of Pidgin and Creole Languages*. John Benjamins, 2004.
Maldonado Torres, Nelson. "On the Coloniality of Being: Contributions to the Development of a Concept." *Journal of Cultural Studies*, vol. 21, no. 2, 2007, pp. 240–270.
———. *Against War; Views from the Underside of Modernity*. Duke UP, 2008.
Neumann-Holzschuh, Ingrid. "Gender in French Creoles: The Story of a Loser." *History, Society, and Variation*, edited by J. Clancy Clements, John Benjamins, 2006, pp. 251–272.
Repko, Allen F. "Assessing Interdisciplinary Learning Outcomes." *Academic Exchange Quarterly*, vol. 12, no. 3, 2008, pp. 171–178.
Valdman, Albert. *Le creole: Structure, statut et origine*. Klinksieck, 1978.
Whitney, William Dwight. *Language and the Study of Languages; Twelve Lectures on the Principles of Linguistic Science*. N. Trübner, 1867.

Teaching about Haitian History and Politics

6

Haiti in the Presidencies of John Adams and John Quincy Adams

Lesson Plans and Course Modules

DARREN STALOFF AND ALESSANDRA BENEDICTY-KOKKEN

Introduction: Why Haiti through John Adams and John Quincy Adams?

This chapter tells a story that focuses on the role of Haiti in the political careers of John Adams and his son John Quincy Adams. It also ineluctably, if somewhat tangentially, addresses issues raised by the presidencies of Thomas Jefferson and Andrew Jackson.[1] In so doing, we offer students and instructors insight into the importance of Haiti in the political imaginary of the first four decades of US-American history. The need to tell this particular story—and to recount it with a pedagogical objective—directly emerges from students' questions, in the context of a variety of our courses. It also comes from conversations between historians of the early United States and historians of Haiti.

The history of the early United States with regard to Haiti means considering some rather vexed and complex facts. It is important to keep in mind that the Haitian Revolution began in 1791 and ended in 1804, with the establishment of Haiti under revolutionary leader Jean-Jacques Dessalines on January 1, 1804. The period from 1791 to 1806 involved many geopolitical shifts. In 1791, the island of Saint-Domingue/Santo Domingo, as the colonial powers named it, was divided into two parts. The western part of the island was under French control while the eastern part was under Spanish rule. In the period leading up to and during the Haitian Revolution, Toussaint Louverture, the Haitian revolutionary leader who is the most influential in the story we tell about Adams and Jefferson, had to deal with drastically changing political contexts in France, from the Girondin government titularly led by Louis XVI to the French Republic under Maximilien Robespierre (which officially outlawed slavery in the colonies, including Saint-Domingue) and the failed attempt to reimpose slavery by Napoleon Bonaparte. During these tumultuous years, John Adams and Thomas Jefferson negotiated their relationship to Saint-Domingue and, later, Haiti in rather different ways. Where Adams engaged in direct diplomacy with Louverture, Jefferson limited interaction to the consular level. Decades later, John Quincy Adams dealt with the legacy of this history.

A second context to hold close as we tell the story of Adams's and his son Quincy Adams's presidencies is that of the mobile episteme of racialization. In a rather short time period, understandings of race changed, and the Haitian Revolution played into this evolving understanding. From the 1600s to the 1800s, there were workers, businesspeople, plantation laborers and owners who were members of the community of free people of color or *gens de couleur libres* in the Caribbean and North America. While enslaved people were commonly imagined as those of African descent, not all those of African descent were enslaved. What existed then in North America and the Americas more broadly was a world in which slavery was largely accepted as an institution while free people of color participated in varying degrees in the civil society of which they were a part.

The Haitian revolutionaries' commitment to abolishing slavery occurred at a moment when plantation slavery played a significant economic role in many North American, South American and Caribbean communities. Both Adams and Jefferson explicitly denounced slavery, yet neither was willing to insist on its complete abolition within the United States. Nevertheless, Adams and Jefferson did differ on the extent of diplomatic engagement of the United States with Haitian revolutionary leaders; Adams favored complete engagement, while Jefferson opted for restricting it to the consular level. Moreover, although both Adams and Quincy Adams understood slavery as a moral wrong, they were unwilling to officially proscribe it within the United States. It must also be noted that Louverture faced similar economic dilemmas and even sought to sustain the plantation system within what would become Haiti, though at the same moment in history, he never accepted the possibility of any course that did not include the complete and immediate abolition of slavery.

Further complicating matters is the fact that the Haitian Revolution contributed in part to a shift in racial thinking in the United States. The success of the Haitian Revolution, and reports of massacres by émigré *gens de couleur libres* and white refugees, fed a rising fear that gripped plantation owners in the

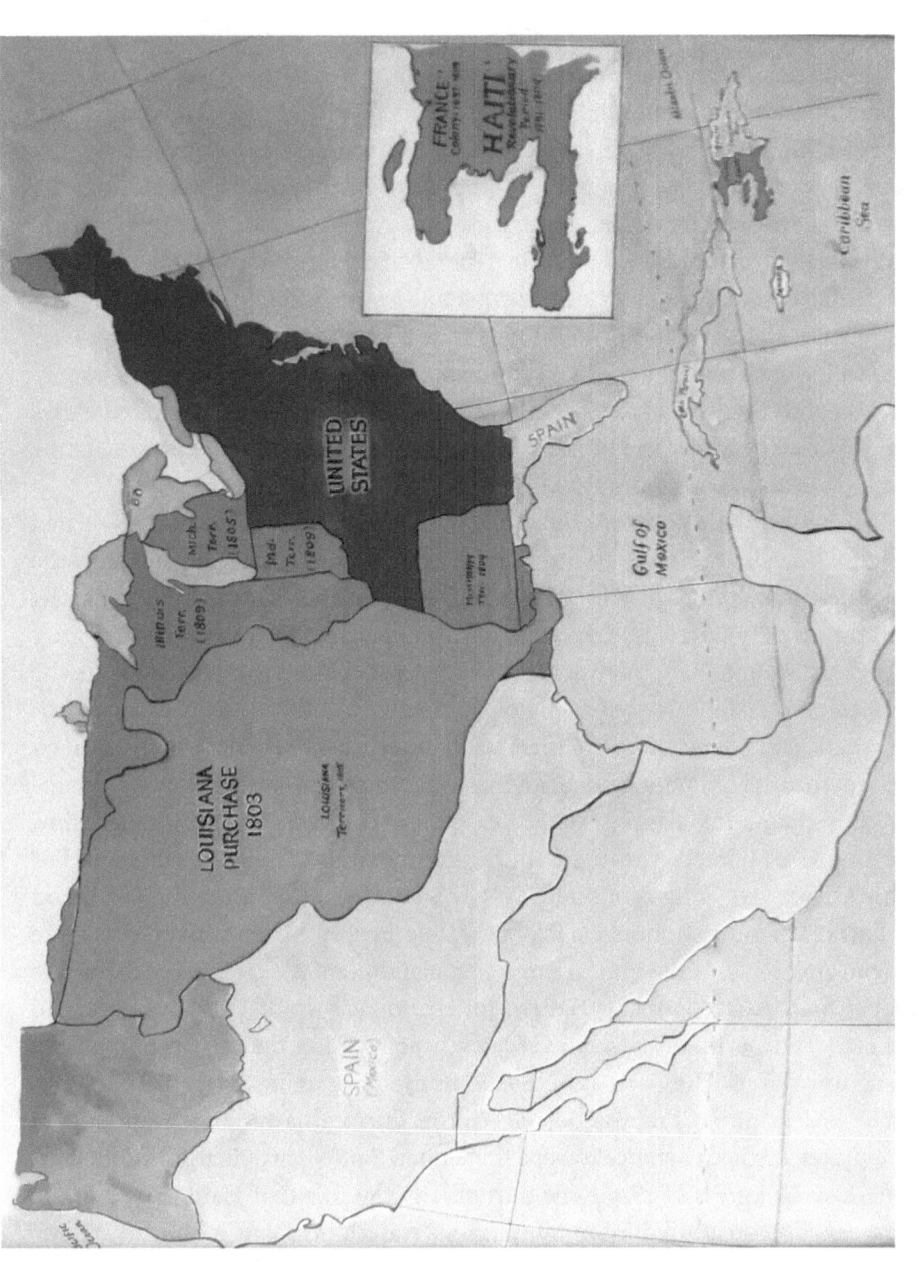

Figure 6.1. Colonial-era map of the island of Saint-Domingue/Santo Domingo with the French territory of Louisiana in what would become the United States. Ulrick Jean-Pierre, *Haiti-Louisiana Map*. 2018. Oil on canvas. 48 × 60 inches. Collection of the artist.

United States. Part of this fear was that if they were to allow free people of color to have status in society, they might, inspired by the example of Haiti, encourage all people of color to rebel. This fear became all the more palpable when it seemed to materialize in Gabriel Prosser's planned insurrection of 1800.

This article would not have been possible without the past two decades' proliferation of excellent scholarship in English, which brings US and Haitian histories into dialogue with each other. This chapter provides specific suggestions as to course modules and readings. For each reading, we indicate the particular readership(s): i.e., undergraduate, graduate, and/or instructors. In addition to these tools, we provide general historical background as well as particular contexts necessary to understanding and explaining how the early histories of Haiti and the United States were particularly intertwined. We have chosen to focus on the father and son presidents because they serve as human bookends to the period that we might consider to be the early United States (the birth of the father in Quincy, Massachusetts, in 1735 and the passing of the son in 1848 in Washington, D.C.).

What comes through most forcefully in the many and varied sources related to John Adams and John Quincy Adams is their absolute commitment to the documents that undergird the US government (Traub xvii), and more generally the ethos that "all men are created equal" (Declaration of Independence 1776). Yet both statesmen saw themselves as pragmatists whose role was to assure the political and economic well-being of the United States of America, and such pragmatic considerations were ineluctably imbricated in and compromised by the fact that the Union included a number of states whose economy was predicated on plantation slavery. Tragically, this meant that some of the decisions they made conflicted with their constitutional and republican principles. For John Adams, engaging economically with Haiti meant securing the livelihood and safety of US merchants (Fick 31). While he and his administration were in conversation with Louverture in an official diplomatic capacity, Adams was well aware that recognizing Haitian independence would pose a problem to the early prosperity of the United States, a new nation that was economically reliant on slavery (Johnson 176). For John Quincy Adams, Haiti played a decisive role in how Congress perceived him during his time as president. In fact, Quincy Adams's stance toward the United States' participation at the Pan-American Congress of 1825—and particularly the role that Haiti played in the conference—constituted Quincy Adams's "Waterloo," costing him his bid for re-election: in 1828, he was defeated by Andrew Jackson (Traub 345).

In its most general sense, then, as historians such as Jean Casimir, Marlene Daut, Laurent Dubois, Carolyn Fick, Ronald Angelo Johnson, Darren Staloff, and James Traub point out, for the early US statesmen, Haiti represented an inconvenient truth, which compromised the ideals of the new state. They saw themselves as having no choice: they felt they had to accept the ethical wrong so as to guarantee the United States' economic livelihood as well as ensure that it would not be threatened by the interests of secessionists and advocates for civil war. In focusing on Haiti in narrating the early history of the United States, it becomes clear that statesmen of the first republic in the Western Hemisphere struggled between principle and what they understood to be pragmatism. On the one hand, politicians such as Adams and his son saw themselves as endowed with the duty to uphold the principle of freedom for all. On the other hand, they also understood themselves as realists who had to preserve—both economically and politically—a precarious new Federal Republic.

Moreover, both Haiti and the United States were vulnerable. Both countries came into being within a politically unstable context, a Western Hemisphere in constant turmoil, wherein European colonial powers attempted to preserve a certain amount of hegemony over territories that were now increasingly asserting themselves as independent nation-states. Even more troublesome to Adams and Quincy Adams was the fact that the outcome of "radical" (Nesbitt 23) revolutions such as those of France or Haiti had not led to stability, but to quite the opposite: violence, as in the Reign of Terror in France immediately following the French Revolution in 1793 and 1794; or the dissolution of revolutionary forces that were once united, as in Haiti in the last three years of Louverture's leadership of the Haitian Revolution, from 1799–1802 (Dubois *Avengers of the New World*, 233–235, 274). While the case might be made that both Adams and Quincy Adams were morally open to the idea of a nation such as Haiti that outlawed slavery, it also can be argued that both presidents feared that were they to have conceded to such a political reality in the United States, they would have compromised its political and economic stability.

Our Students' Questions, or the Challenge of Pedagogy

Whereas scholars usually focus their work on a particular figure, John Adams or Toussaint Louverture, for example, or a particular time period, such as the revolutionary period and its immediate aftermath, students—or more generally those who are not specialists in a given field—often want to understand a phenomenon more holistically, asking questions that span decades and even centuries: How did Haiti go from being rich to poor? If the US Declaration of Independence is considered one of the foundational texts in a history of human rights, how is it that slavery remained legal for so long? Why did the US initially help Haiti in its revolutionary struggle, and then a few years later cut diplomatic ties with Haiti? Why are we not taught about the Middle Passage and slavery in a more systematic way? Why did Steven Spielberg make first a film about the Holocaust (*Schindler's List* 1993) and then just a few years later a film about the slave trade (*Amistad* 1997), in which John Quincy Adams plays a major role?

From these questions, the two course modules emerged, which we include at the end of this chapter. And while our chapter most certainly does not answer all of the above questions, it emerges from an effort to address them. The particular challenge in composing such a chapter dedicated to the pedagogical imperative to understand a phenomenon more comprehensively is to propose a storyline that takes into account the more *longue durée* [long view] approach while at the same time maintaining academic rigor. To this end, we offer one course module that is more straightforward, which makes connections between and among primary sources, historiography, and literary and cinematic renditions of early US and Haitian history. The other, which is more conjectural, uses scholarly work on race to deliberate on the evolution—or rather the regression—of race discourse as a result of how representatives of the early United States government perceived Haitian independence.

Ultimately, the focus on Adams and his son Quincy Adams shows how two men at different times felt that the new nation could only be fortified by expansion, and that such expansion constantly undermined the universalist principles of the founding documents. For example, Quincy Adams lost the presidency to Andrew Jackson, under whose aegis the Cherokee were forcefully evicted from their fertile agricultural lands to arid land to the west in order to allow an influx of European settlers to re-occupy their farms. The dispossession of the Cherokee in turn led to an increased justification of the large-scale use of slavery in the US South. It is also perhaps not a coincidence that in February 1848, Quincy Adams suffered a stroke on the House floor from which he later died while allegedly arguing in favor of honoring US soldiers who had died in the Mexican-American war. Although Quincy Adams opposed the war, believing it would expand the implementation of slavery, he felt the soldiers' service should be recognized.

In short, the first half of the nineteenth century constitutes a period in which the US government worked to invalidate, contain, and reduce those communities and nation-states, such as Haiti, that threatened its ability to assure its power during a time in which it was particularly vulnerable, a period in which weakened European colonial powers had not yet abandoned their prospects and aspirations for the Americas. The accounts below examine US history through a specific but revelatory lens: that of Haiti in the presidencies of Adams and his son. In so doing, they shed light on the fraught tension between the idealism of service to one's country and the inequalities that undergird the project of establishing a powerful nation-state.

John Adams and Saint-Domingue

On July 2, 1799, President John Adams wrote of his befuddlement with the diplomatic strategies of Saint-Domingue's revolutionary leader. "Toussaint [Louverture] has evidently puzzled himself, the French government, the English cabinet, and the administration of the United States," he informed his secretary of state. "All the rest of the world knows as little what to do with him as he knows what to do with himself" (Adams and Pickering). By this point, the United States had established full consular and trade relations with the government of Toussaint Louverture and entered into an unofficial three-way military alliance with it and Great Britain against France. Roughly one year later, in part as a result of prior naval support by the United States, Toussaint had defeated his domestic rivals and consolidated his power over the island. Had he declared independence at that point, the Adams administration would certainly have recognized the new republic and established full diplomatic relations. Yet Toussaint declined to take this step, and in many ways the US president dreaded it. Both wanted and feared the independence of Saint-Domingue because both were caught in the crossfire of the ongoing rivalry between the great Atlantic powers of revolutionary France and Great Britain.[2]

For Adams, the dominant issue was an undeclared naval war with France known as the "Quasi-War," which he inherited upon assuming office in 1797. The roots of this conflict lay in the Jay Treaty, which the previous administration had made with Great Britain, granting that country commercial privileges that seemed to conflict with the previous terms of the treaties that the United States has signed with France in 1778. The Directory (as the government of France was known at the time) responded by issuing orders in the summer of 1796 authorizing the seizure of American shipping to Great Britain, and extended that authorization to commerce throughout the Atlantic the following spring. In addition, they refused to treat with the American representative in Europe, clearly expecting their assaults on American commerce to force the United States to capitulate to their demands. This was a very promising strategy because by the time this conflict erupted, Saint-Domingue was the second-most important source of mercantile trade for the new nation. In short order insurance rates skyrocketed as American ships were seized by French privateers (by the end of the Quasi-War, over one-third of America's merchant fleet had been captured).

Adams adopted a two-pronged response upon assuming office in March 1797. On the one hand, he prompted Congress to support a rapid and dramatic buildup of American naval forces, while on the other, he sent a fresh diplomatic embassy to negotiate a settlement. The latter project faltered when the French foreign minister sent intermediaries to demand bribes and forced loans before negotiations could begin, demands that were curtly refused and, when exposed to the Congress and American public in the spring of 1798, became known as the XYZ Affair. The consequence of this development was not merely the cessation of diplomatic relations with France, but a growing popular pro-war sentiment against the former revolutionary ally. By contrast, the military buildup paid fairly large dividends, as American commanders scored several impressive victories against French military and mercantile vessels. By the summer of 1798, the United States was caught in an increasingly hot if undeclared war with France with few opportunities for resolution. The French were pinned down by British forces that had captured Napoleon Bonaparte's fleet at the battle of the Nile, and Britain's attempt to capture Saint-Domingue, the jewel of the French empire in the Americas, had faltered in the face of Toussaint's military leadership.

It was at this point that Toussaint took the initiative. In November 1798 he wrote to Adams, offering friendly assurances that US shipping to ports under his control would be protected. Toussaint desperately needed military supplies in his struggle for control over the island as well as a market for exports of sugar and coffee, and the United States was the only reliable venue for both. He also understood that Adams could use the leverage of this alliance, one that shortly included the British as well, to force the French back to the negotiating table (Adams proposed a French embassy to Paris within one month of receiving Toussaint's letter). In early 1799, Adams signed legislation that authorized him to resume trade with what would become Haiti as soon as he could determine that such shipping would be protected. He dispatched a consul general, Edward Stevens, to negotiate just such an agreement. By the early summer of that year trade had been resumed with two of the leading ports under Louverture's control, and the other ports were cleared for US shipping before the end of the year. In early 1800, a US blockade and bombardment of Jacmel had reduced the last stronghold of Toussaint's rival, André Rigaud. By early April, negotiations for what would be known as the Treaty of Mortefontaine had begun, officially beginning the end of the Quasi-War. The United States had, at least for the time being, extricated itself from the ongoing struggles of Britain and France, and Toussaint had established the conditions for declaring the independence of Saint-Domingue.

It was a step, however, that Louverture never took. Had he done so, as noted above, the Adams Administration would certainly have recognized his government. But it would have done so with great reluctance. Not only would such recognition have complicated relations with France, but the president feared that independence for Saint-Domingue would trigger anti-colonial movements throughout the Caribbean (Adams 634). This in turn would have led to more intrusions by the European colonial powers of the Netherlands and Spain, both of which the United States needed as friendly trading partners, but it would also have disrupted trade within the "New World." For his own part, Toussaint faced a similar dilemma. Independence might have given his regime legitimacy, but it would have made him increasingly dependent on his US and British allies, limiting his options for independent maneuvering. As long as he remained ostensibly loyal to France, he could play one side against the other, but without independence there was always the threat that France would try to recapture the island from his grasp, the very thing that the new first consul Napoleon Bonaparte endeavored to do shortly after Adams left office. The problem of independence for what would become the nation of Haiti puzzled both Adams and Toussaint because, faced with the challenge of European imperial states, neither had the means or power to steer an independent course in the war-torn Atlantic.

John Quincy Adams, Haiti, and the *Amistad*

Twenty-five years later, John Adams's son John Quincy Adams faced twin challenges: a continued—even if mitigated—wariness of European imperial states, but also that of emerging American nations' quest for sovereignty and independence (such as the Republic of Bolivia). As such, Haiti continued to play an essential role in the US presidency. Traub writes, in "the spring of 1825, the foreign ministers of Colombia and Mexico invited the United States to attend a Pan-American Congress to be held October 1 in Panama, then part of Colombia" (Traub 342). The invitation came in the immediate aftermath of the Monroe Doctrine, articulated by President James Monroe in his annual address in December (1823), which Quincy Adams himself had worked to draft in his role as President Monroe's secretary of state. Quincy Adams was reticent about attending the Pan-American Congress for two reasons. First, he did not want to be directly involved in confrontations among Britain, Spain, Colombia, and Mexico unless these conflicts were to affect the United States directly. Before the Haitian Revolution, Saint-Domingue had been one of Europe's and the United States' most lucrative trading partners. However, following the Haitian Revolution and Haiti's independence in 1804, Cuba had replaced Haiti as a more profitable trading partner. By 1825, it was clear that France would not regain Haiti as a colony (Traub 342). Quincy Adams was not interested in annexing Cuba unless France or England were to try to take it over from Spain. In other words, for Quincy Adams, the Monroe Doctrine meant that European powers could keep their extant colonies, but they could not acquire new territories or transfer them to each other. At the time of his invitation to the Pan-American Congress in 1825, Quincy Adams felt that it was unlikely that France would try to acquire Cuba from Spain. Instead, it was his secretary of state Henry Clay, "the great champion of the infant republics" of Colombia and Mexico (Traub 342), who wanted to attend the Pan-American Congress to show US solidarity with their cause.

The second reason that Quincy Adams was wary of attending the Pan-American Congress was that he wanted to avoid upsetting congressional interests that perceived any US engagement with Haiti as indicating an abolitionist stance. During his presidency as well as later in his political career, Quincy Adams wanted at all costs to avoid appearing as an abolitionist, not because he approved of slavery (in terms of his personal beliefs), but because his main objective was to preserve the union and avoid secession or civil war. In the end, Quincy Adams's administration attended the conference; yet, for many politicians and pundits, a presence at the conference indicated to the US public that his presidency had engaged in official diplomatic relations with Haiti.

It is perhaps Henry Clay's stance in regard to the attendance at the Pan-American Congress that is most indicative of the inconsistencies associated with the United States' principle of "freedom." More particularly, the disagreement between President Quincy Adams and Secretary of State Clay reveals how both statesmen underestimated the power of the emerging slavocracy in the United States. Clay, "himself a slave owner" (Traub 430), felt that the American public would read Quincy Adams's attendance at the Pan-American Congress as a forceful statement that England and France should retreat from meddling in Western hemispheric affairs. Clay was convinced that the president's attendance at the Congress in Panama would demonstrate the United States' "hemispheric fraternity" to other nascent republics trying to assert their sovereignty against Europe. Most interestingly as regards Haiti is that Clay "had tried, and failed, to persuade Quincy Adams to recognize Haiti" (Traub 351). In other words, Clay thought it was the United States' role to acknowledge other

American nations' sovereignty regardless of what their stance on slavery was. Moreover, he believed the American people also felt this way. On the other hand, Quincy Adams, who was morally against slavery, maintained a political record that illustrates that he considered that if slavery indeed fell under governmental dominion, its jurisdiction lay less with the federal government than with state governments. More directly stated, Clay owned slaves but took the political position that the US should recognize Haitian sovereignty, whereas Quincy Adams never owned slaves, but demonstrated himself to be extremely reticent to make any move that might appear as an indicator of US recognition of Haiti.

Most importantly, the disagreement between Clay and Quincy Adams over their attendance at the Pan-American Congress demonstrates two facts. First, Haiti mattered enormously to both the US Congress and the US public. Most tangibly, the event led to "a new Washington newspaper, the *United States Telegraph*, designed to counteract the pro-Adams *National Journal* and the mostly nonpartisan *National Intelligencer*" (Traub 355). Second, the controversy between the two statesmen suggests that there was little consensus regarding what exactly constituted the US ideal of freedom. Was freedom about the right for a nation-state to be recognized as a sovereign republic regardless of the republic's stance on slavery? Was freedom about "permitt[ing] restricted white, male republicanism to masquerade as universal" (Dillon and Drexler 4), or about exposing such racial inequality? Or was freedom about assuring economic and political stability even at the cost of keeping a significant part of the population enslaved?

Quincy Adams never admitted that he was an abolitionist, even if his political and legal record, as well as his journals, corroborate the opposite. For the majority of his career, he felt that whether or not one chose to own slaves was primarily of private moral rather than political concern. His primary goal, then, in his five-decade career as a public servant was to preserve the unity of the United States. In other words, his political decisions—and his private journals—show that he unambiguously wanted to avoid the division of the union. Both the threat of secession of emerging new states such as Texas as well as the imminent possibility of civil war threatened the existence of a nation conceived in 1776, which when Quincy Adams became president was not yet six decades old.

Even when Quincy Adams successfully argued in front of the Supreme Court in favor of the freedom of the Mende, who after insurrection aboard the schooner *Amistad* had made their way from Cuba to Long Island on August 24, 1839, he did so avoiding discussions of abolitionism. He had to deliberate on the case bearing in mind that five of the Supreme Court justices "were Southern slaveholders" (Traub 477). Instead, he based his litigation around the urgency to preserve the integrity associated with the principles that undergird the Declaration of Independence. The irony is palpable: to be successful in convincing the Supreme Court justices to return the Mende to West Africa, Quincy Adams had to devise an argument that distanced itself as much as possible from conversations around human rights. Instead, he had to argue on the principles of US sovereignty. In other words, as Roger Sherman Baldwin had previously argued before the federal magistrate, the Mende were not to be tried under US jurisdiction because they were not US property. They were not the property of anyone in the United States, nor were they US citizens, for they had not been born in the United States. In addition, the Treaty of 1795, which bound the US to return "shipwrecked or disabled vessels and cargo" to Spain, did not apply, since it had been proven in the initial federal case presided over by Judge Andrew Judson that the Mende men were not the legal property of Spain, but rather kidnapped illegally from the Gallinas Coast (Traub 472, 478). In other words, Quincy Adams was able to win the case because he convinced the Supreme Court justices on two points. First, that by appealing the case at the federal level, the executive branch of the US government had impinged heavy-handedly on the judicial process. Second, and more importantly, the Spanish crown seemed to impose its will on the US government. The entire ethos of the Monroe Doctrine was to assure US sovereignty with respect to foreign, and notably, former European colonial powers in the Americas (Traub 280–81).

Despite the fact that Baldwin had argued using similar premises as Quincy Adams, it was Quincy Adams's stature and pedigree that played the most important role in advocating for the Mendes' freedom. Traub explains that upon "his death in 1848 at the age of eighty, [John Quincy] Adams was mourned, and revered, as the last remaining link to the heroic generation of the [US] founders" (Traub xii). Quincy Adams's political career is remarkable in that he was quite unpopular among many politicians, never really belonging to any one party or faction of politicians. As disliked as he was in Congress, success before the Supreme Court in the case of *United States v. The Amistad* had as much to do with the respect the Supreme Court justices had for him as a guardian of the original founding tenets that undergird(ed) US government (as they understood them) as it did with how he argued the case.

If Quincy Adams was the last living link to the founding fathers, by the same token, he was also the last US president to be consciously aware of the role that Haiti had played in the imaginary of the early United States. In other words, for Americans who were not abolitionists, the memory of Toussaint's legacy as an essential ally to the United States for a brief but crucial moment in US history was soon to be forgotten (Johnson 175). While Quincy Adams did not mention Haiti in his litigation of the *Amistad* case, the spirit of Haiti was present, for as Marcus Rediker notes, wherever "contemporaries debated the meaning of the *Amistad* rebellion, the ghosts of Walker, Toussaint Louverture, and Turner hovered above their heads" (Rediker 9). Whether or not abolitionists, Federalists, or members of the slavocracy agreed on which humans belonged in the category of "all," the varying biographies and historiographies of the younger Quincy Adams's lifelong political career attest to his commitment to the Declaration of Independence within what he understood as pragmatism: a republic whose policy-making was motivated by expansionism and whose leaders refused to denounce slavery. And as Elizabeth Maddock Dillon and Michael J. Drexler argue in their edited volume *The Haitian Revolution and the Early United States: Histories, Textualities, Geographies* (2016), the choice to bring Haiti back into a discussion about the history of the United States has to do with emphasizing the important role that Haiti played in the imaginaries of the early United States (Dillon and Drexler 1–16).

Two Course Modules

To facilitate the role of the teacher, we offer the below chart, which explains sources readily available to instructors teaching at varying levels. While the focus is on undergraduate and graduate students, we have also included sources for elementary and junior high school. It is essential to note that the below material, and notably literary fiction and Steven Spielberg's narrative film *Amistad* (1993), can be extremely upsetting to students. For some students, the overwhelming emotional labor that it takes to discuss slavery in an intellectual space that does not allow (much) for the affective is harrowing. For students who understand themselves as post-racial or race neutral (Hawthorne, Nimako, Wekker), realizing how sedimented and institutionalized racialized practices are can be very challenging. As such, these discussions are difficult ones, and they invoke Gayatri "Spivak's old adage, 'unlearning one's privilege as loss' . . . [which] describes precisely the process of dismissing 'the conviction that I am necessarily better, I am necessarily indispensable, I am necessarily the one to right wrongs'" (Mascat 90). To this end, we have been mindful to include accompanying readings that are grounded in fact and at least help students to better understand the contexts out of which such a history emerged.

Table 6.1. Sources readily available to instructors teaching at varying levels

"Haiti in the Presidencies of John Adams and John Quincy Adams"

A 4- to 8-hour lesson plan, on one day or across multiple class periods.

Teaching Outcome

To understand the important role that Haiti played in the presidencies of John Adams and John Quincy Adams.

Leading Questions

What does "freedom" mean in the US context?
How are Haiti and the United States of America related historically?

Suggested Activities

- Before beginning the module, the instructor might ask students what they know about the Declaration of Independence, John Adams, John Quincy Adams, Toussaint Louverture, the *Amistad*, and/or Lomboko.

- Before beginning the module, the instructor might request that students keep a journal about what they think about when they examine the words "freedom," "slavery," and "race." The journals may be exchanged. For example, students might type up a part of the journal they find interesting, upsetting, or troubling without identifying themselves on the typed-up journal entry excerpt. They can then turn the pages into the professor to redistribute among the students. In this way, a discussion can take place in a more anonymous space, relating the historical context of the course to a more contemporary context of geopolitics and race in North America and the Caribbean.

Primary Sources for Students

Students might read the relevant primary documents, that is, the Declaration of Independence, Adams and Pickering's proclamation on US vessels in Haitian ports, or the Supreme Court decision in the *Amistad* case, all easily available online (see bibliography). These are relatively short texts, and interesting to read as an introduction to the lesson plan, but also exciting to re-consult at the closure of the module to show students how much "more" they understand.	Lower- and upper-division BA and MA/PhD
Sibylle's Fischer's chapter titled "Foundational Fictions: Postrevolutionary Constitutions I" in *Modernity Disavowed: Haiti and the Cultures of Slavery in the Age of Revolution* (2004) offers a textual analysis of Toussaint Louverture's Constitution of 1801, which banned slavery. As an appendix, she also includes the full text of Jean-Jacques Dessalines's *Imperial Constitution of Haiti*, dated 1805. In her chapter titled "Liberty and Reason of State: Postrevolutionary Constitutions II," Fischer compares Dessalines's constitution to the French constitutions as well as to Louverture's 1801 constitution. These work best for the second proposed teaching module on race (see below).	Upper division BA and MA/PhD

Scholarly Readings for Students

For John Adams: The section titled "The Adamsian Practice" (pp. 194-217) in Darren Staloff's *Hamilton, Adams, Jefferson: The Politics of Enlightenment* (2005) as well as Ronald Angelo Johnson's *Diplomacy in Black and White: John Adams, Toussaint Louverture, and Their Atlantic World Alliance* (2014). Both are extremely readable.	BA (all levels) and MA/PhD
For John Quincy Adams: See Chapter 34, titled "The Captives Are Free" (pp. 462-483), in James Traub's *John Quincy Adams: Militant Spirit* (2016). The entire book is readable but it is 600 pages long. Another chapter that may be of interest to students is the chapter titled "A Great Man in the Wrong Place at the Wrong Time" (pp. 341-352).	BA (all levels) and MA/PhD
For a very accessible history of the Haitian Revolution, see Laurent Dubois's *Avengers of the New World: The Story of the Haitian Revolution* (2004). As regards John Adams's support of Toussaint Louverture, Chapter 11, titled "Territory," deals directly with Adams. Reading Chapters 11 to 13 helps students to understand Louverture's tragic downfall (Girard pp. 549-82).	BA (all levels) and MA/PhD
For information about the *Amistad*, see "Introduction: Voices" (pp. 1-12) in Marcus Rediker's *The Amistad Rebellion: An Atlantic Odyssey of Slavery and Freedom* (2012). The book offers a history of the *Amistad* from the point of view of the captives, including a remarkable sixteen-page inlay of archival images of paintings, sketches, and drawings of the ships on which the captives were transported and portraits of the men aboard the ship, as well as John Quincy Adams and Roger Sherman Baldwin.	BA (all levels) and MA//PhD
Karen Zeinert's *The Amistad Slave Revolt and American Abolition* is a young adult book. It is exactly one hundred pages on smaller-than-standard pages with larger-than-standard font.	Young adult book
Monica Edinger's children's book, illustrated by Robert Byrd and titled *Africa Is My Home: A Child of the Amistad*, is a fifty-seven-page text that takes the perspective of a child captured in West Africa and who survived to return to West Africa after captivity aboard the *Teçora*, and later the *Amistad*.	Children's book

Screening for Students

Steven Spielberg's *Amistad* (1993) brings many of the issues discussed in this article to the fore, notably as they reference John Quincy Adams's career. Although Haiti is not explicitly mentioned, the fact that the Mende captives boarded the schooner *Amistad* in Cuba is essential to understanding the volatile role that Cuba played in the Americas after Haiti's independence. Another angle that the course might take is to lead out of a discussion of the *Amistad* Supreme Court case to a lesson based around Frederick Douglass and his relationship to Haiti. It can be argued that the character of Theodore Joadson (played by Morgan Freeman) is based on historical accounts of Douglass (Newman 218). Douglass was not part of the *Amistad* case; the trial took place when Douglass was still enslaved, that is, four years before he published his autobiography *Narrative of the Life of Frederick Douglass, an American Slave* (1845). Laurent Dubois's article "Frederick Douglass, Anténor Firmin, and the Making of U.S.-Haitian Relations" offers an excellent summary of Haitian–US relations from 1862 (Dubois 96) through the early 1890s, when Douglass travelled to Haiti on a diplomatic mission as a representative of the United States to expand US economic activity in Haiti and the Dominican Republic. (The year 1862 marks the date that the United States under President Abraham Lincoln finally recognized Haiti.)

The second module, "Race, Haiti, and the United States of America," is less traditional. Its purpose is to study how perceptions of race changed significantly in the latter part of the 1700s and the early 1800s, especially as a result of US politics around slavery. Although Eric D. Weitz's work deals more generally with the notion of genocide in the twentieth century, his overall deliberations on the function of race in the modern nation-state resonate with Laurent Dubois's more specific historical work about race in revolutionary Saint-Domingue. Together their scholarship illustrates how the establishment of Haiti as a nation-state took place at a transitional moment in transatlantic thinking about race and nation, one that existed at a time in the Americas when racial thinking had not yet become the dominant organizational mode. Weitz argues that one of the defining factors of the modern nation-state is the imposition of "inheritable and sometimes immutable" variables for citizenship of a nation-state (Weitz 97). If Weitz refers to modernity as the key moment in which the concepts of "race" and the "nation-state" were developed and took hold, then it is not surprising that in the 1790s and the first decade of the 1800s, Haiti's constitutions, as Fischer's work illustrates (Fischer 239), struggled against the "immutability" of the category of race. Dubois traces "both how the meaning of race changed through emancipation and how forms of racial identification and hierarchy were maintained in the midst of a regime in principle based on racial equality" (Dubois "Inscribing Race," 95–96). In describing the revolutionary French Antilles, Dubois historicizes the impossibility, despite the best intentions, of eradicating racializing techniques. In other words, while the rights afforded to specific racial groups might have been provisional, the fact of race as a principle of social organization took root. For a fictional account in English of Haiti during the periods discussed, see Marie Chauvet's novel *Dance on the Volcano* (*La Danse sur le volcan*), re-translated from French in 2016 by Kaiama L. Glover. This is a historical novel that recounts the story of two sisters, both actresses in Haiti at the pinnacle of Haiti's wealth and the tumultuous decades leading up to the Haitian Revolution. Although long, it is a veritable page-turner, which students read quite quickly.

Notes

1. Thank you enormously to Cécile Accilien, Jessica Adams, and Laurent Dubois for their invaluable feedback, time, and patience in reworking this narrative in ways that honor the late Michel-Rolph Trouillot's work, notably in *Silencing the Past*, and Gina Ulysse's call for "new narratives."

2. While perhaps hyperbolic, Adams's 1799 observations about Louverture proved tragically astute: Toussaint's capture and death after Napoleon's ascension to power in France in

1799 and after Jefferson defeated Adams in 1801 marked the end of Louverture's life, diplomatically and literally. Adams had been the only leader in the world to recognize Louverture as a diplomatic equal, offering him naval aid against André Rigaud, his revolutionary rival. Louverture's demise was due to the fact that besides Adams, no other government leader in the world was willing to recognize Louverture as the legitimate head of state. In 1802, Louverture was captured by Napoleon's troops and transferred to a prison in France, where he died in 1803.

Works Cited

Adams, John. *The Works of John Adams, Second President of the United States, Vol. 8*, edited by Charles Frances Adams, 1850–56. Online Library of Liberty. http://oll.libertyfund.org/titles/adams-the-works-of-john-adams-10-vols. Accessed 15 April 2017.

Adams, John, and Timothy Pickering. "'An Act Further to Suspend Further Intercourse . . .': Proclamation to allow US vessels to enter 'Cape Francois' and 'Port Republicain.'" 26 June 1799. *Yale Law School*. avalon.law.yale.edu/18th_century/japroc02.asp. Accessed 15 April 2017.

Amistad. Directed by Steven Spielberg. DreamWorks, 1997.

Casimir, Jean, and Laurent Dubois. "Reckoning in Haiti: The State and Society Since the Revolution." *Haiti Rising: Haitian History, Culture, and the Earthquake of 2010*, edited by Martin Munro, University of West Indies Press, 2010, pp. 120–26.

Chauvet, Marie. *Dance on the Volcano*. Translated by Kaiama L. Glover, Archipelago, 2016.

"Declaration of Independence." 4 July 1776. www.ushistory.org/declaration/document. Accessed 15 April 2017.

Dillon, Elizabeth Maddock, and Michael J. Drexler. "Introduction: Haiti and the United States, Entwined." *The Haitian Revolution and the Early United States: Histories, Textualities, Geographies*, edited by Elizabeth Maddock Dillon and Michael J. Drexler, University of Pennsylania Press, 2016, pp. 1–16.

Dubois, Laurent. *Avengers of the New World: The Story of the Haitian Revolution*. The Belknap Press of Harvard University Press, 2004.

———. "Inscribing Race in the Revolutionary French Antilles." *The Color of Liberty: Histories of Race in France*, edited by Sue Peabody and Tyler Stovall, Duke University Press, (2003) 2006, pp. 95–107.

———. "Frederick Douglass, Anténor Firmin, and the Making of U.S.-Haitian Relations." *The Haitian Revolution and the Early United States: Histories, Textualities, Geographies*, edited by Elizabeth Maddock Dillon and Michael J. Drexler, University of Pennsylvania Press, 2016, pp. 95–110.

Edinger, Monica. *Africa Is My Home: A Child of the Amistad*. Illustrated by Robert Byrd. Candlewick Press, 2013.

Fick, Carolyn. "Revolutionary St. Domingue and the Emerging Atlantic: Paradigms of Sovereignty." *The Haitian Revolution and the Early United States: Histories, Textualities, Geographies*, edited by Elizabeth Maddock Dillon and Michael J. Wexler, University of Pennsylvania Press, 2016, pp. 23–42.

Fischer, Sibylle. *Modernity Disavowed: Haiti and the Cultures of Slavery*. Duke University Press, 2004.

Girard, Philippe R. "Jean-Jacques Dessalines and the Atlantic System: A Reappraisal." *The William and Mary Quarterly*, vol. 69, no. 3, 2012, pp. 549–82.

Hawthorne, Camilla. "In Search of Black Italia." *Transition*, vol. 123, 2017, pp. 152–174.

Johnson, Ronald Angelo. *Diplomacy in Black and White: John Adams, Toussaint Louverture, and Their Atlantic World Alliance*. University of Georgia Press, 2014.

Mascat, Jamila. "Humanities and Emancipation: Said's Politics of Critique Between Interpretation and Interference." *Conflicting Humanities*, edited by Rosi Braidotti and Paul Gilroy, Bloomsbury Academic, 2016, pp. 75–94.

Monroe, James. "Monroe Doctrine." 2 December 1823. www.ourdocuments.gov/doc.php?flash=true&doc=23. Accessed 15 April 2017.

Nesbitt, Nick. *Caribbean Critique: Antillean Critical Theory from Toussaint to Glissant*. Liverpool University Press, 2013.

Newman, Richard. "Not the Only Story in 'Amistad': The Fictional Joadson and the Real James Forten." *Pennsylvania History: A Journal of Mid-Atlantic Studies*, vol. 67, no. 2, 2000, pp. 218–239.

Nimako, Kwame. "Location and Social Thought in the Black: A Testimony to Africana Intellectual Tradition." *Postcoloniality-Decoloniality-Black Critique: Joints and Fissures*, edited by Sabine Broeck and Carsten Junker, Campus Verlag, 2015, pp. 53–62.

Rediker, Marcus. *The Amistad Rebellion: An Atlantic Odyssey of Slavery and Freedom*. Penguin Classics, 2012.

Spivak, Gayatri Chakravorty, Donna Landry, and Gerald MacLean. *The Spivak Reader: Selected Works of Gayatri Chakravorty Spivak*. Routledge, 1996.

Staloff, Darren. *Hamilton, Adams, Jefferson: The Politics of Enlightenment and the American Founding*. Hill and Wang, 2005.

Traub, James. *John Quincy Adams: Militant Spirit*. Basic Books, 2016.

Trouillot, Michel-Rolph. *Silencing the Past*. Beacon Press, 1995.

Ulysse, Gina Athena. "Why Haiti Needs New Narratives Now More Than Ever." In *Tectonic Shifts: Haiti Since the Earthquake*, edited by Mark Schuller and Pablo Morales, 240–244. Kumarian, 2012.

Wekker, Gloria. *White Innocence: Paradoxes of Colonialism and Race*. Duke University Press, 2016.

Weitz, Eric D. *A Century of Genocide: Utopias of Race and Nation*. Princeton University Press, 2003.

Zeinert, Karen. *The Amistad Slave Revolt and American Abolition*. The Shoe String Press, Inc., 1997.

7

Teaching the 2004 Coup in Haiti from a French Perspective

Insights into France's Neocolonial Culture and Practices

SOPHIE WATT

Examining the 2004 coup in Haiti opens a window onto one of the most heated ideological debates in understanding current geopolitics and neo-imperialism. Teaching the political history of Haiti is particularly stimulating because of its implications for understanding the contemporary world order. This chapter focuses on teaching this material through Critical Discourse Analysis, an approach that helps students to draw conclusions from primary materials. The understanding of discourse as a social practice also helps students enter into the history of ideas and concepts, such as neo-imperialism. Using this approach, students can effectively grasp the impact such an ideology continues to have in Haiti. The unit I will describe could be part of a module dealing with French and Francophone Studies, postcolonial and global studies, critical humanitarian studies, or media studies. At the end of the chapter, I include syllabi for a two-semester course as well as lesson plans.

After winning the Haitian presidential election for a second time in 2001, Jean-Bertrand Aristide, the first democratically elected president of Haiti, was forcibly removed from power in 2004 by French, US, and Canadian Special Forces in the presence of US Ambassador Luis Moreno, and escorted to a plane bound for the Central African Republic. Drawing on Peter Hallward's book *Damming the Flood* and Hallward's debate with Lyonel Trouillot, Slavoj Žižek argues that the for/against Jean-Bertrand Aristide discussion among the left distinguishes the "partisan[s] of radical emancipation" from those who are "merely ... humanitarian liberal[s] who want 'globalisation with a human face'" ("Democracy Versus the People"). However, I argue that understanding the impact of the 2004 coup in Haiti also entails recognizing the political, social, and human repercussions of the neoliberal agenda imposed by Western powers such as France, Canada, and the United States and critically assessing the true nature of the current world order.

This chapter offers pedagogical suggestions to help students critically assess French involvement in the military intervention that overthrew Aristide in light of the political and economic context of the coup; the ideological debate among scholars who have written on the topic; and the discourse contained within portrayals of Aristide's government in the press. It pays particular attention to discursive justifications offered by French intellectuals and newspapers that legitimized the intervention. The collusion of the political sphere with the liberal press and intellectuals is at the center of this unit. Indeed, most of the articles published on Aristide after 2001 appeared in *Le Monde* and *Libération*. Furthermore, in the month preceding the intervention (January 2004), Régis Debray, the French intellectual and former advisor to President François Mitterrand, published a widely circulated report on France and Haiti.

This teaching unit is informed by both a research-led teaching approach and a student-led teaching approach. It should be divided into three two-hour sessions and is suited for advanced undergraduates. It could also easily be adapted for a postgraduate module by adding a theoretical framework of analysis related to neocolonial studies and disaster capitalism and global studies. The first session deals with Jean-Bertrand Aristide's two mandates, along with the history of the three coups and their impact on Haitian society; the second session analyzes the historical debate surrounding the nature of the 2004 coup; and the final session deals with press coverage and the power of language. The four main teaching/research questions addressed in this unit are:

1. What were the prerequisite conditions that justified the intervention?
2. Did the press campaign led by the two publications and echoed in Debray's report pave the way for a Franco-US-Canadian military and diplomatic intervention?
3. What were the discursive techniques used to legitimize military intervention and the removal of Aristide, who had been democratically elected in 1991 and again in 2001? Ruth Wodak and Martin Reisigl's Discourse-Historical Approach is pertinent here in identifying and classifying such techniques (Wodak and Reisigl 87).
4. What were the impacts of the military intervention?

Jean-Bertrand Aristide's Two Mandates: A History of Interventionism

The first research/teaching question to be addressed is, What were the prerequisite conditions that justified the intervention? In order to contextualize the 2004 coup in Haiti, it is essential to understand that it was not the first attempt to get rid of Aristide's government. It is also important to note that Haiti's debt as well as its type of government, deemed corrupt under Aristide, were the triggers for French action against the Aristide government from 2003 onwards. Dividing the class into four groups helps in addressing four essential research areas for the students:

1. The history of interventionism and ongoing colonialism in Haiti;[1]
2. The social and political climate that witnessed the rise of Aristide as a popular leader;[2]
3. The similarities and differences between the two coups against Aristide's government in 1991;[3] and
4. The economic and political context that justified the US and European embargo launched against Haiti after Aristide's second election.[4]

These four student groups should lead discussion, with each exploring their main research questions and developing answers to help identify the prerequisite conditions that justified the 2004 coup.

It is essential for students to understand the conditions that Haitian society was experiencing, both economically and politically, when Aristide, the leader of the Lavalas Party and a priest strongly influenced by Liberation Theology, was elected with 67 percent of the popular vote in 1991 on the basis of a radical social program of rebuilding the Haitian state and public sector.[5] Groups 1 and 2 usually report that Haiti was in the midst of a severe economic depression. The dictatorships of François Duvalier and his son, Jean-Claude Duvalier, lasted almost 30 years and opened up the country to US economic domination. With the work of Group 3, students also realize that the ten years of successive military juntas, led mostly by General Henri Namphy, were rooted in the long development of a paramilitary structure that can be traced back to the US occupation (1915–1934), the Macoutes, and the Attachés (Sprague, ch. 2 & 3). With the work of Group 4, the debate turns to the ways in which Namphy's junta finalized the process of liberalizing the economy (also known as the *Plan Meriken*, or American Plan). USAID Development strategy reports helped open Haitian markets by advocating grain imports, cutting and eventually eliminating export taxes, and pushing the development of the assembly industry, which had begun under Jean-Claude Duvalier (USAID 24). This process was imposed via directives like the Structural Adjustment Program (SAP) led by the World Bank and the IMF (International Monetary Fund) and signed by General Namphy. The debate among students will take into account the ways in which this plan resulted in the pauperization of the population, the rise in food prices dictated by low export taxes, and the increase in urbanization. As Alex Dupuy notes, "Haiti's neoliberal agricultural policies had drastic consequences for the country's farmers. Whereas in the 1970s Haiti imported about 19% of its food needs, it now imports 51%. . . . Eighty percent of all the rice consumed in Haiti is now imported" (Dupuy, *The Prophet*).[6] This desperate economic situation worsened with the "Washington Consensus" that pushed neoliberal reform even further (Klein, *Shock Doctrine*). It is worth showing excerpts from the film *Poto Mitan* in class to discuss the worsening of working conditions in factories between the mid 1970s and the mid 1980s.

The work of Group 4 will incorporate ways in which the 1991 election of Aristide threatened to disrupt the neoliberal agenda. When Aristide assumed office, there existed an external debt of over 939 million dollars, inherited from the Duvalier and Namphy regimes.[7] After he agreed to a second Structural Adjustment Program in exchange for grants and loan money, which was needed to keep the economy afloat, opposition to Aristide grew very quickly (McGowan, "Democracy Undermined"). Indeed, this new SAP imposed strict measures on the public sector that were in total contradiction to Aristide's political agenda: redundancies, reduction of import taxes, elimination of custom tariffs, and suspension of licensing requirements for sugar and rice imports (McGowan 10). In relation to these questions, Group 3 should discuss the two 1991 coups against Aristide's government. The political opposition planned a first coup in January 1991. This unleashed an incredibly strong popular response as thousands of people, mostly from the poorer areas like Cité Soleil, charged into the streets of Port-of-Prince and surrounded the presidential palace to protect the president (Hallward 38–39). Here it will be important to underline the ways in which such coups result from a long tradition of paramilitary power and the use of militaristic logistical strategies and weaponry. Learning about the population protecting its president from the January 1991 coup is usually a turning point for students, who realize to what extent the vast majority of the Haitian population was committed to a strong democratic shift. Following this episode, the military organized a second coup in September 1991. The army contained the population of Cité Soleil by shooting on sight anyone attempting to reach the city center. At least 300 people were killed on the first night (Hallward 40). Aristide was then placed under arrest and deported to Venezuela. Raoul Cédras, head of the army, who was also on the CIA payroll (Rossier, *Aristide*), established a military junta that lasted three years, until Aristide's return was organized by the administration of US President Bill Clinton in 1994 under Operation Restore Democracy.

The first half of Group 3's work should examine the junta, a brutal and violent regime that established a reign of terror in Haiti. Almost 5,000 Lavalas supporters were killed, while many other Haitians were forced to flee the country. The army reestablished the old paramilitary structures that Aristide had abolished (Chomsky, *Year 501* 211), the Chefs Seksyon and ex-Macoutes, and with the assistance of the Defense Intelligence Agency (DIA) created the Front for the Advancement and Progress of Haiti (FRAPH) (Sprague 71). The FRAPH incorporated former death squads led by Emmanuel Constant and Louis-Jodel Chamblain that had worked for the Macoutes (Sprague 71). The international community publicly condemned the coup and organized a trade and economic embargo. The embargo was broken, however, by the administration of President George H. W. Bush, which then granted exceptions to 800 US companies (Chomsky, "Democracy Restored"). While the Clinton administration increased trade with the military junta, the embargo had hugely detrimental consequences for the population, and unemployment rose. The unprecedented brutality of the regime led to a record number of forced exiles, who began landing on the shores of Florida. On arrival they were denied political asylum and were detained in Guantánamo Bay before deportation back to Haiti. The students in Group 3 will analyze the impact of the junta, including an examination of the refugee crisis, as well as the negative coverage of the Cédras regime that eventually pushed the Clinton administration to overthrow the junta and allow Aristide to return to power (Girard 70–85).

Finally, Group 4 should analyze Aristide's return to power in 1994. This session will conclude with an analysis of the stringent conditions of his return imposed by the Clinton government. These conditions took the form of another Structural Adjustment Program called the Emergency Economic Recovery Program (EERP), led by the Inter-American Development Bank (IDB), the World Bank, the IMF, and USAID.[8] The terms of the contract were very clear: Aristide had to comply with the EERP plan, which would redirect the economy toward the private sector. This plan involved privatization of state-owned companies, redundancies of most civil servants, a radical reduction in government regulation, a push toward an export-led economy, and cuts to salaries.[9] These measures were later advanced by the René Préval Administration (1996–2000).

The period 1995–1997 was crucial for the Organisation Politique Lavalas (OPL), which split into the factions OPL and Fanmi Lavalas (FL), led by Aristide. Their tensions and disagreements were mainly linked to class issues: the

OPL represented bourgeois civil society, while the FL was a popular movement that supported Aristide's social program. The FL won the legislative elections in May 2000 and Aristide was reelected in November 2000. Aristide won 92 percent of the votes with 60 percent voter turnout. The same year, despite the ratification of IDB loans, the funds were withheld and the World Bank suspended all its grants to Haiti.[10] The US government, as well as the EU, justified the embargo by claiming that electoral fraud had been committed in Haiti during the May 2000 legislative elections and that Lavalas had benefited as a result. However, it was misleading to assert that Aristide was responsible for any alleged fraud and inconsistencies. Aristide had not even been elected at that point; the presidential elections had yet to take place. Once he was elected president, Aristide in fact demanded that the beneficiaries of the alleged fraud step down.

The impact of the embargo on Haitian society was extreme, as the government budget was reduced to $300 million by 2003 and Haiti's GDP fell from $4 billion in 1999 to $2.9 billion. The nature of the embargo and the aid blockage is key to understanding the most brazen aspects of the neoliberal agenda and the tools used in the planning of the 2004 coup.

When introducing the second session, it is important for students to view and/or read Aristide's speech during the bicentennial commemoration of Haitian revolutionary Toussaint Louverture's death that took place in April 2003.[11] Aristide reminded France of its colonial past and asked for the return of the 90 million gold francs that Haiti had paid France in exchange for its independence. Because of the exorbitant interest rates applied to this infamous debt, Aristide made a case for the sum to be paid back with interest ($21.7 billion). Following Aristide's demand, in October 2003, Prime Minister Dominique de Villepin put together an "independent committee of reflection and propositions on the Franco-Haitian relationship" and appointed two representatives, Régis Debray and Véronique Albanel. The commission's report was published in January 2004 and Aristide was overthrown the following month.

Historiographical Debate

Historiography is particularly revealing in understanding the 2004 coup. Chris Bongie, Noam Chomsky, Michael Deibert, Alex Dupuy, Robert Fatton Jr., Paul Farmer, Philippe Girard, Peter Hallward, Nick Nesbitt, Randall Robinson, Lyonel Trouillot, and Christophe Wargny are among the most significant scholars who have contributed to the historiographical debate. The debate highlights the fact that the notion of the historian's neutrality is a myth and that the work of writing history is often highly ideological. It also reveals what was at stake with the coup in Haiti and situates what happened at the core of a series of neo-imperial and military practices. Students are thus able to articulate a better understanding of the process of writing and representing history.

Students present the two main sides of this debate, putting forth the two sides' interpretations of the coup as legitimate or illegitimate depending on their understanding of, and level of agreement with, Aristide's political agenda. Students' presentations of the arguments used by both sides are a very productive way of addressing this material. Students should be able to present the scholars' work and summarize each perspective along with the sources scholars used to support their arguments.

The two groups should present the different sides of the history of the coup to a third group, which is in charge of the intermedial representations. The two main foci should be the nature and practices of Aristide's government and Aristide's own evolution as a highly contested political leader. This exercise is pedagogically extremely useful because students take note of different interpretations of the same event, concentrating on each scholar's argument. Rather than allowing or encouraging them to take sides, it helps them to evaluate their sources and the concrete examples used to substantiate each position. It also enables students to critically examine the practice of historiography, which often presents distinct ideological stances.

The first group presents the pro-Aristide arguments. Michael Deibert's book *Notes from the Last Testament* takes the format of a file made up by the series of lawsuits against Aristide and Lavalas. However, since the book's publication, the evidence presented in the book has been proven erroneous and all charges against Aristide have been dropped. Alex Dupuy's book *The Prophet and Power* elaborates a much more subtle critique of Aristide's administration. Aristide's social program was inevitably going to alienate the dominant class, Dupuy argues, and Aristide's unwillingness to compromise pushed him to resort to the repression of the elites' dissent. The repression of dissent and the fear of yet another coup were, according to Dupuy, the two principal reasons why Aristide relied on the armed group Chimère as a paramilitary force. This perspective is shared by Robert Fatton Jr. in his 2007 book *The Roots of Haitian Despotism*. Christophe Wargny also laments the gradual corruption of the regime in *Haïti n'existe pas: deux cents ans de solitude*. The issue of armed groups is at the heart of the debate related to the practices of the Aristide government. Examination of this issue can also be advanced further by the third group, which deals with the intermedial representations and the concept of "fake news."

Peter Hallward's *Damming the Flood* and Justin Podur's *Haiti's New Dictatorship*, along with Paul Farmer's "Who Removed Aristide? Paul Farmer Reports from Haiti" and Noam Chomsky's "US-Haiti," share similar perspectives. They argue that the Aristide government was weakened and destabilized by a combination of factors because he was trying to establish a popular democracy. These factors included economic pressure due to the embargo, a national and international media campaign of vilification, paramilitary violence, and co-optation of civil society organizations. None of these authors denies that corruption also existed under Aristide, but they note that the scale of this corruption was different than it had been previously, and that it was not institutionalized to the same extent as it had been under the military juntas or the Duvaliers.

The second group presents Lyonel Trouillot's attack on Hallward's *Damming the Flood* in his article "Hallward, or The Hidden Face of Racism." Trouillot openly launches an ideological attack on Hallward ("Hallward" 128–136). He accuses Hallward of corruption, of being Aristide's ghostwriter; he also accuses Hallward of racism because he claimed "the right to name the other's reality in the other's stead" (132). He concludes by calling Hallward a "fanatic." In an newspaper article published by *L'humanité* in March 2004, Trouillot reasserts that the overthrow of Aristide was orchestrated by the population (Trouillot Interview). Trouillot tries very hard to legitimize Aristide's fall as the result of popular action and never acknowledges the actions taken by the G184 against the Aristide government, or its links with the *Collectif NON*, led by Trouillot. This "collective" was a group of artists and intellectuals who in December 2003 took a public stance against Aristide and began denouncing violence and abuse.

A series of concluding arguments from both groups should take into consideration Hallward's response to Trouillot's attack in his article "Lyonel Trouillot, or The Fictions of Formal Democracy." Here, Hallward underscores Trouillot's class affiliation, reaffirming the popular support enjoyed by Aristide even months after the coup and despite associated risks of being killed. Hallward rejects the charges of authoritarianism and corruption against Aristide's regime as being a construct to discredit and thwart popular democracy while acknowledging that gangs were responsible for some of the political violence under Aristide. However, both Sprague and Hallward draw a comparison among the number of murders committed by FL from 2000 to 2004 (around 30), the murders of Lavalas supporters during the military junta from 1991 to 1994, and the killing of between 30,000 and 50,000 people during the Duvalier dictatorships (1957–1986) (Sprague 29).

It is important to note that the international community did not at any point suggest overthrowing either of the Duvaliers. One should also recall that instead, the French government hosted Jean-Claude Duvalier during his exile in France for 25 years. Furthermore, according to a study published by the University of Miami School of Law, around 4,000 people were killed after they were accused of being Lavalas supporters (Griffin, "Haiti Human Rights"). Although this question of casualties is important to assess factually, also at stake in both sides of the historiography is the question of an emphasis on race versus class when writing history. This issue could be addressed by students as part of an examination of the concept of neutrality in historical works.

As a conclusion to this hour-long session, it is important to take note of the ways in which this debate was received among historians and political scientists. Chris Bongie discusses the Trouillot and Hallward debate and concludes by reaffirming US friendship toward Haiti, particularly in the face of the tragedy of the January 2010 earthquake: "How can one speak of enemies, when the self-styled 'Friends of Haiti'—the U.S. government and its military first among them—are so visibly engaged in benign acts of 'reconstruction and stabilization'" (Bongie 14). Peter Hallward and Naomi Klein, on the other hand, implore the public and the international community to stay vigilant and to protect "human rights" at all costs. Both Nesbitt's and Hallward's arguments are reinforced by a detailed narration of the coup from a close personal friend of Aristide: Randall Robinson, author of *An Unbroken Agony*.

In the second hour-long session, a third group of students can present the intermedial representations of the coup via a comparative analysis of the documentaries directed by Kevin and Nicolas Rossier (*Haiti: We Must Kill the Bandits* and *Aristide and the Endless Revolution*, respectively). They are perhaps the most influential journalists who have engaged with the coup and its aftermath. Their documentaries are based on Randall Robinson's version of the facts, included in the form of an interview by both directors, so excerpts of Robinson's text could also be used. One of these two documentaries could then be compared with *Ghosts of Cité Soleil* by Asger Leth. This comparison would allow students to consider the concept of "fake news." Such analysis pushes students to dig deeper into the questions around the Aristide government's practices and the use of armed forces such as the Chimères by the Aristide government. The comparison of these texts and visual images of the coup is extremely important, as students can thus comprehend the power of historiography and representation. Students can also be paired to discuss the concept of how conflicts are represented. The analysis of visual discourse in this session leads to problematizing the notion of discourse in written language that is central to the last two-hour session.

A Critical Discourse Analysis of the French Media Campaign

A brief introduction to the methodology used to analyze this form of media is important. Remind students that the Discourse-Historical Approach outlined by Ruth Wodak is useful here as a methodological approach for two reasons:

1. "Discourse always involves power and ideologies . . . and no interaction exists where power relations do not prevail" (Wodak and Ludwig 12).
2. "Discourse . . . is always historical, that is, it is connected (synchronically and diachronically) with other communicative events which are happening at the same time or which have happened before" (Wodak and Ludwig 12).

Students should research the context in which Aristide's demand for reparations was made and link it to the results of the work done by the focus group on the embargo. They should also research the background of the main actors: Dominique de Villepin, Régis Debray, Véronique Albanel, and the G184. In October 2003, as a result of Aristide's demand for reparations, Prime Minister Dominique de Villepin commissioned Régis Debray and Véronique Albanel to write a report on the Franco-Haitian relationship. The report was published by the prestigious conservative publishing house Les Éditions de la Table Ronde.

The two French newspapers used here are *Le Monde* and *Libération* because of their liberal reputation and their tradition of intellectual resistance, with figures like Hubert Beuve Méry and Serge July. These voices of authority are joined and reinforced by Régis Debray, a former student of Louis Althusser (École Nationale Supérieure). Debray was a professor of philosophy at the University of Havana in the 1960s and developed a close relationship with Che Guevara during his time in Bolivia. By 1981, he was an adviser to the government of President Mitterrand. Until his report on Haiti, his reputation was that of left-wing intellectual à *la française*. Véronique Albanel is the sister of then–Prime Minister Dominique de Villepin and was also part of the administrative council of the NGO Association Fraternité Universelle en Haïti (AFU), whose partners are Bouygues Telecom and Air France. The intellectual credibility of these newspapers and the reputation of the intellectual figure of Régis Debray are symbolic, and are firmly rooted in French national identity.

Once this context has been established, students should be put into three groups in order to identify the different discursive techniques at hand, following the approach laid out in Critical Discourse Analysis. According to Ruth Wodak's argumentation theory, topoï correspond to "conclusion rules which connect the argument or arguments with the conclusion, the claim. . . ." This methodology allows the reader to identify what constitutes a topos in the texts being studied. The topos of threat is particularly interesting because it provokes an emotional reaction: "[I]f there are specific dangers and threats, one should do something against them" (Wodak and Reisigl 74). Students can read both newspapers online and then list the different topoï they are able to identify. Once all the different topoï have been identified, the groups should analyze the three major ones (as I note below, these are fear/threat, fraud, and urgency).

In the April to December coverage, the general discursive structures apparent in all the articles published on Aristide (76 in *Le Monde* and 50 in *Libération*, as I outline in the lesson plans at the end of this chapter) and Debray's report are very similar. They develop three general topoï to portray the ongoing situation in Haiti: the topos of fear, which is developed around the political chaos in Haiti; the topos of fraud, which accompanies the theme of the aid money poured into the country despite ongoing level of poverty; and the topos of urgency/emergency, with Aristide portrayed as the new tyrant, a discursive construction that paves the way for the eventual "necessity" of military intervention. Although these are the main topoï that students tend to identify as examples of discourse analysis, this list is not exhaustive, and this section should be the object of class discussion.

The following are a few examples of the rhetorical structures that students usually identify as being part of the topos of fear, involving political and social chaos. In Denis Tillinac's "Preface" to Debray's text, Haiti is introduced as a Francophone country whose population deserves France's clemency (7). A condescending recognition of the importance of Haitian culture is immediately followed by an infantilization of the population. "This beautiful country," Tillinac laments, "tyrannizes itself constantly." The juxtaposition of opposing and contrasting ideas represents the figure of speech called antithesis. This rhetorical tool is constantly used to remind the reader that the richest colony in the world became one of the world's poorest countries following independence. Antithesis is reinforced and thematically developed in Debray's first chapter, where the use of metaphorical language centers on the figure of apocalypse. Debray uses words like "chaos" and "anarchy," and verbs that reinforce the decline from the colony's golden age, such as "to deepen into" and "to continue to sink into." Vocabulary and semantics thus paint a picture of wretchedness. Terms like "tragic history," "corruption," and "social misery" are reinforced through the use of numerous superlatives as well as by data and statistics, such as the fact that life expectancy is on average 52 years for women and 48 for men, and unemployment is about 70 percent. Some 85 percent of Haitians live on less than one US dollar per day. Yet the structure of Debray's argument always places responsibility for Haiti's situation firmly in the hands of the population, as is visible in the following passage:

> May our Haitian friends assume their part in the responsibility in the incredible descent that in two centuries took Haiti from being "the pearl of the Antilles," the richest colony in the world, which provided a third of France's import commerce—the Kuwait of the time of Voltaire—to a level equivalent to the Sahel and with similar conditions. (Debray 20)

Debray uses an optative mood that is conveyed almost like a prayer. He ends his account of Haiti's chaotic situation by blaming the population for not "even" being self-sufficient "any longer" in terms of food production.

It is useful to ask students what Debray has left out of his text that they have learned about during their preliminary research sessions. One example would be that Debray fails to explain the disastrous impact that the US export–led economy had on the food industry as of 1981, when the Clinton Administration forced Haiti to drop tariffs on imported, subsidized US rice. This policy destroyed Haitian rice farming and jeopardized Haiti's ability to be self-sufficient. Even Bill Clinton, when he became UN envoy to Haiti, apologized before the US Senate Foreign Relations Committee for this disastrous policy.[12]

Another main topos is that of fraud, usually linked to aid money. The second group usually discusses it along with themes such as debt. They may also note that the theme of humanitarian aid is a similarity between Debray and the liberal press. "Haïti," Debray writes, "is one of several extreme cases: it has received billions in foreign assistance, yet persists as one of the poorest and worst governed countries in the world." Debray reminds us that between 1994 and 1999, European aid was 487 million Euros, a fifth of which was provided by the French government (30). But again Debray fails to explain that in 1994, after Aristide's return, most of the aid money came via the Emergency Economic Recovery Program (EERP) imposed as a condition of his return by the International Development Bank, IMF, the World Bank, and USAID, and included the privatization of a series of state-owned companies, flour and cement mills, the ports and airports, banks, and electricity and telecommunications services, as well as cutting the jobs of the majority of civil servants.

According to Debray, following the return of Aristide in 2001, the international community poured about 2 billion Euros into the country, 200 million of which came from France (25). And yet Haiti's situation did not improve. Regarding the 2001–2004 period, Debray also fails to explain the difference between bilateral and multilateral aid. No bilateral aid was disbursed to the Haitian government between 2000 and 2004 from the US, Canada, or the EU.

According to economist Jeffrey Saxe and US Representative Maxine Waters, in April 2001 six loans were approved by the IMF, the Inter-American Development Bank, and the World Bank, but these loans were blocked. Nonetheless, the Aristide government still had to service interest on Haiti's debt to these international institutions, which drained the government of the foreign external reserves to pay for loans it had never received. As a result, the exchange rate collapsed, inflation rose, and the economy collapsed. However, for Debray and the French liberals, only Aristide is to be held responsible. Two reasons are invoked repeatedly: Aristide's refusal to implement the EERP after 1995 and the senatorial elections of November 2000, which were declared fraudulent, although, as I mentioned previously, Aristide was not even in power at that time. Debray goes into more detail about Haiti's debt when discussing reparations, arguing that the demand for reparations served as a diversion from real issues with Aristide's presidency and its failure to use aid money successfully for the country (Debray 30).

The other principal topos, urgency/emergency, implies that Aristide was a threat to democracy in Haiti. The process that brought Aristide into power twice, with 67 percent of the electorate in 1991 and 92 percent in 2000, was rigorously monitored by the international community. These percentages, verified by the international community itself, are virtually unheard of in the West, where low voter turnout and political disengagement characterize most general elections, yet Debray dismissively refers to the process as "a populist shortcut" (36). He calls Aristide's regime an "anarcho-authoritarian mess" (34), claiming that the Restore Democracy operation led by Clinton in 1994 to bring Aristide back into power had failed.

It is worth asking students to compare the tone of the articles written before and after Debray and Albanel's visit to Haiti. They went to Haiti in December to put pressure on Aristide to force him to resign, and usually students notice that in the articles published both in *Le Monde* and *Libération* following the visit of Debray and Albanel, the discursive structure intensifies and the demonization is pushed to the extreme. Consider these examples, which were typical of French media coverage: "the Slum's prophet" (*Le Monde*); "from the slums to the luxurious villa" (*Le Monde*); "from the prophet to the dictator"(*Le Monde*); "the defrocked priest" (*Le Monde*); "Aristide has become a Bokassa" (*Libération*); "he dilapidated everything" (*Libération*); "fear has changed sides like with Duvalier" (*Le Monde*). The religious references are used as metonymies of Aristide's illegitimate power. Aristide is increasingly referred to not by his name, but rather by pejoratives related to his subjectivity: "the ex-priest," "the Voodoo dictator," "the Voodoo priest that brings death," "le dictateur vaudou mortifère" (this sensationalist language is particularly prominent in *Libération*).

Another exercise that can be led by students is to compare French with US press coverage and to discuss the use of similar or different topoï. Peter Hallward discusses a few of these articles, but students can find more; students can even compare the mainstream US press coverage of Aristide's government with the Haitian press coverage (Spencer).

Once some of these discursive constructions have been identified, it is crucial to discuss the performative nature of the press reports in order to understand the role that the press and intellectuals played in justifying the military intervention. With the publication of Debray's report in January 2004, the intervention is clearly announced, as well as the absurdity of the debt repayment. The closing paragraph of the report's preface reaffirms the objectivity of the report as a whole, which seeks to justify decisions already taken and to make sure that they are acted upon quickly: "May this report—as detailed as it is objective—incite our authorities to hasten the implementation of the decisions just taken." This language conveys to the reader the clear idea that the intervention has already been decided upon, and reinforces a sense of urgency even before the reader has had a chance to read the report. Again, the use of the optative mood reinforces the almost religious or prayer-like language. Around the same time, *Le Monde* affirms that "Aristide's departure is imminent."[13]

Constant references to the humanitarian crisis are reinforced by several interviews and quotations from the opposition and the use of UN reports, as well as by the lobbying of NGOs that have a clear interest in not allowing the Haitian government to rebuild its public sector as Aristide had proposed. The combination of reports on the presence of a "tyrant," demonstrations, and the active presence of the rebel army in the north of the country are the three main arguments used to outline the "humanitarian crisis," which in turn legitimized intervention. Media and intellectual production before the 2004 coup in Haiti thus provides an insightful example of this dialectical relationship, as outlined by Wodak and Reisigl in their discussion and definition of discourse as social practice, and highlights how this process in turn impacts political decision-making. This issue can be the object of a debate among students as a conclusion to the three sessions.

Conclusion: The Power of Language

As a conclusion to the session, it is a useful and interesting exercise to ask students to label some of the quotes found in the articles studied using George Orwell's critique of political language. They may find that the 2004 coup narrated by the French and US press becomes the perfect example of George Orwell's slogan from 1984, "War is peace." The following are a few examples that were used by students to exemplify Orwell's categories. The neo-Duvalierist Guy Philippe, who led several coup attempts against Aristide and was the leader of the February coup, armed by the US and trained by US forces in Manta, Ecuador, is described by *Le Monde* as "a chance for peace."[14] Raoul Cédras, who took power after the first coup in 1991 and imposed a brutal military dictatorship, is similarly quoted unchallenged in *Le Monde*: "We will free Haiti from Aristide's slavery."[15]

In the two weeks that followed "the humanitarian intervention," 600 corpses were found in Cité Soleil. After the coup, Boniface Alexandre was sworn into office; Gérard Latortue was flown in from Miami to take the head of the new government, and a committee of seven men chosen by US, Canadian, and French authorities was put in place to help him govern. It is important to discuss how students view this process and the legitimacy of this new government. It is worth asking the class to reflect once more on the historiographical debate around the coup and to assess its impact.

As part of the same exercise, it is important for the class to identify all the main actors behind this coup—not just the foreign forces but also the corporate forces—and to consider the ways in which they are portrayed in the press. For example, the G184 is referred to as the "democratic opposition"; Debray calls it "the national consciousness (neither nationalist nor *noiriste*) ready to assume its rights and civic duties." It is also frequently described in both newspapers as "the democratic platform," "the pacifist option," and "the Haitian opposition," and characterized as "pacifist and legal." Students usually do not need to do much research to find out that the G184 is a conglomerate of the richest families in Haiti, the largest corporations, and a few elite "intellectuals." The leader of the G184, André Apaid, is also the CEO of Alpha Industries, which is the biggest sweatshop operator in Haiti, with about 15 garment-assembly plants where workers sew clothing for the Canadian and US firms Gildan Activewear, Disney, and Walmart. It is perhaps not surprising that Apaid so fervently opposed Aristide's increase in the minimum wage. After the coup, he once again managed to keep the minimum wage down. Professionals and businesses declared that Apaid is "the real government in Haiti" (Griffin, "Haiti Human Rights"). Keeping these quotes in mind in relation to the excerpts from the film *Poto Mitan* studied in class, Orwell's "Freedom is slavery" seems particularly relevant.

Since the summer of 2004, the Comité des Avocats pour le Respect des Libertés Individuelles (CARLI) has denounced the massacres, political killings, arbitrary/political arrests, and the withholding of due process under the Latortue government. CARLI has also denounced the active return of the army to power and killings by former soldiers. As a result of their recent work, members of the staff have received death threats, mostly from former soldiers and members of FRAPH, the paramilitary organization that terrorized Haiti during the 1991–1994 military junta. CARICOM has asked the UN repeatedly to investigate the 2004 coup, but to no avail.

Neither *Le Monde* and *Libération* nor Debray fully explain the crisis in Haiti. A final discussion on the role of the liberal media and their affiliation with certain ideologies is crucial and corresponds with the last of Orwell's concepts: "Ignorance is strength." Certain questions that students have developed usually become central to this part of the unit, such as, "Are the media's objectives still to inform, or has their power of persuasion transformed this goal?" Chomsky and Herman analyze this kind of media representation in the United States in their "propaganda model," in which they identify several filters that shape the news and that construct and/or reinforce the dominant discourse (Chomsky and Herman 2). In his recent work on the media coverage of wars in Francophone Africa, François Robinet argues for the emergence of common transmediatic techniques to cover these conflicts. Analyzing recent military interventions in Rwanda, Congo, Ivory Coast and Darfur, Robinet demonstrates that transmediatic techniques such as strategic coproduction of narratives, dominant representations and/or dismissal of certain conflicts disclose a strong common national imaginary among the journalistic discourse that is based on a polarized vision of France's relationship with its former colonies (Robinet 2016 359).

It is important to finish this unit by asking students to question whether or not what happened in Haiti during the 2004 coup can be seen as a modus operandi that has been used elsewhere, or if it was symptomatic of the Haitian context.

Syllabus

Haiti: History of a Tragedy

Semester 1

Course Objectives

This course consists of two consecutive modules that consider the intricate history of Haiti and France from the colonial period to the present day. The focus of the course will be to analyze the historical development of the Haitian nation via the prism of Western imperialism and especially French colonial and postcolonial history. Through the analysis of historical works, but also of works of political science and works of fiction, this module will review elements of Haitian history and the ways in which it is closely intertwined with French imperialism and the development of global capitalism. The course is taught in French.

By the end of the unit, the student should be able to demonstrate

an ability to conduct close readings of fiction and non-fiction texts, with emphasis on issues of nation building, colonial and postcolonial history, and global capitalism;
a critical understanding of the history and the political background of Haiti and France from the colonial period to the present day;
the ability to analyze and show an understanding of the relationship between sociocultural phenomena and their representations in texts of fiction, political science, and history;
an enhanced linguistic competence overall and with specific relevance to the disciplines studied

WEEK 1: INTRODUCTION

WEEK 2: THE COLONIAL PERIOD

C.L.R. James, *The Black Jacobins: Toussaint L'Ouverture and the San Domingo Revolution*, The Dial Press, 1938 (Chapters I to V)

WEEK 3: THE BEGINNING OF THE HAITIAN REVOLUTION

Yves Benot, *La Révolution française et la fin des colonies*, Éditions de la Découverte, 1987, 2004 ("Introduction: Pouvoir ou impuissance de l'idéologie")
C.L.R. James, *The Black Jacobins* (Chapters VI to IX)
https://colonyincrisis.lib.umd.edu/category/historical-background-notes/

WEEK 4: THE HAITIAN REVOLUTION (1791–1801) AND DESSALINES VERSUS NAPOLÉON (1804)

First Hour:
C.L.R. James, *The Black Jacobins* (Chapters X to XI)
Nick Nesbitt, *Universal Emancipation: The Haitian Revolution and the*

Radical Enlightenment, University of Virginia Press, 2009 (Chapter 2, "The Idea of 1804")

Second Hour:
C.L.R. James, *The Black Jacobins* (Chapters XII and XIII)
Cécile Accilien et al., eds., *Revolutionary Freedoms: A History of Survival, Strength and Imagination in Haiti*, Caribbean Studies Press, 2006 (Chapter 11, "Dessalines")
Philippe R. Girard, "Jean-Jacques Dessalines et l'arrestation de Toussaint Louverture," *Journal of Haitian Studies*, vol. 17, no. 1, Spring 2011, pp. 123–138, https://www.jstor.org/stable/i40080389

WEEK 5: THE INDEPENDENCE AND THE DEBT (1825)

Jean-François Brière, "L'Emprunt de 1825 dans la dette de l'indépendance haitienne envers la France," *Journal of Haitian Studies*, vol. 12, no. 2, Fall 2006, pp. 126–134
Paul Farmer, *The Uses of Haiti*, Common Courage Press, 2003 ("The Template of a Colony")

WEEK 6: THE AMERICAN OCCUPATION (1915–1934)

First Hour: The American Occupation
Les chemins de la mémoire (Haiti Before Duvalier) part 1/5
http://www.youtube.com/watch?v=28cUSZQeGfM&list=PL559E49D6DEF2C833
Suzy Castor and Lynn Garafola, "The American Occupation of Haiti (1915–34) and the Dominican Republic (1916–24)," *The Massachusetts Review*, vol. 15, no. 1/2; *Caliban*, Winter/Spring 1974, pp. 253–275

Second Hour: Jacques Roumain's poetry
"Bois d'ébène" de Jacques Roumain (selected poems)
Reading by Jenny Salgado
https://www.youtube.com/watch?v=fHCpN8MDUdk

WEEK 7: READING WEEK

https://colonyincrisis.lib.umd.edu/category/historical-background-notes/

WEEK 8: THE 1937 MASSACRE

Richard Lee Turits, "A World Destroyed, a Nation Imposed: The 1937 Haitian Massacre in the Dominican Republic," *Hispanic American Historical Review*, vol. 82, no. 3, 2002, pp. 589–635

Philip Martin, Elizabeth Midgley and Michael S. Teitelbaum, "Migration and Development: Whither the Dominican Republic and Haiti?" *International Migration Review*, vol. 36, no. 2, Summer 2002, pp. 570 of 570–592

WEEK 9 & 10: LOUIS-PHILIPPE DALEMBERT, L'AUTRE FACE DE LA MER

Emanuela Cacchioli, "Départs volontaires, faux-départs, retours impossibles dans l'œuvre de Louis-Philippe Dalembert," *Convergences francophones*, vol. 1, no. 2, 2014, pp. 34–47
http://mrujs.mtroyal.ca/index.php/cf/inde

Elena Pessini, "Présences insulaires dans l'œuvre de Louis-Philippe Dalembert," *Des îles en archipel . . . Flottements autour du thème insulaire en hommage à Carminella Biondi*, edited by Carmelina Imbroscio, Nadia Minerva and Patrizia Oppici, Peter Lang, 2008.

Syllabus

Haiti: History of a Tragedy

Semester 2

Week 1: Introduction

Week 2: Papa Doc, a "traditional dictatorship" (1957–1971)

First Hour: Papa Doc and Noirism, a new ideology

Wien Weibert Arthus, "L'aide Internationale ne peut pas marcher: évaluation des relations Américano-Haïtiennes au regard de l'alliance pour le progrès (1961–1963)," *Journal of Haitian Studies*, vol. 17, no. 1, Spring 2011, pp. 155–177

James Ferguson, *Papa Doc, Baby Doc: Haiti and the Duvaliers*, Blackwell, 1987, pp. 30–60

Second hour (debate): Haiti 1969 ("Papa Doc" Duvalier interview by Christian Bernadac)

Haiti 1969 ("Papa Doc" Duvalier interview) – Screening in class
https://www.youtube.com/watch?v=iLxwh9KtppQ
http://www.youtube.com/watch?v=msi_Ox4DQsA

DEBATE QUESTIONS:

What were the particularities of François Duvalier's regime?
How can we describe Haitian society at the time?
What are the roots of *Noirisme*?

Week 3: Baby Doc's dictatorship (1971–1986)

First hour: Baby Doc

Jean-Claude Duvalier interview (1981), screening in class, http://www.youtube.com/watch?v=5J5R8CRsLKE; http://www.youtube.com/watch?v=XLRSFTFAXFQ

Second Hour: "Jean-Claudisme"—A "liberal" dictatorship

David Nicholls, "Haiti: The Rise and Fall of Duvalierism," *Third World Quarterly*, vol. 8, no. 4, October 1986, pp. 1239–1252
James Ferguson, *Papa Doc, Baby Doc: Haiti and the Duvaliers*, Blackwell, 1987, pp. 60–90

Week 4: The post-Duvalierist era

Paul Farmer, *The Uses of Haiti* ("Duvalierism Without Duvalier," pp. 91–107)
Paul Farmer, *The Uses of Haiti* ("Duvalierism Without Duvalier," pp. 107–120)
Christophe Wargny, *Haïti n'existe pas*, Autrement, 2004 (Chapter 7)

Week 5: Historical context of Aristide's two mandates

First hour: The first two coups

Jeb Sprague, *Paramilitarism and the Assault on Democracy in Haiti* (Chapter 2, "Popular Democracy and Attempts to Turn It Back")
Philippe R. Girard, "Operation Restore Democracy?" *Journal of Haitian Studies*, vol. 8, no. 2, A Special Issue on Politics & Grassroots Organizing, Fall 2002, pp. 70–85
Paul Farmer, *The Uses of Haiti* ("The Coup of 1991," pp. 149–187)
Christophe Wargny, *Haïti n'existe pas* (Chapter 8)

Second Hour: The 2004 Coup

> National Coalition for Haitian Refugees and Americans Watch: https://www.refworld.org/docid/3ae6ac7c44.html
>
> Mats Lundhal, *The Political Economy of Disaster: Destitution, Plunder and Earthquake in Haiti* (Chapter 4, "Descent into Crisis"), and Eirin Mobekk & Spyros I. Spyrou, "Re-evaluating IMF Involvement in Low-income Countries: The Case of Haiti," *International Journal of Social Economics*, vol. 29, no. 7, 2002, pp. 527–537
>
> Alex Dupuy, "Disaster Capitalism to the Rescue: The International Community and Haiti After the Earthquake," *NACLA*. https://nacla.org/article/disaster-capitalism-rescue-international-community-and-haiti-after-earthquake. Accessed 5 September 2015.

Week 6: Historiographical debate and intermedial representations

First Hour: Historiographical debate

> Interview exclusive de Jean-Bertrand Aristide par Claude Ribbe, https://www.youtube.com/watch?v=4vcbGjIUu9U
>
> Peter Hallward, *Damming the Flood: Haiti, Aristide, and the Politics of Containment* (Chapter 9)
>
> "Hallward, or The Hidden Face of Racism," Lyonel Trouillot & Nadève Ménard
>
> Entretien de Lyonel Trouillot et Françoise Escarpit, "Ce sont bien les Haïtiens qui ont renversé Aristide (*L'Humanité.fr*, 9 Mars 2004)
>
> "Lyonel Trouillot, or The Fictions of Formal Democracy," *Small Axe: A Caribbean Journal of Criticism*, vol. 13, no. 3, pp. 174–185

Second Hour: Intermedial representations

> Nicolas Rossier, *Aristide and the Endless Revolution*, 2005
> https://www.youtube.com/watch?v=1h2MYoWBidc
> Kevin Pina, *Haiti: We Must Kill the Bandits*, 2007
> http://www.youtube.com/watch?v=25Mf7Lv5Qo8
> Asger Leth, *Ghosts of Cité Soleil*, 2007
> https://www.shoutfactorytv.com/ghosts-of-cite-soleil/5db74c9d8b34365ca3ab154b

Week 7: Critical Discourse Analysis of the French Media Campaign

Régis Debray, *Rapport au Ministre des affaires étrangères M. Dominique de Villepin*, Janvier 2004 (selected chapters, pp. 15–60)
http://www.ladocumentationfrancaise.fr/var/storage/rapports-publics/044000056/0000.pdf
Newspaper articles from *Le Monde* et *Libération*

Week 8: Raoul Peck, *Haiti, Le profit et rien d'autre*, 2001

First hour: Screening of the film

Second hour: Discussion

Christopher McAuley, Claudine Michel, and Raoul Peck, "Filmer sans compromis: Interview avec le cinéaste, Raoul Peck/Filmer sans compromis: An Interview with Raoul Peck," *Journal of Haitian Studies*, vol. 9, no. 2, Fall 2003, pp. 128–140

Jana Evans Braziel, "Profit and Nothing But!" (Le profit et rien d'autre!): Raoul Peck's Impolite Thoughts on the (Haitian Diasporic) Class Struggle," *Journal of Haitian Studies*, vol. 9, no. 2, Fall 2003, pp. 141–176

Antony Loewenstein, *Disaster Capitalism*, Verso, 2015 (Chapter 3: "Haiti: If Anybody Here Says They've Had Help, It's a Lie," pp. 105–153)

Week 9: Louis-Philippe Dalembert, *Les Intouchables*

"Les Intouchables," *Les Chaînes de l'Esclavage* (collectif), Florent-Massot, 1998, pp. 135–149; *Île en île*, 2000; *Dernières nouvelles du colonialisme* (collectif), Vents d'ailleurs, 2006, pp. 25–47

Week 10: Haïti since the earthquake

Peter Hallward, *Damming the Flood: Haiti, Aristide, and the Politics of Containment* (Chapter 11)

Justin Podur, *Haiti's New Dictatorship: The Coup, the Earthquake and the UN Occupation*, Pluto Press, 2012 (Chapters 2 & 3)

Paul Farmer, *Haiti After the Earthquake*, Public Affairs, 2011 (Chapter 5)

Noam Chomsky, "Haiti Post-Earthquake: Aid Should Go to Haitian Popular Organizations, Not to Contractors or NGOs," http://www.zcommunications.org/haiti-post-earthquake-by-noam-chomsky.html

Lesson Plans

Session 1 (50 min x 2): Historical Context of the 2004 Coup

Mini lecture on the 2004 coup and presentations of the research questions (10 min)
Four student-led presentations and debate (20 min for each group)
General research question: What were the prerequisite conditions that justified the intervention?
Activities: Divide the class in four research groups and assign the work a week in advance
Group 1: Ask students to compare the histories of the coups with the US Occupation (1915–1934) and the Duvalier regimes.
Suggested Corpus: The DLOC: Digital Library of the Caribbean at FIU (http://dloc.com/) and the website "Haiti: Island Luminous" (http://islandluminous.fiu.edu/); Jeb Sprague, *Paramilitarism and the Assault on Democracy in Haiti* (Chapters 2 & 3)
Focused questions and reflexion: What was at stake with the creation of the US's modern institutionalized military force? How did this force shape coercive structures via both Duvalier regimes and the paramilitary forces of the Macoutes and the Attachés?
Group 2: The students in the second group are in charge of explaining the social and political climate during the rise of Aristide.
Suggested Corpus: Read and compare the work of Paul Farmer and Christophe Wargny related to the rise and election of Aristide; Paul Farmer, *The Uses of Haiti* ("Duvalierism Without Duvalier," pp. 91–120); Christophe Wargny, *Haïti n'existe pas* (Chapitre 7)
Focused questions and reflexion: What were the characteristics of the post-Duvalier era? Define the concept of Liberation Theology. In what ways was Aristide's political program viewed as a threat?
Group 3: This group will first concentrate on the two coups against Aristide in January and September 1991 and discuss the history of paramilitary forces in Haiti.
Suggested Corpus: Jeb Sprague, *Paramilitarism and the Assault on Democ-*

racy in Haiti (Chapter 2) and some reports from National Coalition for Haitian Refugees and Americans Watch, https://www.refworld.org/docid/3ae6ac7c44.html. These sources should be contrasted with Paul Farmer, *The Uses of Haiti* ("The Coup of 1991," pp. 149–187).

The second half of the group's work will involve reporting on Philippe R. Girard, "Operation Restore Democracy?" *Journal of Haitian Studies*, vol. 8, no. 2, A Special Issue on Politics & Grassroots Organizing, Fall 2002, pp. 70–85, and reflecting on the work done by Lawrence P. Rockwood.

Focused questions and reflection: What do we learn from the two 1991 coups against Aristide? What were the characteristics of the regime that replaced Aristide's government? Why was Aristide brought back into power by the US government?

Group 4: This group will focus on the neoliberal project in Haiti and the terms and conditions of Aristide's return to power in 1994. Students will prepare a debate on the reasons given for imposing an embargo on Haiti just after the election of Aristide in 2004, and their legitimacy.

Suggested Corpus: Mats Lundhal, *The Political Economy of Disaster: Destitution, Plunder and Earthquake in Haiti* (Chapter 4, "Descent into Crisis") and Eirin Mobekk & Spyros I. Spyrou, "Re-evaluating IMF Involvement in Low-income Countries: The Case of Haiti," *International Journal of Social Economics*, vol. 29, no. 7, pp. 527–537, https://doi.org/10.1108/03068290210431551, can serve as a basis for understanding the work of the IMF and World Bank in Haiti via the Structural Adjustment Programs (1991, 1994). These two sources can also be compared to Alex Dupuy, "Disaster Capitalism to the Rescue: The International Community and Haiti After the Earthquake," *NACLA*, https://nacla.org/article/disaster-capitalism-rescue-international-community-and-haiti-after-earthquake

Session 2 (50 mins x 2): Historiographical Debate & Intermedial Representations

Projections (10 min): Aristide's speech in 2003 https://www.youtube.com/watch?v=S8ywg8YOJhE

Interview exclusive de Jean-Bertrand Aristide par Claude Ribbe https://www.youtube.com/watch?v=4vcbGjIUu9U

First hour: Two student-led presentations (10 min for each group) and debate (20 min)

Second hour: Student-led presentation on visual representations of the coup

General research question: What does historiography mean? Does history writing have an impact on real life?

Group 1: Ask students to present the pro-Aristide debate.

Suggested Corpus: Hallward, *Damming the Flood* (Chapter 9); Alex Dupuy, *The Prophet and Power: Jean-Bertrand Aristide, the International Community and Haiti*; Noam Chomsky, *Year 501: The Conquest Continues*; Paul Farmer, *The Uses of Haiti*

Group 2: Ask students to present the anti-Aristide debate.

Suggested Corpus: Michael Deibert *Notes from the Last Testament: The Struggle for Haiti*; Christophe Wargny, *Haïti n'existe pas: deux cents ans de solitude*; "Hallward, or The Hidden Face of Racism," Lyonel Trouillot & Nadève Ménard, Entretien de Lyonel Trouillot et Françoise Escarpit, "Ce sont bien les Haïtiens qui ont renversé Aristide"

Debate between the two groups: After reading Hallward's response to Trouillot, the students can debate among themselves to try to understand what is really at stake with the interpretation of the 2004 coup.

Suggested Corpus: "Lyonel Trouillot, or The Fictions of Formal Democracy"

Group 2: During the second hour of the class, the third group should present a comparative analysis of three visual representations of the coup (20 min) and plan a debate around the notion of "fake news" in the context of the 2004 coup (30 min). Students could also be paired to discuss the concept of representation of a conflict. The analysis of the visual sources in this session leads to the problematizing of the notion of discourse that is central to the next session.

Suggested Corpus: Nicolas Rossier, *Aristide and the Endless Revolution*; Kevin Pina, *Haiti: We Must Kill the Bandits*; Asger Leth, *Ghosts of Cité Soleil*

Session 3 (50 min x 2): Critical Discourse Analysis of the French Media Campaign

Mini lecture: A brief introduction to the methodology used to analyze the press—Discourse-Historical Approach outlined by Ruth Wodack (10 min)
  Three student-led presentations and debate (30 min for each group)
  General conclusion of the three sessions (10 min)
  General research questions: Do the newspaper articles and Debray's text present similar linguistic and stylistic features? Does the tone of the articles change after Aristide's speech in 2003? Is the general message supportive of an armed intervention?

Group 1: This group will focus on the topos of fear/threat. Students will make a list of vocabulary and syntactical structures used to convey a feeling of fear/threat.

Group 2: This group will focus on the topos of fraud. Students will make a list of vocabulary and syntactical structures used to convey a feeling of fraud and corruption.

Group 3: This group will focus on the topos of urgency/emergency. Students will make a list of vocabulary and syntactical structures used to convey a feeling of urgency.

Suggested Corpus:

Régis Debray, *Rapport au Ministre des affaires étrangères M. Dominique de Villepin*, pp. 15–60
http://www.ladocumentationfrancaise.fr/var/storage/rapports-publics/044000056/0000.pdf

Le Monde

>April 2003: 1 article (retribution 21.7$)
>Mai 2003: 1 article
>June 2003: 2 articles
>September 2003: 1 article (death of Amiot Metayer)
>October 2003: 5 articles
>November 2003: 1 article
>December 2003: 5 articles
>January 2004: 12 articles
>February 2004: 48 articles

Libération

>October 2003: 2 articles
>November 2003: 1 article
>December 2003: 10 articles
>January 2004: 6 articles
>February 2004: 33 articles

A final session could be held for postgraduate students linking the study of the 2004 coup with a wider theoretical framework of analysis dealing with neocolonialism, global capitalism, and media analysis.

Suggested Corpus (excerpts): Kwame Nkrumah, *Neo-Colonialism: The Last Stage of Imperialism*, International Publishers, 1965; Naomi Klein, *The Shock Doctrine: The Rise of Disaster Capitalism*, Penguin, 2007; Derek Gregory, *The*

Colonial Present, Blackwell Publishing, 2004; Edward S. Herman & Noam Chomsky, *Manufacturing Consent: The Political Economy of the Mass Media*, Vintage Books, 1995.

Notes

1. Ask students in this first group to compare the histories of the coups with the US occupation (1915–1934) and the Duvalier regimes. The DLOC: Digital Library of the Caribbean at FIU (http://dloc.com/) and the website "Haiti: Island Luminous" (http://islandluminous.fiu.edu/) provide excellent sources for research. These documents could be compared to Jeb Sprague, *Paramilitarism and the Assault on Democracy in Haiti* (Chapters 2 & 3). A major question that the students can address is the creation of the US modern institutionalized military force and the ways in which this force shaped modern-day coercive structures via both Duvalier regimes and the paramilitary forces of the Macoutes and the Attachés.

2. In order to get a good understanding of the social and political climate during the rise of Aristide, students in the second group should read and compare the work of Paul Farmer and Christophe Wargny. See Paul Farmer, *The Uses of Haiti*, pp. 91–120, and Christophe Wargny, *Haïti n'existe pas*, Chapitre 7.

3. The first half of this group's work will concentrate on the two coups against Aristide in January and September 1991, and they will discuss the history of paramilitary forces in Haiti using Jeb Sprague, *Paramilitarism and the Assault on Democracy in Haiti* (Chapter 2) and some reports from the National Coalition for Haitian Refugees and Americans Watch (https://www.refworld.org/docid/3ae6ac7c44.html). These sources should be contrasted with Paul Farmer, *The Uses of Haiti* ("The Coup of 1991," pp. 149–187). The second part of the group's efforts will involve reporting on Philippe R. Girard's "Operation Restore Democracy?" and reflecting on the work done by Lawrence P. Rockwood.

4. This group will focus on the neoliberal project in Haiti and the terms and conditions of Aristide's return to power in 1994. The work of Mats Lundhal and Eirin Mobekk and Spyros I. Spyrou can serve as a basis for understanding the work of the IMF and World Bank in Haiti via the Structural Adjustment Programs (1991, 1994). These two sources can also be compared to Alex Dupuy's "Disaster Capitalism to the Rescue." Students will present a debate on the reasons used to impose an embargo on Haiti just after the election of Aristide in 2004.

5. Ask students to brainstorm on the symbolic meaning of this name (it means "landslide," as in "avalanche") in the context of the broad-based popular support of Aristide's social agenda.

6. It is worth showing the students a clip of Bill Clinton admitting his responsibility. See http://www.democracynow.org/2010/4/1/clinton_rice

7. http://data.worldbank.org/indicator/DT.DOD.DECT.CD?locations=HT

8. Alex Dupuy, "Globalization, the World Bank and the Haitian Economy."

9. United Nations,"Emergency Economic Recovery Programme," *International Report* 1.A1, 1995. http://www.hartford-hwp.com/archives/43a/050.html. Accessed 10 June 2015.

10. Dan Beeton, "What the World Bank and the IDB Owe Haiti."

11. https://www.youtube.com/watch?v=S8ywg8YOJhE

12. "Bill Clinton's Heavy Hand on Haiti's Vulnerable Agricultural Economy: The American

Rice Scandal," http://www.coha.org/haiti-research-file-neoliberalism%E2%80%99s-heavy-hand-on-haiti%E2%80%99s-vulnerable-agricultural-economy-the-american-rice-scandal/. Accessed 10 June 2015.

13. "Le départ d'Aristide ne devrait pas tarder," *Le Monde*, 18 December 2003.
14. "Une chance pour la paix," *Le Monde*, 27 February 2004.
15. "Nous libérerons Haïti de l'esclavage d'Aristide," *Le Monde*, 25 February 2004.

Works Cited

Beeton, Dan. "What the World Bank and the IDB Owe Haiti." ZNet, August 2, 2006. https://zcomm.org/znetarticle/what-the-world-bank-and-idb-owe-haiti-by-dan-beeton/. Accessed 5 September 2015.

Bergan, Renée, and Mark Schuller. *Poto Mitan: Haitian Women, Pillars of the Global Economy*. Tèt Ansanm Productions, 2009.

Bongie, Chris. "Universal Envy: Taking Sides in the Trouillot-Hallward Debate." *Bulletin of Francophone and Postcolonial Studies*, vol. 1, no. 1, 2010, pp. 8–14.

Chomsky, Noam. *Year 501: The Conquest Continues*. Verso, 1993.

———. "Democracy Restored." *Z Magazine*, November 1994, https://chomsky.info/199411__/.

Debray, Régis. *Haïti et la France*. Les Éditions de la Table Ronde, 2004. http://www.diplomatie.gouv.fr/IMG/pdf/rapport_haiti.pdf. Accessed 15 September 2013.

Deibert, Michael. *Notes from the Last Testament: The Struggle for Haiti*. Seven Stories Press, 2005.

Dupuy, Alex. *The Prophet and Power: Jean-Bertrand Aristide, the International community and Haiti*. Rowman and Littlefield, 2007.

———. "Disaster Capitalism to the Rescue: The International Community and Haiti After the Earthquake," NACLA. https://nacla.org/article/disaster-capitalism-rescue-international-community-and-haiti-after-earthquake. Accessed 5 September 2015.

Farmer, Paul. *The Uses of Haiti*. Common Courage Press, 2003.

Farmer, Paul, M. Smith Fawzi, and P. Nevil. "Unjust Embargo of Aid for Haïti." *The Lancet*, vol. 361, no. 9355, 2003, pp. 420–423. doi.org/10.1016/s0140-6736(03)12380-x.

Girard, Philippe R. "Operation Restore Democracy?" *Journal of Haitian Studies*, vol. 8, no. 2, A Special Issue on Politics & Grassroots Organizing, Fall 2002, pp. 70–85.

Griffin, Thomas M. "Haiti Human Rights Investigation: November 11-21." *The University of Miami School of Law*, 2004. http://www.ijdh.org/CSHRhaitireport.pdf. Accessed 5 September 2015.

Hallward, Peter. *Damming the Flood: Haiti, Aristide and the Politics of Containment*. Verso, 2007.

Klein, Naomi. *The Shock Doctrine: The Rise of Disaster Capitalism*. Penguin, 2007.

Leth, Asger. *Ghosts of Cité Soleil*. Image/Thinkfilms, 2007.

McGowan, Lisa. "Democracy Undermined, Economic Justice Denied: Structural Adjustment and the AID Juggernaut in Haiti." The Development Group for Alternative Policies, January 1997.

Nesbitt, Nick. "Turning the Tide: The Problem of Popular Insurgency in Haitian Revolutionary Historiography." *Small Axe*, vol. 27, October 2008, pp. 14–31.

Pina, Kevin. *Haiti: We Must Kill the Bandits.* Kevin Pina Production Company, 2007.
Podur, Justin. *Haiti's New Dictatorship: The Coup, the Earthquake and the UN Occupation.* Pluto Press, 2012.
Robinet, François. *Les Conflits africains au regard des médias français (1994–2008). Construction, mise en scène et effets de narration médiatiques.* 2012. Versailles St-Quentin-en Yvelines University, PhD Dissertation.
Rossier, Nicolas. *Aristide and the Endless Revolution.* First Run Features, 2005.
Spencer, Amar N. "A Comparative Analysis of the US Mainstream Press and Black Press Coverage of Jean-Bertrand Aristide from 1991–2011." *Journal of Mass Communication and Journalism,* vol. 2, no. 11, 2012. https://www.omicsgroup.org/journals/a-comparative-analysis-of-the-us-mainstream-press-and-black-press-coverageof-jean-bertrand-aristide-from-1991-2011-2165-7912.1000136.pdf. Accessed 10 May 2017.
Sprague, Jeb. *Paramilitarism and the Assault on Democracy in Haiti.* Monthly Review Press, 2012.
Trouillot, Lyonel. "Hallward, or The Hidden Face of Racism." translated by Nadève Ménard. *Small Axe,* vol. 13, no. 3, 2009, pp. 128–136.
———. Interview by Françoise Escarpit, "Ce sont bien les Haïtiens qui ont renversé Aristide." *L'Humanité.fr,* 9 March 2004. http://www.humanite.fr/node/301661. Accessed 10 October 2015.
United Nations. "Emergency Economic Recovery Programme." International Report 1.A1, 1995. http://www.hartford-hwp.com/archives/43a/050.html. Accessed 1 July 2020.
USAID. "Haiti: Country Development Strategy Statement." FY 1984, 24. http://pdf.usaid.gov/pdf_docs/PDAAM917.pdf. Accessed 16 February 2015.
Wodak, Ruth, and Ludwig Christoph, editors. *Challenges in a Changing World: Issues in Critical Discourse Analysis.* Passagen Verlag, 1999.
Wodak, Ruth, and Martin Reisigl. "The Discourse-Historical Approach (DHA)." *Methods for Critical Discourse Analysis,* edited by Ruth Wodak and M. Meyer, 2nd revised edition, Sage, 2009, pp. 87–121.
Žižek, Slavoj. "Democracy Versus the People." *New Statesman,* 14 August 2008. http://www.newstatesman.com/books/2008/08/haiti-aristide-lavalas. Accessed 10 May 2014.

8

Peck's *Fatal Assistance*

A Filmic Lesson on the Failures of Aid

AGNÈS PEYSSON-ZEISS

Haiti, a nation that had been fighting for years for its right to exist on the social, human, and political map, trembled on January 12, 2010, when "Goudougoudou"—the onomatopoetic term Haitians have given the earthquake—brought the island to its knees. An estimated 316,000 lives were lost and nearly three million people were affected. The disaster generated an immediate international response and many rushed to Haiti's aid: governments, NGOS, nonprofit organizations, and individuals, among them Raoul Peck, who returned to help his compatriots confronted with tragedy. Mainstream media became another responder to the Haitian tragedy, telling a story of the island in situ, representing the victims and informing their listeners and readers about emergency responses, reconstruction efforts, and progress on the ground. They became translators for the world of what was happening in Haiti, working with NGOs, private donors, and governments to provide support and to encourage money to pour in.

This study aims to tell another story, the one Raoul Peck witnessed, which he filmed during the two years following the earthquake. Peck realized, as he states in his film *Fatal Assistance*, that "despite the billions of dollars flushed into it," the help was chaotic, disorganized, and disproportionate (*Fatal Assistance*). As a result, he embarked on a different path, electing to bring a different kind of aid, a visual and in-depth, gut-wrenching exploration of the humanitarian situation in Haiti. His analysis presents a devastating balance sheet of the aid following the earthquake and exposes diverse and competing spheres of power.

As I teach this film, I guide students to an understanding of how the example of post-earthquake aid in Haiti exposes many of the failures of international aid, and how Peck's film, with its unique approach to documentary, by contrast promotes questioning and dialogue. In this chapter, I will outline how this film can be used in a 200-level general study course on Haitian culture and society or a course on the politics of international aid, interspersing my pedagogical approach with an analysis of the film. As companion pieces in the course, I use data from the USAID website as well as chapters from Dambisa Moyo's *Dead Aid: Why Aid Is Not Working and How There Is a Better Way for Africa*. Students focus on the multiplicity of perspectives offered by Peck's camera, the use of epistolary voiceover and effects, and the reasons for the lack of chronology.

According to literature professor Sarah Johnson, "Foreign intervention [in Haiti] today no longer looks like colonization, but . . . [i]nternational aid organizations are pre-occupied with planning long-term business developments more than providing emergency humanitarian relief" (Minato). Johnson's analysis of Haiti echoes Dambisa Moyo's words about the African continent in *Dead Aid*, as "even the IMF—a leading provider of aid—has warned aid supporters about placing more hope in aid as an instrument of development than it is capable of delivering" (Moyo 47). Departing from the traditional victim's perspective, Peck reverses the gaze, filming the "aiding" parties looking for answers, challenging the measures taken, and enabling the spectator to investigate in his wake. He focuses on the different types of assistance that exist (Moyo 7). Students read about and explore those differences.

Between solidarity politics and inequality politics, several questions arise. For example, how does Raoul Peck's inquisitive eye explore abuses and identify gaps in the humanitarian blanket thrown over Haiti in an attempt to recalibrate the meaning of aid on the ground? How does his lens focused on humanitarian work become a teaching tool, and allow his spectators to embark on a visual and sensory voyage to unearth prevalent issues concerning the welfare of Haiti? These are just some of the questions addressed in the course.

I begin by offering a brief study of documentary filmmaking in "Third Cinema" as a genre in order to help students understand Peck's theoretical framework. Third Cinema is a concept of revolutionary filmmaking first proposed by Fernando Solanas and Octavio Getino. This genre, Solanas and Getino argued, was "*the most gigantic cultural, scientific, and artistic manifestation of our time, the great possibility of constructing a liberated personality with each people as the starting point—in a word, the decolonisation of culture*" (Solanas and Getino 2, emphasis in original). Solanas and Getino advocated for a cinema that was both art and action, that became a transformational social practice, an instrument of change and consciousness-raising. Teshome Gabriel expanded on this notion in *Third Cinema Updated,* asserting that Third Cinema has transformed due to new power dynamics, and thus it "continues to live on [but] it cannot stay the same" (Gabriel). This modified form of cinema denotes larger structural problems within society and as such it can

> no longer be defined as a singular, univocal idea if, indeed, it ever could. It has become more complex, multifarious, heterogeneous. Third Cinema, in other words, has [developed into] Third Cinemas . . . becoming based less on oppositional strategies than on more complex, more mixed, more ironic, forms of resistance. (Gabriel)

This complexity led him to revisit his theory, seeing the new cinemas of the early 2000s as Third Cinemas, more adapted to relating the issues, tragedies, and challenges of today's world.

Raoul Peck's work reflects perfectly these cinematic goals. He moves away from a unilateral gaze, tackling issues from a multiplicity of perspectives. *Fatal Assistance* is to be an instrument of change, to recalibrate and bring new perspectives in the hope that they can lead to new practices. Frank Ukadike, speaking about transcultural modernities, noted that "the legacies of colonialism and Africa's own political ineptitude, coupled with a dubious agenda for 'development,' IMF policies, the privatization vogue, and 'globalization' have inaugurated new discourses on culture, postcoloniality and 'modernity'" (Bekers et al. 297). In class, I provide quotes on Third Cinema from Solanas and Getino and have students, in pairs, offer their understanding of the genre by selecting a scene and explaining whether or not they consider that it exemplifies Third Cinema.

Influences of the Third World Film Movement on Peck

Peck's approach offers a new discourse on the aid dilemma that overlaps, juxtaposes, and blends a variety of techniques to inform his spectators. His polyvocal lens provides "an alternative third space where we can engage in ideas about imagination, about dreams, tales, and magical vision" (Gabriel). Students examine Peck's use of flashbacks, interruptions, music, and silences and see how these techniques allow the spectators to reflect on the situation at hand. When asked by Olivier Barlet about his methodology and use of flashbacks, Peck replied: "You say flashback, I call that different levels of stories, different levels of narrative that I superimpose, that I switch around so that the inversion itself can create something else" (Barlet). These various stories are those of the protagonists on the ground, and the purpose of analepsis is to interrupt the chronological sequence, raising enough questions that the spectator must inquire as to the veracity of the official, mainstream story. Additionally, through these "various levels of different narratives," the filmmaker captures the story from different perspectives, creating a space to question what is being told, emphasizing the value of individual as well as collective stories. Once Peck has found the necessary, the just distance that brings reality to the screen, he subverts it, filming the absent images. Haitian stories come to life as the camera unearths the situation on the ground, bringing the hidden pieces to the screen. In addition to the multilayered stories highlighting the complexity of the situation, Peck involves the spectator in a quest of discovery through voiceover commentaries, poetry, and music; he also uses graphs and archival footage to document the tragedy. In the process, his overlaps and inversions create a space for the spectator's thoughts and disrupt the concept of "neutral" aid. This critical engagement incites viewers to ponder the following statement: "The essential question on the rational repartition of the aid is not and can never be asked" (*Fatal Assistance*). Peck then proceeds to leave silence on which the spectator can reflect. Thus Peck structures his narratives using frames and fragmentation that create spaces in which the spectator can pause and ponder, and these moments of silence allow students to discuss and analyze the situation as it plays out, through fact sheets on the aid. They also create themed vignettes and write down what they understand of the situation, leading to discussions and debates on the value or role of foreign aid. The silences that Peck introduces contribute to the suspension of judgment and reflection on the viewer's part. It is at the moment when Peck films the unspeakable, the untold, when the story is displayed through frames that "fracture both time and space, offering a jagged, staccato rhythm of [seemingly] unconnected moments" that spectators can start to decipher, deconstruct the official story and reconstruct the unofficial one (McCloud 67). Examining Peck's filming technique closely, looking at the modes of investigation that he uses, the viewer can see that the multiplicity of approaches, far from weakening his focus, actually strengthens it. The proliferation of modes of resistance on the screen in conjunction with the spaces left for the spectator to contemplate make for a more powerful film and analysis of the tragedy. As Paul Ricoeur suggests, "the meaning or the significance of a story wells up from the intersection of the world of text and the world of the reader" (430). This approach applies to Peck's documentary filmmaking as well, as the stories on the screen not only re-present events but also provide a variety of experiences wherein ideas can be explored. Peck scrutinizes interviews, focuses on graphic images of devastation, listens to discussions, and analyzes voiceover commentaries about the aid dilemma to bring the viewer to reflect on the situation.

Footage of Destruction and Dead Aid

Fatal Assistance opens with an expositional scene, a mise en récit, starting with Minister of Public Works Joséus Nader's retelling of what happened when the earthquake occurred, supported by archival footage of destruction while the death toll appears. The film projects this shocking information slowly, as a metaphor of the slow response to the tragedy. In gray and red letters we read, 230,000 dead, 300,000 injured, 1,500,000 homeless. The multiplicity of perspectives and the lack of results echo the deficiency of structure and utter chaos the earthquake produced, reinforcing the multiple levels of disorder occurring in Haiti. The visual and auditory stimuli create a frame of reference for the spectator, who witnesses an overload of numbers, graphs, names of agencies working on the ground, people helping, waiting, asking questions. The filmic reflection of the physical experience of these events is deliberately overwhelming and difficult to comprehend. The documentary will end with the same image, the arrival of the earthquake, as it obliterates what looks like a library, highlighting the failure of the aid, returning to that fateful January 12 to indicate the lack of progression, the lack of results. The instructor should have students take notes as numbers appear on the screen, recording who the actors are, and they should investigate the source of the funding using USAID factsheets to help. Departing from the point of erasure, Peck hopes that spectators will investigate in his wake and come up with their own conclusions, generating a space to think that the Haitian people did not have at the time. The objective flashback technique transports the spectators back to earlier events to show their relationship to the present. Even though students do not have all the necessary facts, it is important for them to understand who the actors are and what those humanitarian gifts mean: "As Naomi Klein explains in *Shock Doctrine*, disasters are generally opportunities for capitalists but not the victims of disasters" (Pressley-Sanon and Saint-Just 53). Peck's film, which begins and ends with the same frame of reference, insists on the failure of this fatal aid that serves only a few. The lack of closure shown on the screen accentuates the failures of resolutions taken by the government and the various agencies on the ground. Silences, empty shots, and empty discussions mimic the aid that agencies and governments offer without any concrete results. Projecting numbers onto the screen is another effective means of deconstructing the myth of the aid and the dysfunctionality of its applications. The visual effect of the amounts of funds offered, zooming in and out of the screen, is powerful and ignites dialogue about the aid promised. The audience can start evaluating how international aid is administered, distributed, and managed. We find out that "[t]he Brazilian president announced $100 million dollars, South Korea $10 million, Belgium $8.9. Japan promised $100 million. The World Bank insures a participation of $227 million." The verbs projected on the screen—announce, promise, guarantee, propose to give—leave some uncertainty as promises are made. Assurances and the reality of the aid are very different, as are the requests from the Haitian government that fall on deaf ears.[1]

Peck continues filming the failure of the aid through additional discussions filled with empty words. In one of the segments, he announces the players in the aid game starting with a shot of then–Secretary of State Hillary Clinton, who in 2011, a year after the events, met with President Préval. The conversation shows that not much has been done, that words have lost their meaning, and no useful, concrete work is happening on the ground. Secretary Clinton's remarks are highlighted by the camera, which films endless conversations with no solid results. The frustration felt by the actors and aid workers in this tragedy is transferred to the viewers as the narrator adds that a lot of good could have resulted from all the aid: "Such sincere energy, such individual devotion wasted by a machine that surpasses the protagonists. On one side, attrition, on the other, anger, frustration and those truly responsible are absent" (*Fatal Assistance*).

It is at this moment that Peck re-sets the stage, adds other approaches, mixes genres, takes the discussion out of its existing diegesis and frames the query another way, displaying the ongoing epistolary exchange in which his "chère amie" (dear friend), his partner in uncovering the tragedy, declares, "International agents ceased a long time ago to be impartial intermediaries. They fight ferociously; they intervene for their own profit, supplanting local agencies" (*Fatal Assistance*). Examining the role of the agencies on the ground with a close reading of the meetings Peck filmed will allow students to gain a more comprehensive understanding of humanitarian aid in Haiti. By transcribing some of the exchanges that occur among the existing parties, students can examine the language they use and decide whether it is meaningful or purely rhetorical.

The History of Foreign Aid

To contextualize the events in Haiti, students read about the history of foreign aid from its inception at the Bretton Woods Conference in 1944 and the development of the concept since the 1960s.[2] After reading Andy Baker's book *Shaping the Developing World*, they will be able to identify the different kinds of aid and can cast an informed eye on the roles of the IMF and World Bank as they apply to the Haitian context.[3] Though development assistance has been in existence for 60 years, "poor people don't believe in it anymore. . . . One needs to know how to put a stop to it. Let's stop pretending" (*Fatal Assistance*). Peck's goal is to use his film as a tool, a model to examine and evaluate aid in countries affected by disaster. The eye of the camera speaks for itself and the voiceover denounces the failure and frustration as we see that real aid is not happening: "Everything is there. Technical means, a minimum of political will, urgency, leadership," but to no avail (*Fatal Assistance*). Ready to unearth the reasons behind this lack of progress, Peck's camera, privy to many meetings, brings the spectator closer to negotiations between NGOs and Interim Haiti Reconstruction Commission (IHRC) members. With his use of close-ups, we become voyeurs in what he calls the "pornography" of aid. Even if they do not partake of the decisions made around the table, students gain a sense of what the aid represents. In bringing us behind closed doors, Peck does away with the presumed objectivity and distance evoked earlier to offer an intimate look at what aid negotiations involve. The discussions in the films are devoid of emotion and involve only financial decisions based on capital and not on people's needs.[4] These moments in the film put names and faces to the entities behind the aid. For example, Peck films a meeting between ICRC members and NGOs discussing how to use the money allocated to the 16/6 rehabilitation project,[5] and Priscilla Phelps, a post-disaster recovery specialist, senior advisor for Housing and Neighborhoods in the IHRC, wonders what the money is buying since there is nothing concrete, no job creation, no economic developmental strategy. She adds: "I feel like we are being played" (*Fatal Assistance*).[6] Projecting clips of the discussions is a useful way to set up debates in the classroom as to the pros and cons of international aid in Haiti. Class discussions can focus on questions such as, What is the visible impact of aid on civil society? What are the economic limitations of the aid? How can we do away with aid dependency?[7]

Epistolary Exchanges on Dead Aid: Classroom Discussions

After the first descriptions of the situation on the ground narrated by Joséus Nader, Peck picks up his camera and begins an epistolary exchange in voiceover: "Dear friend, I will not talk to you about the 75 seconds of hell that destroyed everything . . . about the shouts and clamors. I will no longer show you the fixed stares . . . asking for answers that will not come. . . ." (*Fatal Assistance*). The narrator struggles with how to describe the inexpressible. The narrator and his female interlocutor, his "chère amie" as she will be referred to throughout these epistolary exchanges, give the audience the opportunity to partake of the "meaning-making process" as they try to make sense of the situation.

Examining the role of the epistolary exchanges in creating a narrative framework that binds the story together allows for meaningful class discussions. In class, groups can present on the different exchanges, looking at the function of spaces and silences. Furthermore, it is imperative to examine the way the epistolary discussion gives life to the letters and thoughts as the exchange takes place outside of the existing diegesis between a frustrated relief worker—the chère amie played by Céline Salette—and a member of the Haitian diaspora—Raoul Peck—expressing individual subjective voices out of the rubble. How does the use of these two techniques, the voice-over narration using the epistolary medium and the silences used by Peck's camera, ensure a variety of perspectives? This is a question that opens a dialogue, and pushes the spectator to dig deeper to find what is concealed under the rubble of politics. We find that there is not just one story but many as we work to understand "what on earth was happening/*ce que diable il s'y passait*" in a country where relief organizations are behaving as "entrepreneurs" (*Fatal Assistance*). To emphasize this fact, the instructor can ask students to create a grid of the major actors in distributing the aid, their roles, and their requests or offers, and also show how the aid has stalled, the absence of results.

The overlapping images and blending of stories in the film mimic the stories told by various actors on the ground. An examination of the problems of coordination of the aid programs and their lack of coherence can be effected by making lists of the tasks or projects that the film depicts and the results that ensue. Students can also do research on the various camp sites where people displaced by the earthquake were living, as they work on an interactive map of aid projects and follow NGO worker Bryan Castro's efforts while in Haiti.[8] In an interview a year later, Castro, filled with sadness, says, "The larger context has not changed. The Camp Corail site is still on the fringes and there are no jobs" (*Fatal Assistance*). Camp Corail-Cesselesse was a transitional shelter camp located on an arid expanse of land 18 kilometers from Port-au-Prince (*Fatal Assistance*). It was home to between 65,000 and 100,000 people (Haiti Grassroots). The stories embedded in Peck's film are a mise en abyme depicting a tale of absence: the absence of organization, absence of communication, absence of concrete, absence of useful help that hinders relief work.

In class, it is important to select clips showing the aid provided, examine the way Peck films the scenes, and mark a pause on various projects that reveal the disorganization of the aid distribution. For example, Peck films a scene in which we discover that four NGOs worked on the same canal at the same time without coordinating or communicating at all. Students can examine various examples of this lack of coordination from the film and reflect on this potent exercise in futility, for example looking at the image of mud being brought up by laborers and eroded again by the rains. Peck's lens zooms onto the feet of a worker, covered in mud, trying to empty the canal, even as Haiti's prime minister, Jean-Max Bellerive, states that with more rain, the dirt would eventually find its way back in, a comment that serves as a metaphor for the people drowning under the murky waters of the aid. Additionally, Laura Graham, Bill Clinton's cabinet director, interjects that removing debris, which should come first before any type of reconstruction happens, is not deemed "sexy" enough by donors, who prefer giving to more appealing causes such as rebuilding because they want a photo op, or tangible proof of progress (*Fatal Assistance*). Peck reveals that if money is given to the cause in the wrong order, nothing will be done; the financial aspect of the aid is extremely structured and can only be applied to what donors assign. The IHRC members interviewed are very candid: if the rubble is not removed, reconstruction cannot start. The aperture of the camera closes on Jean-Max Bellerive's comment as he compares Haiti to a city and concludes ironically, "If we cannot solve the problem of a city, a metropolis, what do we expect to solve elsewhere?" (*Fatal Assistance*).

Peck's Political Commentary on Glamour Aid

Peck continues to address this issue as he focuses on glamour aid and its consequences in relation to modernity and postcoloniality. Peck intersperses political comments with emotional and poetic declarations: officials, celebrities, international and local agents, and camp residents appear; some are asking questions while others are stating facts or announcing what they will do. The film raises the question of the well-meaning "glamour aid" that started in the 1970s with George Harrison's concert for Bangladesh. Immediately following the earthquake, many celebrities and politicians came to Haiti's aid: Presidents Barack Obama and Nicolas Sarkozy, the Clintons, the Jolie-Pitts, George Clooney, and Sean Penn, among others, gave their time and energy to help the situation. Amounts of money are projected onto the screen; journalists talk about what is being done while reports fade in and out or overlap while the narrator says, "This is the way this story starts" (*Fatal Assistance*). Students can research glamour aid as defined by Moyo and see how it applies to Haiti. People mean well, but does this type of aid actually make people's lives better, especially when decisions are not made in consultation with the local population? In this exercise, students examine the way the process worked in Haiti and write blog posts about their findings. The results will be discussed during roundtables organized in class.

Language and Aid

Peck then proceeds to talk about the creation of the now-defunct IHRC, as he was able to film their meetings. His camera travels from people's faces to graphs to houses and information about whether these structures will remain standing or are slated for demolition.[9] The four-tiered storytelling is impregnated with reality, forcing the spectator to better grasp this lived reality. Students will focus on the use of the conditional mood used by many interviewees to express their frustration. The film shows an amalgam of people, entities, and "aid," but no true relief, no organization, no long-term goals—a state of affairs reinforced by the leitmotiv "*on n'avait pas prévu*/we had not planned" (*Fatal Assistance*). Students will follow a series of vignettes of disillusioned aid workers on the ground who communicate feelings of frustration that can be analyzed in class through the use of indicative and conditional moods used in the French language. An Oxfam Québec representative, Philippe Mathieu, in a lucid assessment of the situation, reiterates the refrain: "*aucun plan prévu*/ there are no plans" when speaking of Camp Corail. Nothing has been done, in spite of the promises and plans. In the film, some of Camp Corail's residents affirm that the NGOs have underestimated the extent of the damage: "They calculated badly or funding was poorly used. If only they had taken time to speak with the inhabitants. It would have been better" (*Fatal Assistance*). There were many meetings but not many positive outcomes. The past conditional mood of the French language reinforces the lack of perspective and is used in several parts of the documentary, reflecting what could have been but did not happen. Joël Boutroue, former UN coordinator, admits, "We should have given a bigger role to the local population . . . we should have thought of that" after the fact (*Fatal Assistance*). At Camp Corail, Priscilla Phelps sighs and says, "This is going to be like putting toothpaste back into the tube. When the story of the Haitian reconstruction will be written, the international community will admit its guilt about this site" (*Fatal Assistance*). In this instance, the use of the simple future tense shows definite failure. Not only do forces/ entities on the ground lack forethought, they also fail in communicating what is happening. If Peck is trying to give viewers a different sense of or relationship to reality, he is also highlighting the connections that are not happening as he films the gaps in the story. There was no true involvement of the Haitian community in the reconstruction process. Haitians did not have a real voice; they were "accompanied" by someone from the outside. Peck highlights a neocolonial mindset in which Haitians are viewed as "wards of the state," just as they were during the US Occupation (1915–1935).

Why do economically developed countries feel that they can and must decide what is best for Haiti? To explore this issue, the instructor can have students listen to Dr. Ernesto Sirolli, a consultant who promotes local entrepreneurship and local self—determination, as he distinguishes between paternalistic and patronizing aid in his TED Talk titled, "Want to Help Someone? Shut Up and Listen!" Sirolli argues that the first principle of aid is to sit, listen, and "become a servant to the local people" (Sirolli). Peck's *Fatal Assistance* shows meetings where 12 Haitians, 13 international partners, co-presidents for the IHRC, Bill Clinton, and Jean-Max Bellerive seem to have an apparent equality of voices. The engineer from Myamoto International does comment on the rebuilding effort, "This is a Haitian operation; I am only an assistant," but is that truly the case (*Fatal Assistance*)? Peck follows a number of Haitians, such as Suzy Percy Filippini, a representative of the Haitian executive at an IHRC meeting, who feels that the Haitians are "*débranchés de la CIRH*" [disconnected from the IHRC] and feel as if they have a "*rôle de figurant*" [role of extras] (*Fatal Assistance*). On the surface, there is a certain equality at the IHRC, but the filming reveals a different reality. When Onaville camp leader Jean-Ronald Merisma is interviewed, he expresses the same sentiment: "*Pourquoi les étrangers font ce qu'ils veulent . . . Si elles [les ONG] avaient pris le temps de poser des questions aux habitants, les résultats auraient été meilleurs.*" [Why do foreigners do what they want? . . . If NGOs had taken the time to ask questions of the occupants, results would have been better] (*Fatal Assistance*). This reality is strengthened by Peck's voiceover comment: "*Le pays est meurtri, fatigué, déplacé, accablé . . . qui les sauvera des sauveurs?*" [The country is scarred, tired, displaced, worn down . . . who will save them from their saviors?] (*Fatal Assistance*).

This heaping visual, sensory, verbal overload added to the subversion of linear time and space calls attention to ideas, as the spectator focuses not only on the unfolding of the story, but also on the questions that arise from the images as a new reality is surfacing. In the face of the chaos, disorganization, and tensions displayed on the screen, students will think critically as they enter the discussion and imagine how the story Peck tells could be given a different ending. The film begins and ends with the same archival footage; it is given a rhythm by the letters sent between the female narrator, the "chère amie," and Peck, as he receives information from her in which she documents her frustrations. He provides us with a multiplicity of perspectives, as seen by a Haitian from the diaspora and a Westerner on the ground. The exchange opens up the closed proceedings of the aid to examine it from another angle. This aid that has created a "dictatorship" has become "a paternalistic monster that sweeps everything in its path. It pretends to solve problems that it creates," states Peck, paralleling his comments with earthquake footage that sweeps everything into oblivion (*Fatal Assistance*). Each comment is supported via another medium to give a multiplicity of perspectives that reinforce one another, underscoring their importance. Raoul Peck's camera reverses the preconceived ideas that the world may have of Haiti. Students in their turn will be in charge of rethinking the notion of aid in practical terms. A disheartened Phelps states that "money should have been given directly to the people on the ground. Yes, some of these may have disappeared, but it would have disappeared with NGOs as well" (*Fatal Assistance*). Phelps comments on the fact that some corruption takes place, but the camera encourages the spectators to place their trust in the local people, and encourages talking with them to see a different result emerge. That is the tacit pact that Peck establishes with his audience from the very beginning. He entrusts his viewers with a mission to look at what is happening and come up with their own interpretation. Students' final projects will have that same aim. Peck's arguments, supported by reflections, images, statistics, and comments by officials, offer a way to negotiate chaos and make sense of it, exposing the process of the "reconstruction" of Haiti the way it has been done as deeply flawed, indeed denouncing aid as "humanitarian pornography" (*Fatal Assistance*). In doing so, he engages viewers to join in the conversation, questioning the conditions of the aid. As a final project, students can work in groups to try to develop alternative approaches to aid distribution. Each group will select an area of their choice, such as a school, a canal, a transit shelter, or a hospital, and create a case study for it. Their task will be to imagine an innovative plan emulating Sirolli's model of "shut up and listen." They will think of donors, accountability for both sides, questions that local people may have, and ways in which the local community can participate actively in the project.

Syllabus

This 200-level course examines the 2010 earthquake in Haiti from a political, historical, and societal perspective. Students will read texts on the topic, view the documentary, and imagine a plan for aid as a final project.

Week 1: Introduction to Haitian culture and society

Week 2: Excerpts from Andy Baker's book *Shaping the Developing World*, in which he uses a threefold framework of the West, the South, and the natural world to categorize and analyze the factors that cause underdevelopment—from the consequences of colonialism, deficient domestic institutions, and gender inequality to the effects of globalization, geography, and environmental degradation.

Week 3: Read about documentary filmmaking in Third Cinema as a genre to understand Peck's theoretical framework, using Solanas and Getino's *Toward a Third Cinema,* and examine how Teshome Gabriel expanded on this notion in *Third Cinema Updated,* asserting that Third Cinema has transformed due to new power dynamics, and as such it "continues to live on [but] it cannot stay the same."

Week 4: Aid: Dambisa Moyo's *Dead Aid: Why Aid Is Not Working and How There Is a Better Way for Africa*. Students will focus on the multiplicity of perspectives offered by Peck's camera and compare and contrast these perspectives with the arguments in Moyo's book.

Weeks 5–6: discussion of the following texts:

a) Dany Laferrière's *The World Is Moving Around Me: A Memoir of the Haiti Earthquake* (2013), his own take on what happened.
b) Danticat's foreword to *Tales of Port-au-Prince: Letting Haitians Speak for Themselves* (2017)
c) Students who read French can report on Yanick Lahens' *Failles* (2013)

Week 6: History of Interim Haiti Reconstruction Commission (IHRC) and pros and cons associated with it. Students research the history of the organization. They can also look at the letters from the Haitian members of the IHRC to its co-chairs, protesting their marginalization and silencing within the organization.

Week 7: Research on NGOs on the ground and their work at the time in order to understand Peck's comments. Web research. (See the lesson plan for this week below.)

Week 8: Look at "glamour aid"

Weeks 9–10: Work on the Haitian Recovery Project (http://haiti.si.edu/)

Week 11: Potentialities—Dr. Ernesto Sirolli. Listen to the TED Talk and discuss the solution to prepare for the final project.

Weeks 12–13: As a final project, the instructor will ask students to create their own aid plan for Haiti. Each group will select an area of their choice—a school, a canal, a transit shelter, or a hospital, for example—and create a case study of it. Their task will be to imagine an innovative plan emulating Sirolli's model of "shut up and listen." They will think of donors, governance accountability for both sides, questions that local people may have, and ways that the local community can participate directly in determining the details of the project and in helping it to unfold.

Lesson Plan for Week 7

NGO Research

Day 1:

1. Research the types of NGO working in Haiti after the earthquake (haiti.ngoaidmap.org/) and evaluate the use value of their type of work.
2. Create groups and do computer research on the types of NGOs that exist.
3. Students will select a particular NGO that was working in Haiti during the earthquake to profile. They will create an outline for a presentation about this organization and do research at home.

Day 2:

1. Each student researches a specific aspect of the NGO their group selected.
2. Students will identify the history, funding, type of work, and members of the NGO.
3. Students will identify the current status and criticism of the NGO.

Day 3:

1. Presentations
2. Q&A
3. Reflection on the work of each of the NGO presented
4. Critical reflection on each group's NGO (to turn in)

Notes

1. Préval's requests for Haiti were to provide shelter for those living in the ruins as Haiti's rainy season approached, and getting seed to farmers in time for spring planting. "Our priorities are, first and foremost, protection of those people who today are homeless and who must be relocated," Préval said after meeting with President Obama at the White House. "And in parallel, we must prepare for the rainy season." Préval identified two priorities for the broader

task of rebuilding Haiti: encouraging people to move from the overcrowded capital by providing education, health care, and jobs in the provinces; and setting up a donors' trust fund to be overseen by an agency that would track the spending (*Fatal Assistance*).

2. State Government Archives, 20 January 2001, 2001-2009.state.gov/r/pa/ho/time/wwii/98681.html.

3. By focusing on Chapter 6, students will gain a better understanding of the various agencies and their agenda.

4. It may be interesting to watch excerpts of Peck's *Profit and Nothing But* (2001), in which economy and capital are global oppressors.

5. Haiti Reconstruction Fund. www.haitireconstructionfund.org/NewsFeed

6. The World Bank, 2017, blogs.worldbank.org/team/priscilla-m-phelps.

7. See Moyo's *Dead Aid*, Chapter 5, "A Radical Rethink of the Aid-Dependency Model," p. 75.

8. InterAction. 2017, haiti.ngoaidmap.org.

9. The World Bank, 30 July 2010, www.worldbank.org/en/news/feature/2010/07/30/haiti-homes-safe-100000-families-finds-assessment.

Works Cited

Baker, Andy. *Shaping the Developing World: The West, the South, and the Natural World*. CQ Press, 2014.

Barlet, Olivier. "Interview with Raoul Peck." *Africultures*, 30 Sept. 2000, africultures.com/interview-with-raoul-peck-by-olivier-barlet-5466/.

Bekers, Elisabeth, Sissy Hekff, and Daniela Merolla, editors. *Transcultural Modernities: Narrating Africa in Europe*. Brill Rodopi, 2009.

Daney, Serge. "'Le Travelling de Kapo.'" *Persévérance*. P.O.L., 1994.

Gabriel, Teshome. "Third Cinema Updated: Exploration of Nomadic Aesthetics & Narrative Communities." teshomegabriel.net/third-cinema-updated.

Haiti Grassroots. https://grassrootsonline.org/who-we-are/partners/haiti/, accessed May 18, 2021. https://grassrootsonline.org/who-we-are/partners/haiti/, accessed May 18, 2021

McCloud, Scott. *Understanding Comics: The Invisible Art*. HarperCollins Publishers, 1993.

Minato, Jasmine. "Detrimental Development: How International Aid Organizations Failed Post-Earthquake Haiti." Prospect. April 16, 2015. https://prospectjournal.org/2015/04/16/detrimental-development-how-international-aid-organizations-failed-post-earthquake-haiti/.

Moyo, Dambisa. *Dead Aid: Why Aid Is Not Working and How There Is a Better Way for Africa*. Douglas & Mcintyre, 2009.

Profit & Nothing But! Or, Impolite Thoughts on the Class Struggle. Dir. Raoul Peck. Icarus Films, 2001.

Fatal Assistance [Assistance mortelle]. Dir. Raoul Peck. Velvet Film, 2013.

Meurtre à Pacot. Dir. Raoul Peck. Velvet Film, 2017.

Pressley-Sanon, Toni, and Sophie Saint-Just. *Raoul Peck: Power, Politics, and the Cinematic Imagination*. Lexington Books, 2015.

Ricoeur, Paul. *A Ricoeur Reader: Reflection and Imagination*. University of Toronto Press, 1991.

Solanas, Fernando, and Octavio Getino. "Toward a Third Cinema." *Cineaste*, vol. 4, no. 3, Winter 1970–71, pp. 1–10.

Sirolli, Ernesto. "Want to Help Someone? Shut Up and Listen!" TED Talk, 20 Nov. 2012, www.ted.com/speakers/ernesto_sirolli.

Teaching about Haiti in American Studies, Latin American Studies, and General Studies Contexts

9

Rendering Haiti Visible in an Introductory American Studies Course

ELIZABETH LANGLEY

This essay centers on teaching Haitian texts in dialogue in an introductory American Studies course. I use the word "text" to refer to an article or object of cultural or scholarly production that can be interpreted. Visibility and the discourse on exceptionalism inform curriculum choices, and I argue that these lenses are particularly relevant to teaching Haitian and/or Haitian American texts or texts relevant to Haitian Studies in an interdisciplinary context. I will first offer a description of the class and its goals to enable readers to better understand how teaching Haiti through and beyond literature is germane to this approach to American Studies. I will then consider three lessons along with their keywords and texts to analyze how particular texts treating the Haitian/Haitian American experience work in conversation with other course texts. I will also demonstrate how students are able to move past singular understandings of these keywords, even as they develop a richer understanding of the transnational relationship between Haiti and the United States. At the end of the chapter, I provide a lesson plan, a sample syllabus, and additional recommended resources.

The three texts treating Haitian experience from the class sessions that I will analyze here are Edouard Duval-Carrié's *Imagined Landscapes*, an art exhibit that considers the Caribbean and its relationship to imperialism, expansion, and tourism; Alex Stepick's "Just Comes and Cover-Ups: Haitians in High School," an academic article that explores the Haitian/Haitian American experience in a high school in Miami in the '80s and '90s; and excerpts from Edwidge Danticat's *Create Dangerously*, a collection of autobiographical essays that treat art and exile. The first is viewed through the lens of empire along with excerpts from Nelly Rosario's *Song of the Water Saints* and the "Roosevelt Corollary." The second is considered in conjunction with keywords such as ethnicity and race among works such as *SNL*'s "White Like Me" featuring Eddie Murphy, and clips from David Oyelowo's *Fresh Air* interview. Lastly, the excerpts from Danticat's essay appear in the class session on diaspora with extracts from Roberto Fernández's *Raining Backwards*.

Before entering into these particular lessons and keywords, it is useful to ponder what American Studies actually is. It is neither American history, as many students assume from its name, nor is it American literature, but it certainly relies on both disciplines.[1] The nomenclature American Cultural Studies describes more clearly what the field encompasses, which is an interdisciplinary and increasingly transnational approach to US cultures. The American Studies Association, for example, describes itself as "the oldest and largest scholarly institution devoted to the interdisciplinary study of US culture and history in a global context," which, in turn, defines the field in a broad sense ("What the ASA Does").

I am writing this description of American Studies from the perspective of teaching an introductory course and the confusion that arises among students unfamiliar with the field. Nonetheless, the purview of American Studies and the debates within it are more complex than I am stating here. For more about the questions of nomenclature, history, inclusion and exclusion, exceptionalism, and difference germane to American Studies, please see the presidential addresses from American Studies' conventions past and present (e.g., Radway, Washington, and Limerick from the late 1990s).

Introductory American Studies courses at the University of Miami utilize a central construct or umbrella concept along with a series of related keywords to structure lessons, although that central theme and the additional keywords chosen vary by course. This class, then, employs this approach, emphasizing language as a central construct, and studies its intersections with a variety of terms pertinent to American Cultural Studies, including ethnicity, race, class, gender, identity, and diaspora. Some language questions that are raised include language attitudes and perceptions; linguistic profiling; mono-, bi-, and multilingualism as lived experiences; and minority and majority languages and the debates that surround them. Although the course considers many cultural spaces, there is a primary focus on Miami—as the city of instruction—and its cultures.

Students rely on keyword texts from *Keywords in American Cultural Studies* to contextualize their reading and begin their foray into the keyword(s) at play (i.e., empire, ethnicity, race, and diaspora), learning about the conceptualization of these terms across time and context as well as how they might be represented in particular texts. This keywords approach and the interdisciplinary nature of American Studies engender four major student outcomes based on Bloom's taxonomy:

- Students will be able to summarize and explain the meaning(s) and usage(s) of several keywords in American Studies.
- Students will be able to compare and contrast how different authors and artists employ or represent keywords from American Studies.
- Students will be able to analyze and evaluate a variety of texts and determine their intended audiences, as well as interpret their objectives.
- Students will be able to construct a digital story based on a keyword and its relationship to Miami.

The goals of the class, then, ultimately rely on the reading, evaluation, and interpretation of many different types of texts as well as putting those texts in conversation.

Texts related to Haitian Studies are germane to this class for several reasons. One is that Miami is a primary space of study for the course, and in recent years, the Miami metropolitan area has "become home to the largest number of Haitian-born immigrants in the U.S." (Carter and Lynch 379). Additionally, the course focuses on language questions, especially where they intersect with other key terms such as identity. The questions of bi- and, at times, multilingualism are relevant to Haitian and Haitian American experience. That is, in Haiti, Haitian Creole (or Kreyòl) is by far the majority language (spoken by all Haitians), yet French, spoken by a small minority, has been the language of prestige and of the elite, associated with class status and a high level of education. Despite major inroads, including the recognition of Haitian Creole as an official language, a significant body of literature written in Haitian Creole, and the increased (albeit gradual) use of Haitian Creole in schools, French continues to enjoy significant privilege. It is the principal language used in government and is still an important, if not the primary, language of instruction in Haitian schools.

In some ways, this dichotomy is recreated in the US, as Haitian Creole again becomes marginalized in comparison to English (although the small number of speakers of Haitian Creole is the major factor in the US). Furthermore, questions of class, race, and ethnicity come to bear in the Haitian American experience with language. Specifically, while highlighting the work of Flore Zéphir, Arthur K. Spears points out that Haitian Americans sometimes use French as a status marker and as a way of differentiating themselves from African Americans in the US. In communities where few Haitian Americans speak French, Haitian Creole is, instead, utilized as a marker of difference (14).

In the case of Miami, this is further complicated, as Spanish enjoys some privilege in terms of its dominance, although it is not a primary institutional language. Although Haitian Creole is increasingly used for official documents and in public spaces such as the Metrorail in Miami, it remains a minority language, both in number of speakers and in its sphere of influence in the area, in comparison to English and Spanish. Ultimately, the inclusion of Haitian texts in this course provides an interesting point of comparison with other immigrant communities in South Florida.

Lastly, Haitian texts are important for this course because both American Studies and Haitian Studies have been characterized by a discourse of exceptionalism. In the case of American Studies, Donald E. Pease has stated:

> The discourse of exceptionalism may be best characterized by its account of the United States' unique place in world history. . . . But this discourse drew its structure out of its difference from the historical trajectories that it attributed to Europe, the Soviet Union, and the Third World. The exceptionalist paradigm represented U.S. uniqueness in terms of absent and present elements—the absence of feudal hierarchies, class conflicts, a socialist labor party, trade unionism, and divisive ideological passions; the presence of a predominant middle class, tolerance for diversity, upward mobility, hospitality toward immigrants, a shared constitutional faith, and liberal individualism. (np)

Haiti, similarly, has often been described in exceptionalist terms, with the success of the Haitian Revolution on the one hand and its economic difficulties on the other. That is, it is often referred to as the first Black Republic and the poorest nation in the Western Hemisphere. As to the former, Asselin Charles elaborates:

> The awareness Haitians have of the exceptional circumstances in which their nation was born and how they became a people shapes their view of themselves and of their place in the world. The dramatic singularity of their history naturally has fostered in them, particularly as their country was isolated by the colonialist powers during most of the 19th century, a sense of their own singularity, of their uniqueness. Theirs is, after all, the land where the first and only successful slave revolt in history took place. (116–117)

This ethos of Haitian exceptionalism, however, is not limited to cultural production, research, and other media produced by Haitians; instead, it appears internationally via other actors, where it may vary from the positive to the negative end of the spectrum of exceptionalism. Nadège T. Clitandre has described, for example, the degrading way in which international media presented Haiti and its history in the aftermath of the earthquake of 2010:

> From reducing the Haitian Revolution to a "pact with the devil," to calling for an intrusive paternalism that combats so called progress-resistant cultural influences, to describing the survivors of the quake as looters inciting violence, to blaming the natural disaster on the victims and their inability to use birth control, the unimaginable, unprecedented catastrophe in Haiti was being made legible through a recognizable long-standing master narrative of degradation. (146–147)

Clitandre has further sought to reframe and complicate the discourse of Haitian exceptionalism by rethinking it outside of or beyond the nineteenth century (147).

Ultimately, exceptionalism and its rethinking are central to the work of American Studies and Haitian Studies alike. Thus, the inclusion of texts from Haitian Studies in the syllabus allows students to further investigate how exceptionalism works across different geo-cultural spaces and historical contexts and make productive comparisons. At the same time, students are able to reflect on the transnational relationship between the US and Haiti, and the inclusion of Haitian Studies texts is further justified by the strengthened role of Ethnic Studies within American Studies.

Given the centrality of language questions to this course, the focus on Miami, and the contested exceptionalist discourse that has informed Haitian Studies and American Studies alike, I contend that Haitian American texts are pertinent to this class. The challenge is in finding a balance among texts that treat different influences in Miami, as a key space of analysis, without overshadowing particular experiences. This is where visibility is important in a broad sense in the course. My use of the term visibility draws on Armin Paul Frank's and Daniel Dayan's work. Frank defines visibility in reference to the literary canon:

> A literary work is visible in this sense when it has a place—preferably a prominent one—in a literary history or other comprehensive compendium of a country's literature which serious students consult in order to obtain a survey of their chosen field.... The idea of *canon* presupposes an authority that aims at perpetuating both the norm and itself; visibility, by comparison, connotes a measure of prominence which a work may have in one compendium but need not in the next. (1)

Certainly, a single syllabus does not a compendium make, but a series of syllabi containing a text would approximate something akin to a compendium. The goal, ultimately, is to increase the visibility of Haitian Studies texts vis-à-vis other texts relevant to American Studies and those relevant to Miami (such as Cuban Studies works).

In reference to the media, Dayan refers to the issue of visibility and the questions we must ask: "The issue at hand is therefore one of calling attention to something by showing it. You are showing me this? Why are you showing it this way? What is it? Where is the rest of it? What have you chosen not to show? These are naive questions. These are key questions" (146). He further claims that media or the "authorized managers of collective attention" manage visibility through monstration:

> Monstration is typically performed by individuals. But it also involves groups, "moral" persons, and institutions such as museums, festivals, monuments, movie theaters, galleries, zoos, world fairs, installations, and fashion shows. The Venice Film Festival calls itself La Mostra (the monstration). Of course, the media are eminently concerned since they are society's major institution of monstration. (146)

Although they are not generally part of the media, I contend that teachers and professors play a role in monstration as parts of institutions that incorporate monuments, galleries, and installations, but also, and perhaps more importantly, they participate in a type of monstration by curating their syllabi. This renders texts—including those that may be marginalized—visible to students, and the interpretation of those works can go into greater depth, in many cases, than a news report. That said, professors' choices about their syllabi may be limited to single classes, and so they admittedly do not have the same size "audience"; yet, as Dayan points out, "the simple act of showing or not showing" is a powerful decision (147). As he is referring to the media, this choice to show states that an event exists. For professors, placing particular texts in a syllabus pronounces their existence for students and their relevance to the themes and goals of the course. The converse is to "strike it out of existence" (147). Thus, my goal in constructing this syllabus is to avoid the kind of "silencing wall" that can occur in media (147). I do admit, however, that curriculum choices based on an ethos of visibility always result in some experiences remaining invisible to students, at least as far as the texts in the course calendar are concerned. Nevertheless, allowing students to explore their own topics in certain projects, such as in the digital story project assignment of this course, is a way to help combat invisibility where it relates to student interests.

The first lesson at hand concerns the keyword *empire*. Edouard Duval-Carrié's *Imagined Landscapes* is viewed through that lens, along with excerpts from Nelly Rosario's *Song of the Water Saints* and the "Roosevelt Corollary." Each of these texts treats empire in distinct ways and for different audiences. This is key in the context of the course, considering that one of its student outcomes relates to the interpretation of a variety of different types of texts along with an understanding of the different audiences that the texts attempt to reach. Reading the "Roosevelt Corollary" helps establish context for empire and connects well with the general overview of the term provided in the keyword text. Students gain an awareness of how this text establishes the US as a hemispheric police force that can intervene—a text that would help justify invasion and even occupation—when it deems its presence necessary. With the context of early twentieth century US-Caribbean relations established through a close reading and discussion of the "Corollary," the discussion turns to an excerpt of *Song of the Water Saints*, a novel that treats the lives and experiences of four generations of Dominican (and, eventually, Dominican American) women. The narrative considers several significant moments in Dominican history. It begins in 1916 during the US Occupation of the Dominican Republic and examines questions of violence, collaboration, and resistance along with the personal experiences of Graciela, the initial protagonist, and her family. This fictional account of occupation increases students' engagement with the term empire as it increases their identification with the tensions created between Dominicans and US soldiers in the text.

Finally, we turn to *Imagined Landscapes*, a collection of paintings and statues in which Duval-Carrié recreates nineteenth-century works with an eye to exploiting their expansionist leanings. That is, he recreates them with a sense of humor, yet he criticizes their intentions. One of the paintings that elicits many responses from students is "After Bierstadt: The Landing." As this collection draws from paintings from the nineteenth century that promoted expansion and exploration in the Caribbean as a point of departure, this painting recreates a work by Albert Bierstadt entitled "Columbus: The Landing" and depicts his arrival on an island, probably in the Caribbean, where a group of people on the beach who are presumably Indigenous await Columbus and his companions with anticipation (*Imagined Landscapes*). Duval-Carrié comments on this representation of history by changing it and mocking it. In his version, the boat carrying Columbus transforms into a canoe that brings Columbus along with Marie Antoinette, accompanied by figures from popular culture: Batman, Bugs Bunny, Mr. Potato Head, Mickey and Minnie Mouse, and Daffy Duck. The colors in the Bierstadt painting are rather bright, and the sunlight as well as the shape of the trees create a frame around the arriving party and their boats, whereas the inhabitants of the island remain in the background in the shade (even if the colors are still relatively bright). On the other hand, Duval-Carrié, as in the other paintings of the collection, reimagines the texts from which he takes inspiration, and he paints them at night. In this way, the colors are somber and unclear, but the size of the paintings as well as the usage of mixed media, including glitter, render this painting and the others of the collection very striking. These changes criticize the expansionist and Paradisiacal vision that the paintings of inspiration evoke in their representations of the Caribbean, partially through color. Tobias Ostrander, the curator of PAMM (Pérez Art Museum Miami), where this collection was shown, affirms that the use of black and shadow in several works of the collection serves to recall the silences of the more difficult and dark history of the Caribbean (*Imagined Landscapes*).

Similar to Bierstadt, the arriving party remains the focal point in Duval-Carrié's painting, but contrary to Bierstadt's work, no one awaits them on the island. Despite this, a gunboat in the distance assures their safe arrival, and its presence links the previously mentioned histories with the occupations and the imperialist project of the United States during the nineteenth century and especially during the twentieth. This text, consequently, becomes a visual hypertext (of images) that simultaneously evokes variable histories of colonization, expansion, and exploration, criticizes them, and encourages the viewer to think about history that is both unspeakable and rarely spoken about. One way that this painting renders this type of silence or absence is through the erasure of Native Americans in the recreation of the text. Within other texts in the collection, this question of the loss of Native Americans through epidemics (illnesses to which they were previously unexposed) and extermination, the suffering of slavery, and other tragedies of Caribbean history are represented through spirit figures that lack facial features.

With this lesson, students read the keyword text on empire, "The Roosevelt Corollary," and excerpts from *Song of the Water Saints* prior to coming to class. They also take an online quiz prior to each class to encourage reading. I first present the paintings to the students in class where I ask them to describe what they see and to compare the nineteenth-century source images and twenty-first century recreations. This promotes conversation, as many of the students I have taught have had relatively limited experience analyzing paintings. Students are then asked to compare and contrast how empire works or is represented across these different texts.

The second lesson relevant to this discussion is a larger one occurring across two class days, which treats several keywords, including ethnicity and race on the one hand, and Black and racialization on the other. The key texts for this lesson include *SNL*'s "White Like Me" featuring Eddie Murphy; clips from *Do You Speak American?*, a documentary treating accents, language variations, attitudes and perceptions in the United States; clips from David Oyelowo's *Fresh Air* interview; and Alex Stepick's "Just Comes and Cover-Ups: Haitians in High School." We also look at excerpts from Gayle Wald's work on passing and Silvio Torres-Saillant's work on global Blackness.[2] This conglomeration of texts allows students to think critically about the deployment or representation of keywords in these texts, including which keywords are most appropriate or clearly engaged in the work of the authors or creators at hand. For example, the keyword *Black* may initially seem like the most appropriate keyword for analyzing and thinking about Alex Stepick's article because the text deals, in part, with Haitian high school students passing as African American. However, it is difficult to understand the cultural expectations and differences at play (including vocabulary use, accent, clothing, behavior in school, involvement in particular school activities) in the article without also contemplating the role of ethnicity.

The biggest potential pitfall for students working with these texts relates to their focusing on a singular aspect of a work. This means that with "White Like Me," students may find Murphy's performance to be exaggerated and comical, relaying a particular perception of whiteness. If their analysis is limited to the question of performing whiteness, they may miss the meaningful inclusion of spaces such as the bus, a key site of protest in the US civil rights movement, as well as the obvious privilege that Murphy enjoys in whiteface. With Oyelowo's interview, some students tried to delineate his description of Blackness in a limiting way. That is, when students in North London called Oyelowo a coconut (like an oreo in the US) because he did not meet their expectations of Blackness (i.e. being disrespectful to teachers, getting into trouble with the authorities, etc.), he states that this is due to their culture's tarnished concept of Blackness and how it has been projected on them. There is also considerable irony to this experience, as he has just returned from living in Nigeria, where his family originates ("David Oyelowo"). A careful reading of this text is, therefore, required to avoid recreating this tarnished projection of Blackness. With Stepick's article, too, students may believe that Haitian American students cannot identify as African American, or that if they do, they are passing. This is a reductionist viewpoint based on a particular cultural moment in the article. With all of these texts, then, it is important to establish the historical and cultural context at least in a perfunctory way in order to ground class discussion of the texts. There are different ways of doing this: a student presentation, a mini-lecture, a videoclip, etc. This exercise usually helps minimize the aforementioned pitfall.

The third lesson and its corresponding class session deal with the keyword *diaspora*. Students read excerpts from Danticat's *Create Dangerously* that deal with the experience of Haitians from the diaspora who feel "in-between" because they are considered American by Haitians and Haitian by Americans. This text allows students to encounter the complications of diaspora and to see how one is usually a part of multiple diasporas (e.g., one could be a part of the Haitian and African diasporas simultaneously). These extracts also serve as a unique text of analysis as the essays in this book can also be read as memoir. Students also read extracts from Roberto Fernández's *Raining Backwards*, which treats the Cuban American experience in South Florida. The initial part of the text deals with a boy named Eloy whom an older woman manipulates through his interest in his Cuban history and identity. That is, she exchanges his spending time with her in questionable situations for sharing information, which is often erroneous, about Cuba, the fatherland he has never known. The two texts in conjunction permit students to compare the diasporic and immigrant experiences of Cubans and Haitians in Miami, and to reflect on Miami as an immigrant city, at least to the extent that one can with two texts.

I should also point out that the texts discussed in this essay are not the only Haitian texts used in the class. I also include short stories and opinion pieces related to immigration and internment in Miami, such as Edwidge Danticat's "Children of the Sea" and "Detention Is No Holiday."[3] The inclusion of this variety of texts from Haitian Studies—from paintings to academic articles to short stories to autobiographical essays—challenges students to engage with works of different genres with different goals. These texts also invite productive comparative conversations with texts from other disciplines, such as Cuban Studies, concerning their myriad ways of representing keywords from American Studies. This set of texts ultimately serves to render Haiti visible in an introductory American Studies course, and it simultaneously challenges the imperial "American" of American Studies, revealing a transnational America extending well beyond the US.

Sample Lesson Plan on the Keyword "Empire"

I. Lesson Plan Objectives

- Students will be able to summarize and explain the meaning(s) and usage(s) of the keyword "empire."
- Students will be able to compare and contrast how different authors

and artists employ or represent the keyword "empire" within American Studies.
- Students will be able to analyze and evaluate a variety of texts, and determine their intended audiences as well as interpret their objectives.
- Students will be able to construct and/or evaluate a digital story based on a keyword and its relationship to Miami.

II. Prior to class:

1. Students are expected to have read the "Roosevelt Corollary" and excerpts from Nelly Rosario's *Song of the Water Saints*.
2. Students will take an online open-book quiz on Blackboard before class to encourage reading and to check comprehension.

III. During class:

1. A student previously assigned the keyword "empire" will show their completed digital story presentation to the class. Students will have the opportunity to comment and ask questions. I will briefly lecture on the keyword in accordance with its usage in *Keywords for American Cultural Studies* and check student comprehension by referencing the student digital story presentation.
2. I will briefly lecture on the "Roosevelt Corollary," providing context for the speech and its relevance to US foreign policy in the early twentieth century. Students will be asked to find in the text and read aloud with the class quotes that are relevant to the keyword "empire." Students will then reflect on the ramifications of this document/speech for US foreign policy today.
3. Students will be assigned to work in small groups on sections of *Song of the Water Saints* to answer comprehension and critical-thinking questions about the text (two to three questions per group). Students will present their answers to the class.
4. I will show a PowerPoint presentation with images of paintings from the *Imagined Landscapes* exhibition and/or show images from Edouard Duval-Carrié's or the Pérez Art Museum Miami websites. Students will describe what they see and compare and contrast related images. For context, Duval-Carrié reimagines several nineteenth-century paintings, so seeing the "source" images makes for a more interesting discussion. Students are asked to reflect on how these

images relate to "empire" as well as compare and contrast the different texts we have encountered and their relevance to the discussion of this term. (I am using the word "text" to refer to a cultural product that students interpret in class.)
5. I will close the class with a review of what we considered today as well as a reminder to the students of upcoming homework and other assignments.

IV. After class/Subsequent classes

1. This keyword will continue to be reviewed in class with specific questions. Students will often be asked to compare and contrast different keywords or the relevance of diverse keywords with varying texts as the course progresses.

V. Relevant Resources/Materials

1. *Keywords for American Cultural Studies,* keywords.nyupress.org/american-cultural-studies/
2. "Roosevelt Corollary to the Monroe Doctrine, 1904," www.ourdocuments.gov/doc.php?flash=false&doc=56&page=transcripthistory. state.gov/milestones/1899-1913/roosevelt-and-monroe-doctrine
3. Excerpts from *Song of the Water Saints,* www.amazon.com/Song-Water-Saints-Nelly-Rosario/dp/0375725490; www.penguinrandomhouse.ca/books/157131/song-of-the-water-saints-by-nelly-rosario/9780375725494/excerpt (I had students read a longer excerpt than this, but this portion of the text is relevant to the keyword in question)
4. Images of Duval-Carrié's work, www.pamm.org/exhibitions/edouard-duval-carrié-imagined-landscapes; duval-carrie.com/category/exhibition/curatorial-projects/

Syllabus

In this class, we will foster an understanding of American Studies or American Cultural Studies through an interrogation of many keywords that are pertinent to the field. We will emphasize ethnicity, race, class, gender, identity and diaspora as well as their intersections with questions of language. In addition to initial brief readings that define these terms in the field, we will read and view a variety of texts that relate to or represent these keywords, including fiction (short stories, novel excerpts, film and television), academic articles (from cultural theory to sociolinguistics), documentaries, essays, visual art and even satirical skits. Although we will treat many different cultural spaces, there will be a primary focus on Miami and its cultures.

In different iterations of this course, students have completed digital stories in different ways. In one version, students created ethnographic digital stories in which they visited a neighborhood in South Florida and reported on the sights, sounds, and their experience. The other version involved a presentation on a keyword, which included key debates, definitions, and a consideration of related current events and the local environment. In both versions, students would generally incorporate images, including photos they took, voiceover, and music of their choice. For more on digital stories, please see "Educational Uses of Digital Storytelling."

Luz Ainaí Morales Pino's work on visibility and invisibility with respect to *entre siglos* or turn of the twentieth century narratives in Latin America has been a helpful point of departure for considering canon and extrapolating that to curriculum and syllabus design. See, for example, "*El Perú Ilustrado*: las visualidades en competencia en la articulación de un imaginario de nación."

Torres-Saillant, "One and Divisible: Meditations on Global Blackness," and Gayle Wald, "Race, Passing, and Cultural Representation."

"Children of the Sea" is a short story that appears in Danticat's masterful collection *Krik? Krak!* (1996). It reflects the experiences of the Haitian "botpipèl" or boat people, which is similar to the Cuban term "balseros" or rafters, who attempt to immigrate to the United States, often by traveling to South Florida by boat or raft.

"Detention Is No Holiday" is an op-ed in which Danticat describes her uncle's detention and death in the Krome detention center in Miami, and she also highlights the experiences of other detainees in detention centers across the United States. She further delineates issues with accountability of employees at these centers when their actions result in inadequate medical care or the mistreatment of detainees.

Table 9.1. American Studies or American Cultural Studies syllabus

1	"Exceptionalism"	"America" & "Space"
	Introductions & Objectives	Excerpts from Nirmal Puwar's *Space Invaders*
		José Martí, "Our America"
	Comedy, College and PC Culture	Rosario Ferré, "Amalia"
2	"Empire"	"Capitalism" and "Class"
	Theodore Roosevelt, "Roosevelt Corollary"	Director Jacob Kornbluth's *Inequality for All*
	Excerpts from Nelly Rosario's *Song of the Water Saints*	Benjamin Grant, "What is Gentrification?"
		Richard Florida, "Class-Divided Cities: Miami Edition"
	Edouard Duval-Carrié's *Imagined Landscapes* (viewing in class)	
3	"State" and "Nation"	"Border" and "Culture"
	Excerpts from Michel-Rolph Trouillot's *State Against Nation*	*Dexter*: Season One, Episode One (Director: Michael Cuesta)
	Gullah-Geechee clips	Excerpts from Gloria Anzaldúa's *Borderlands*
4	"Globalization" and Migration"	"Literature" and "Modern"
	Guest speaker: Antoni Fernández	"What Is Literature" from the Norton Anthology
	Excerpts from *Rotten English* (Edited by Dohra Ahmad)	Roland Barthes, "From Work to Text"
		Mary B. Sellers, "Why the Short Story Matters"
	"Tech Talk: Iphone 5" from *SNL* (in class)	
5	"Ethnicity" & "Race"	"Black" and "Racialization"
	Gayle Wald, "Race, Passing and Cultural Representation"	Alex Stepick, "Just Comes and Cover-Ups: Haitians in High School"
	Clip of "White Like Me" from *SNL*	Clips from David Oyelowo interview on *Fresh Air*
	American Tongues (Filmmakers: Louis Alvarez, Andrew Kolker)	Torres-Saillant, "One and Divisible: Meditations on Global Blackness" (in class)
		Paper 1 due
6	"Digital" and "Time"	"Neoliberalism" & "Science"
	Nate Stulman, "The Great Campus Goof-Off Machine"	Short articles on education (e.g., "Medical Humanities, Neoliberalism and the University")
	Director Rachel Dretzin's *Digital Nation*	Michael Menser and Stanley Aronowitz, "The Cultural Study of Science and Technology: A Manifesto"
		Jorge Luis Borges, "The Lottery in Babylon"
7	"Neoliberalism" & "Science"	
	Guest Speaker: Omar Vargas	Exam 1
	Review	

8	"Immigration"	"Identity" and "Subject"
	Edwidge Danticat's "Children of the Sea" Marc Silver's *The Invisibles*	Ana Lydia Vega, "Pollito Chicken" Stuart Hall, "Ethnicity: Identity and Difference" Director Billy Corben's *Cocaine Cowboys*
9	No Class	No Class
	Spring Break	Spring Break
10	"Gender" and "Performance"	"Queer"
	Director Jennie Livingston's *Paris is Burning*	Director Joe Cardona's *The Day It Snowed in Miami* *Whoopi Goldberg Presents Moms Mabley* (clips in class)
11	"Queer," "Gender" and "Performance"	"Latino, Latina, Latin@"
	Guest Speaker: Ellen Davies Paper Idea Due	Luis Santeiro, "¿Qué pasa USA?" (article) Director Bernard Lechowick's *¿Qué pasa USA?* Martin Munro, "Conclusion. The Missing People"
12	"Indian" and "Colonial"	"Internment" and "Asian"
	Excerpts from Susan Orlean's *The Orchid Thief* Noah Billie visual art Excerpts from Linda Tuhiwai Smith's *Decolonizing Methodologies*	Clips with George Takei (in class) Legal text on Japanese-American internment "Not Your Homeland" and "Detention Is No Holiday" by Edwidge Danticat
13	"Diaspora" and "Citizenship"	"Diaspora" and "Citizenship"
	Excerpts from Edwidge Danticat's *Create Dangerously* Excerpts from Roberto G. Fernández's *Raining Backwards* Sandra So Hee Chi Kim on postmemory and diaspora (in class)	Guest Speaker: Donette Francis Student Presentations Begin Benh Zeitlin's *Beasts of the Southern Wild* (watch in class)
14	"Rural" and "South"	"Religion" and "Secularism"
	Director Benh Zeitlin's *Beasts of the Southern Wild* (finish watching in class) Discussion of keywords and diversity of culture in Florida Film discussion	Tedx Talk: "Food Is Our Religion" by Mike Thelin Clips from the Oprah Winfrey Show Discussion of Oprah as Religion Some review, time permitting
15	"Terror" and "Body"	
	Edwidge Danticat's "Nineteen Thirty-Seven" Elizabeth Langley, "Performing Postmemory: Remembering the Parsley Massacre in 'Nineteen Thirty-Seven' and *Song of the Water Saints*" Remaining Review Questions	Exam 2

Additional Recommended Resources

"The Art of Edouard Duval-Carrié." www.edouard-duval-carrie.com.

Danticat, Edwidge, editor. *The Butterfly's Way: Voices from the Haitian Dyaspora in the United States.* Soho Press, 2001.

Dash, J. Michael. *Haiti and the United States: National Stereotypes and the Literary Imagination.* St. Martin's, 1997.

Edmondson, Belinda, and Donette Francis, editors. "American Studies: The Caribbean Edition." *Journal of Transnational American Studies*, vol. 5, no. 1, Summer 2013.

hooks, bell. *Teaching to Transgress: Education as the Practice of Freedom.* Routledge, 1994.

Kaussen, Valerie. *Migrant Revolutions: Haitian Literature, Globalization, and U.S. Imperialism.* Lexington Books, 2008.

Munro, Martin, editor. *Edwidge Danticat: A Reader's Guide.* University of Virginia Press, 2010.

Trouillot, Michel-Rolph. *Silencing the Past: Power and the Production of History.* Beacon, 1995.

Ulysse, Gina Athena. *Why Haiti Needs New Narratives: A Post-Quake Chronicle.* Wesleyan University Press, 2015.

Notes

1. I am writing this description of American Studies from the perspective of teaching an introductory course and the confusion that arises among students unfamiliar with the field. Nonetheless, the purview of American Studies and the debates within it are more complex than what I am stating here. For more about the questions of nomenclature, history, inclusion and exclusion, exceptionalism, and difference germane to American Studies, please see the presidential addresses from American Studies' conventions past and present (e.g., Radway, Washington, and Limerick from the late 1990s).

2. Torres-Saillant, "One and Divisible: Meditations on Global Blackness," and Gayle Wald, "Race, Passing, and Cultural Representation."

3. "Children of the Sea" is a short story that appears in Danticat's masterful collection *Krik? Krak!* (1996). It reflects the experiences of the Haitian "botpipo" or boat people, which is similar to the Cuban term "balseros" or rafters, who attempt to immigrate to the United States, often by traveling to South Florida by boat or raft.

"Detention Is No Holiday" is an op-ed in which Danticat describes her uncle's detention and death in the Krome detention center in Miami, and she also highlights the experiences of other detainees in detention centers across the United States. She further delineates issues with accountability of employees at these centers when their actions result in inadequate medical care or the mistreatment of detainees.

Works Cited

"Bloom's Taxonomy." *Bloom's Taxonomy.* www.bloomstaxonomy.org/Blooms%20Taxonomy%20questions.pdf.

Carter, Philip M., and Andrew Lynch. "Multilingual Miami: Current Trends in Sociolinguistic Research." *Language and Linguistic Compass*, vol. 9, no. 9, 2015, pp. 369–385. doi: 10.1111/lnc3.12232.

Charles, Asselin. "Haitian Exceptionalism and Caribbean Consciousness." *Journal of Caribbean Literatures*, vol. 3, no. 2, 2002, pp. 115–130. www.jstor.org/stable/40986134.

Clitandre, Nadège T. "Haitian Exceptionalism in the Caribbean and the Project of Rebuilding Haiti." *Journal of Haitian Studies* vol. 17, no. 2, 2011, pp. 146–153. www.jstor.org/stable/41715438.

Danticat, Edwidge. "Children of the Sea." *Krik? Krak!* Baldini & Castoldi, 1996, pp. 3–29.

———. *Create Dangerously: The Immigrant Artist at Work.* Vintage Books, 2011.

———. "Detention Is No Holiday." *The New York Times*, 27 March 2012. www.nytimes.com/2012/03/28/opinion/detention-is-no-holiday.html. Accessed 29 July 2019.

Dayan, Daniel. "Conquering Visibility, Conferring Visibility: Visibility Seekers and Media Performance. *International Journal of Communication*, vol. 7, 2013, pp. 137–153. ijoc.org/index.php/ijoc/article/view/1966.

Do You Speak American? Directed by William Cran. PBS, 2005.

Duval-Carrié, Edouard. *Edouard Duval-Carrié: Imagined Landscapes.* Pérez Art Museum Miami. www.pamm.org/exhibitions/edouard-duval-carrié-imagined-landscapes. Accessed 29 July 2019.

Duval-Carrié, Edouard, and Tobias Ostrander. "Imagined Landscapes with Edouard Duval-Carrié and Tobias Ostrander." *Youtube.* 30 April 2014. www.youtube.com/watch?v=2kZQ-kDZEfw. Accessed 29 July 2019.

"Educational Uses of Digital Storytelling." *University of Houston Education.* digitalstorytelling.coe.uh.edu. Accessed 27 July 2019.

Fernández, Roberto. *Raining Backwards.* Arte Público Press, 1988.

Frank, Armin Paul. *Off-Canon Pleasures: A Case Study and a Perspective.* Universitätsverlag Göttingen, 2011.

Limerick, Patricia Nelson. "Insiders and Outsiders: The Borders of the USA and the Limits of the ASA: Presidential Address to the American Studies Association, 31 October 1996." *American Quarterly*, vol. 49, no. 3, 1997, pp. 449–469. www.jstor.org/stable/30041792.

Morales Pino, Luz Ainaí. "*El Perú Ilustrado*: las visualidades en competencia en la articulación de un imaginario de la nación." *Decimonónica. Journal of Nineteenth Century Hispanic Cultural Production*, vol. 12, no. 1, 2015, pp. 151–171.

Oyewolo, David. "David Oyelowo on Acting, His Royal Roots and the One Role He Won't Take." *Fresh Air.* Interview by Terry Gross. NPR, WHYY, 28 May 2015. www.npr.org/2015/05/28/409718943/david-oyelowo-on-acting-his-royal-roots-and-the-one-role-he-wont-take. Accessed 29 July 2019.

Pease, Donald E. "Exceptionalism." *Keywords for American Cultural Studies, Second Edition*, edited by Glenn Hendler and Bruce Burgett, New York University Press, 2014. keywords.nyupress.org/american-cultural-studies/keywords-an-introduction/. Accessed 26 July 2019.

Radway, Janice. "What's in a Name? Presidential Address to the American Studies Association, 20 November 1998." *American Quarterly*, vol. 51, no. 1, 1999, pp. 1–32. xroads.virginia.edu/~DRBR2/radway.html.

Roosevelt, Theodore. "The Roosevelt Corollary to the Monroe Doctrine, 1904." Speech. *Office of the Historian*. history.state.gov/milestones/1899-1913/roosevelt-and-monroe-doctrine. Accessed 29 July 2019.

Spears, Arthur K. "Chapter 1. Introduction: The Haitian Creole Language." *The Haitian Creole Language: History, Structure, Use, and Education*, edited by Arthur K. Spears and Carole M. Berotte Joseph. Lexington Books, 2010, pp. 1–20. www.arthurkspears.com/papers/the-haitiancreolelanguage.pdf.

Stepick, Alex. "Just Comes and Cover-Ups: Haitians in High School." *Pride Against Prejudice: Haitians in the United States*. Allyn & Bacon, 1998, pp. 59–74. wps.prenhall.com/wps/media/objects/12330/12626747/myanthropologylibrary/PDF/NIS_9_Stepick_Foner_146.pdf. Accessed July 28, 2019.

Torres-Saillant, Silvio. "One and Divisible: Meditations on Global Blackness." *Small Axe*, vol. 13, no. 2, 2009, pp. 4–25. https://muse.jhu.edu/article/270122/pdf.

Wald, Gayle. "Race, Passing and Cultural Representation." *Crossing the Line: Racial Passing in Twentieth-Century U.S. Literature and Culture*. Duke University Press, 2000, pp. 1–24.

Washington, Mary Helen. "'Disturbing the Peace: What Happens to American Studies If You Put African American Studies at the Center?': Presidential Address to the American Studies Association, October 29, 1997." *American Quarterly*, vol. 50, no. 1, 1998, pp. 1–23. xroads.virginia.edu/~drbr2/washington.html.

"What the ASA Does." *American Studies Association*. www.theasa.net/about/page/what_the_asa_does/. Accessed 29 July 2019.

"White Like Me." *SNL*, created by Lorne Michaels, performance by Eddie Murphy, season 10, Broadway Video, 1984. www.hulu.com/watch/10356

10

Race and Culture on the Thrift Store Shift

Teaching about Haiti Inside and Outside the Academy

JESSICA ADAMS

As I parsed the racks at the thrift store on the Caribbean island of St. Thomas, I pondered the stories of castoffs, of things rejected and repurposed. The population of St. Thomas, one of the US Virgin Islands, includes many wealthy whites who discard expensive clothing in garbage bags where the arrow points—"Donations." It's a popular spot on weekends, the parking lot often jammed with cars. The customers include a cross-section of the island's population—native St. Thomians along with migrants from the US, Europe, the Dominican Republic, and Haiti. Different stories, lives, cultures are juxtaposed here, failing sometimes to make a whole.

For various reasons, including a congenital impulse to explore the stories told by other people's castoffs, I began volunteering at the thrift store on weekends. My coworkers included white women of a certain age, of whose motives for working with such dedication, weekend after weekend, I was not aware. Their hostility toward customers seemed as palpable as their dedication to their work. Perhaps it is relevant that this thrift store was intended to benefit the local humane society—"All the money goes to the animals," which were indeed in desperate need of help. But in the context of helping the animals, some volunteers seemed to feel for the most part justified in patronizing, denigrating, and verbally berating the Haitian and Dominican customers. For these women, Haitian and Dominican people seemed to be little more than a mass of unintelligible aberrance, objects of anger and frustration distinguished only by the language they spoke.

A world of castoffs presided over by pale-skinned women adding up sales, counting bills—this wasn't my classroom, where I had strategy. In this particular iteration of the Caribbean's long-standing economy of waste, excess, and recuperation, the people in charge saw me as one of them. "Did you see what they did?" "We had so many of them in here." "They always want something for nothing." "They follow you around when you're putting things out, several of them at once." "That one? The pregnant one? She's been here since before we opened." It was afternoon, near closing time—the pregnant Haitian woman had been in the store for nearly five hours. "Maybe she has nowhere else to go," I said—which wasn't much, certainly not enough to make my supervisor change her attitude. I had seen the woman before, spoken to her in French, realizing that she probably spoke Kreyòl, which I could not. I hoped to communicate that I did not share the prevailing stereotype, clearly on display, of Haitians as "fragments . . . bodies without minds . . . or roving spirits," in Gina Ulysse's words (*Why Haiti* 10). We smiled now at each other, had halting conversations in the spaces between the racks.

In the end my attempts to shift the pervasive racism of the thrift store came to nothing. As directed, I made signs in French, Spanish, and English containing messages from the management such as, "Please do not remove the price tags" and "Please do not try on the merchandise." (This was supposed to be a way to head off confrontations with staff.) I chatted with the customers, hoping to project warmth and welcome, and I tried to talk to my coworkers, which resulted in some self-consciousness on their part. Some defensiveness. I don't think I'd call that "success."

When the government of the Dominican Republic began stripping Dominicans of Haitian descent of their citizenship, I was living on the north coast of the country, fairly near the Haitian border—not far from the site of the "Parsley Massacre" (and a place where Trujillo remains in living memory).[1] Here, as in other parts of the country, *antihaitianismo* was commonplace, taken for granted. A vocal march supporting the new law with placards and slogans shouted through megaphones took place as I passed through town on the way to my daughter's school.[2] A Dominican friend who had described his dream of migrating to the United States casually denigrated the Haitian people who lived down the street, commenting, as if offering some final proof of Haitian difference, "The dogs bark at them. They know." "I have to tell you," I found myself saying, "the way you talk about Haitians, people in the US talk about Dominicans. They say exactly the same things about you." The white women in the thrift store were that kind of white person, those who look upon immigrants without empathy even if they are immigrants themselves.

The project of this volume—to offer practical modes of teaching about Haiti—is critical in part because it offers concrete ways to make a difference in entrenched cultural attitudes and assumptions around race. "Haiti" (the stereotype of Haiti) has become a bellwether for expressions of racism, both conscious and unconscious, in the West. In terms of "popular attitudes," Haiti has become arguably the most denigrated, most demeaned, most dehumanized site in the Caribbean, even in the West as a whole. This has everything to do with sometimes deeply buried assumptions about the meaning of foundational concepts in the history of the New World, perhaps most notably freedom. Indeed, the history of Haiti offers keys to understanding so much about the Western world, including the varying meanings of race as well as reasons for the persistence of injustice and the centuries-long reinscription of power relations that serve colonial and neocolonial interests. As Paul Farmer notes in *The Uses of Haiti*,

> The United States and Haiti are something other than the richest and poorest countries in the hemisphere; they are also its two oldest republics. Rarely, in fact, have two countries been as closely linked as the United States and Haiti. Haitians are, by and large, fully aware of this historical fact. But citizens of the United States are, by and large, oblivious to those links. . . . (42)

Farmer underscores the fact that US policy has in large part determined (and undermined) the course of Haitian history. It is not going too far to say that the United States bears a large responsibility for poverty in Haiti.

Thus the version of Haiti that is stigmatized repeatedly in Western journalistic and popular discourse is in part the creation of the very powers that patronize, condemn, and estrange it as either frightening or simply inexplicable. Haiti, for many Americans, is not so much an actual place and an actual people as an idea of what "we" are not. J. Michael Dash writes,

> Images of mystery, decadence, romance and adventure are not arbitrary . . . but constitute a special code, a system of antithetical values which establishes radical, ineradicable distinctions between the Subject and the Other . . . the United States and Haiti. (1–2)

In other words, "The Other is denied its own subjectivity and simply exists so that the Subject can define itself" (Dash 2); in more specific terms, "Haitians are meant to be marveled at, studied, converted, rehabilitated and ultimately controlled" (Dash 3). The consequences of this objectification, as Dash points out, are felt both by the objectified and by the "subject," as this type of subjecthood rests on an unstable foundation in need of constant monitoring and reinforcement, an insatiable monster of self dependent on the objectification of the often African-descended other.[3] We see the consequences of this kind of privileged yet consuming blindness at work in culture all the time. But challenging simplistic views toward Haiti can help to shift the narrative of the effects of slavery as a whole—a narrative that, on the part of whites, has too often been truncated and naive—to create a more accurate rewriting of the story of the New World. In a sense, teaching about Haiti is no less than an attempt to stop a highly destructive cycle that threatens to dismantle not one but two societies. Teaching about Haiti also means teaching about the history of oppression in the West—how it has been effected, and also, perhaps, how it can be stopped—work that has the capacity to remake the vision of the "New World" and to overturn racist stereotypes in general.

In saying this, I hope it is clear that I do not mean to reinscribe Haiti as an "other" (not "us") in order to better understand "ourselves" (whoever "we" may be). Rather, I want to underscore the fact that the Americas are an interconnected system, and to emphasize that in teaching about Haiti, it may be important to ask why and how Haiti has become exceptionalized. What is at stake, for example, in the marginalizing mantra, "Haiti is the poorest country in the Western Hemisphere"?

In what follows, I suggest new combinations of texts and methodologies for teaching about Haiti that can be productively adapted for courses in rhetoric and composition, literature, and Cultural Studies. My approach is shaped by what I have learned teaching in the Caribbean, currently in a department (the English Department in the College of General Studies at the University of Puerto Rico, Río Piedras) that is explicitly interdisciplinary in its focus. At the end of the chapter, I offer a syllabus and ideas for assignments.

• • •

While discussing logical fallacies one day in a writing class at the University of the Virgin Islands, a student raised her hand and offered this example: "Someone said to me the other day, 'You don't look Haitian.'"[4] A raft of prejudices instantly materialized: You don't look (to draw from a list of stereotypes compiled by some of my students) poor. Diseased. Hungry. Uneducated. As if you practice witchcraft. Far too much of the rhetoric that has accompanied the emergence of Haiti as an independent nation has replicated the objectification that turned human beings into objects in the "New World." As Ulysse points out, "Haiti needs new narratives." But how are those new narratives to be created, constructed, revealed? How can public knowledge about Haiti begin to meaningfully integrate the complexity of Haiti rather than regularly stripping it down to stereotypes?

Roxane Gay's very short story "Gracias, Nicaragua y Lo Sentimos" (or, "Thank You, Nicaragua, and We're Sorry") from her collection *Ayiti* takes the typical marginalizing characterization of Haiti head on in a succinct and biting critique, as Gay ironically passes "el título del país más pobre en el hemisferio occidental" ("the title of the poorest country in the Western Hemisphere") to Nicaragua (93). Her story "All Things Being Relative" (again from *Ayiti*) considers both how the US looks from Haiti, and how Haiti looks from the US. Fiction (though perhaps Gay's "Gracias, Nicaragua" would be more accurately cast as creative nonfiction) is uniquely powerful as a way to reach students, for our brains seem to naturally organize information in the form of stories. But I find that in the rhetoric and composition and literature courses I teach, a grounding in the facts of Haitian history is necessary in order to thoughtfully examine specifically *how* and *why* Haiti has been marginalized in the discourse of value (social, cultural) in the west, and perhaps the world. C.L.R. James's classic work *The Black Jacobins*, first published in 1938, explains the conditions that led to the Haitian Revolution, as well as how the Revolution itself took shape, in a way that highlights the perspectives and the humanity of the enslaved—a critical element of any fragmentation of common misperceptions of Haiti.[5] Laurent Dubois's *Haiti: The Aftershocks of History* provides a comprehensive look at the complexities that get radically glossed over in the typical dismissive characterization of Haiti as "the poorest country." And *Libète: A Haiti Anthology*, edited by Charles Arthur and J. Michael Dash, considers the history of Haiti from the first moments of contact between Europeans and Taínos through short pieces from multiple points of view, many from within Haiti. Works such as these can help students critically assess images of Haiti that circulate in literature and popular media.

One must beware even of "classic" works such as Zora Neale Hurston's *Tell My Horse: Voodoo and Life in Haiti and Jamaica*. Like James's *The Black Jacobins*, it was first published in 1938. Unlike James, however, Hurston seems surprised and at times even shocked by what she finds in Haiti. As an outsider armed with the tools of that era's anthropology as well as her own innovative discursive mode, she investigates common sites of fascination for outsiders, such as the figures of zombies and the Vodou religion. This work cannot be taken at face value as a "true account." It's crucial to put it in the context not only of developments in modern anthropology, with its roots in European colonialism, but also of the imperial aggression embodied in US Occupation of Haiti (1915–1934). The assumptions Hurston makes, the stereotypes she brings to bear (but does not admit to), remain live today in part because they are regularly reinforced both in places you'd expect and places you might not expect. They are amply evident in the text about *Tell My Horse* that appears on the "Official Website of Zora Neale Hurston," for example, which describes the book as a "first-hand account of the weird mysteries and horrors of voodoo." "*Tell My Horse*," the blurb continues, "is an invaluable resource and fascinating guide ... [T]his travelogue into a dark world paints a vividly authentic picture of ceremonies and customs of great cultural interest."[6] Clearly, tropes of Haiti as a "dark" and disturbing place "of great interest" are not only present in the book itself, but are (still) being used to promote it.

To halt this reinforcement of the same old images, we might consult travel articles describing Haiti as a destination for luxury tourism, such as those published by *The New York Times* in the 1940s and 1950s, which present an entirely different Haiti than Hurston does (and which also need to be critically analyzed).[7] These accounts of the consumption of Haiti by western tourists can be put in dialogue with Roxane Gay's story "The Harder They Come," told from the perspective of Haitian women who sell sex to US tourists disembarking from the cruise ships that dock in Labadee (the name is trademarked on royalcaribbean.com), a bay on Haiti's north coast that Royal Caribbean Cruises managed as a private resort. "If you just want to kick back and relax, grab our signature drink—the Labadoozie . . ."[8] Students can parse these multivalent images of travel and tourism—images, also, of how stereotypes intersect with concepts of ownership—through Dean MacCannell's theories of sightseeing, which suggest how to become and remain aware of the deep, vertical histories contained within both geographies and things.[9] These works help to both illuminate and change the typical—partial or just wrong—conceptions of Haiti in general, and Haitian people and culture specifically, that tend to haunt discussions of what "Haiti" (as a social, cultural, political entity) means. But perhaps even more importantly, they provide information that will help students participate in constructing "new narratives" of Haiti as they critically assess how it has been valued/devalued over the course of centuries.

Gina Ulysse writes that "Haitians have often been portrayed as . . . fragments"—and maybe in suggesting such a splicing together of different texts, or parts of texts, to coalesce in unpredictable ways in the minds of students, I risk promoting further fragmentation. But perhaps we can revalence the notion of fragments in this context. I find myself returning to the thrift store, an unheralded site of anthropological data and potential inspiration, a collection of things from random and untraceable sources, linked mostly by proximity, capable of creating (if you look at it that way) a thousand different narratives.

Things that have floated perhaps far from their origins and made their way through the world, fragments and castoffs, things considered "trash"—these can be taken seriously as theoretical tools, as sites of potential intervention.[10]

Let's reconsider, for example, the moment at which Columbus arrived on the shores of Haiti (then Ayiti) and encountered people the like of which he had never seen before, who viewed him and his crew, he claimed, as having fallen "from heaven." Leaving aside the fact that we can't know what the Taíno were actually saying—the concept of heaven, if indeed they expressed it, would have been shifted through languages and cultural assumptions and perspectives, or perhaps Columbus simply made it up to please the primary audience for his writing (his financial backers, the Spanish monarchs)—leaving all that aside, with what awareness, with what assumptions and expectations would the natives of Ayiti have viewed the ships rocking at anchor off their shore? It's impossible to say for sure, of course, but the Atlantic currents would have already brought detritus from the Europeans' world to them. Flotsam and jetsam would have washed up on their beaches from Atlantic shipwrecks. Surely they wondered about these things—where they came from, what they had been before. They probably repurposed these objects for their own ends. Imagine, then, that when they saw Columbus's small fleet, they recognized that their curiosity about the source of these fragments was about to be satisfied. The Taíno would have tried to make sense of the ships, the men aboard, in keeping with their own narratives and assumptions. Perhaps the ships were not new, exactly, the Europeans not "heavenly" as Europeans themselves understood this idea, but rather confirmation of something, a piece of a puzzle fitting into place. Perhaps the Taíno had been theorizing the Europeans based on their trash, their fragments.

Pilot charts that show seasonal wind and currents—and therefore the drift patterns of things lost off the coast of Europe—can help students to see quite clearly how this process would have unfolded. These drift patterns have been consistent since the Ice Age. As students examine the information contained in the pilot chart of the North Atlantic, they see clearly the basic conditions that made possible the notorious "triangular trade"—and how the same weather and currents that brought European ships filled with enslaved African people to the Caribbean would have brought any floating goods from shipwrecks, any debris from lost ships themselves, to the shores of Ayiti.[11]

Thus a new narrative of Haiti might begin by understanding the Taíno more viscerally as *subjects*. It might begin by actively rethinking the meaning of that which has been dismissed as irredeemable, of things that were rejected, or lost, or censured centuries ago, including things that typical Western history has labeled valueless. Reconsidering the world that became known as "the poorest country in the Western Hemisphere" before it began to be shaped by European definitions of value, we might imagine Europeans' leavings and failures (their shipwrecks, their flotsam and jetsam) defining *them* for a people they would soon literally objectify as slaves.[12]

There is a currency in objects—objects represent people, objects are people. This is the unique condition of the New World, and it has only been amplified and nuanced by capitalism. Further, the concept of value is connected to the meaning of images of Haitian homes destroyed by natural disasters—which is in turn connected to the meaning of a vulnerable landscape. White planters' narratives of enslaved people's helplessness and disorder, of their need to be governed by the white other, have dominated the discourse of the New World. Such narratives have been repeated endlessly, morphing into a story told over and over by former and current colonial powers gazing upon what they have wrought and disclaiming responsibility for it, and intended to serve as tautological confirmation that Black nations are hopeless. So generating new narratives of Haiti can be aided by both real and imagined listening to the voices of people who have been silenced as they were made to disappear into stereotypes, and into objects and objectification.

Consider the work of the Haitian artists of Atis Rezistans, who use trash to create a radical aesthetics.[13] Sharing this work with students can lead into discussions about the twists and turns that occur as societies conceptualize the meanings of "waste" and "value," and what can happen to these concepts as objects cross cultural, social, national borderlines. N. K. Jemisin's story "The Effluent Engine"—a sci-fi–inspired work set in post-revolutionary Haiti in which a woman transports a sample of waste from the Haitian rum industry to New Orleans, seeking to develop a way to transform it into methane gas that will power industry and everyday life—offers another stunning image of the relationship between waste and the mechanisms (machinery, even) by which value is created.[14] These works can be contextualized using Marx's writing on the commodity fetish, for example, and theories of behavior within a capitalist system such as Peter Corrigan's *The Sociology of Consumption*.[15]

Through methodical yet surprising shifts in perspective, a transdisciplinary series of texts can counter the dehumanizing language and assumptions we find both inside the classroom and outside it, in what people are fond of calling "the real world." But beyond simply putting different kinds of texts in dialogue, what else can we do to stop the cycle of preconceived notions and misknowledge about a place that news media, literature, film, governmental organizations, and NGOs have unremittingly "othered" over the *longue durée*? Ideally, we're using not just texts but also methodologies that can both develop students' knowledge and channel their imaginations as a pedagogical tool. The discipline—or as it's often been called, the "antidiscipline"—of Performance Studies offers a potentially powerful tool for disrupting the insistent rhythm of stereotypes and common assumptions, in part because it focuses on the various meanings and significance of embodiment (Stuckey and Wimmer 3). It grew out of the work of social scientists in the 1940s and 1950s, including Victor Turner and Erving Goffman, who were interested in theater as a mode of understanding social interactions ranging from common everyday conversations to ritual. Using Performance Studies in the classroom, I can comment on and analyze class dynamics, including my own behavior as the instructor, in a way that adds to students' understanding of the process of learning and of "education" (not always the same thing). Moreover, its entire emphasis is on studying "practices, events, behaviors, not objects or things," as Richard Schechner notes (x). Thus Performance Studies offers a way to dismantle processes of objectification, even when applied to actual objects. Take a chair, for example, and consider it as a convergence of forces and histories. We might contemplate the history of its materials—if it's made of plastic, it began as decomposing prehistoric plants and animals, as early life forms. We might consider how far it has traveled, and why it has traveled from the specific place it was made to wherever we find ourselves. In this way, even an actual object may become, in a sense, mobile and fluid. Focusing on motion, ephemerality, the past within the present (in ritual) has the capacity to place objects back into the flow of time—to return them to raw materials, context, influences, history. A theoretical approach that simply refuses objectification can therefore be powerful in dismantling the objectification of Haiti and Haitian people to refocus on individuals and on the specifics of Haiti's long and complex history.

Moreover, Performance Studies' attention to materiality and embodiment can promote an empathic and compassionate response to those who would otherwise be lumped together (consciously or unconsciously) in an inchoate category of "not me." As Nathan Stucky and Cynthia Wimmer write, "Techniques of embodiment increase students' awareness of others' ideological and social subjectivities" (4). Focusing on embodiment in the classroom can help to dismantle stereotypes; it creates a different kind of awareness when, for example, students enter into a dramatic text in which they set their everyday performance of self aside to explore a character, perhaps someone who doesn't externally resemble them. This kinesthetic experience creates knowledge that is not available when simply reading the text. "[P]erformance makes both identification and difference vibrate at a deeper, more resonant pitch," Joni L. Jones asserts, describing classes in which her students embody the roles of "others" (in a form of cross-casting) as they interact to play out situations from a wide variety of cultural and social contexts:

> It does not allow the energetically naive declaration "we're all the same" to hold sway. Doing this would be the same erasure that is found in stereotyping. In the practice of stereotyping, the detail of the individual is overwhelmed, while in the attempt to universalize, the details of difference are deliberately ignored. (Jones 187)

I think this approach may be useful in teaching in general, as well as in considering how to teach about Haiti *outside* Haiti, as a lot of what people outside Haiti think they know is actually just stereotypes, and Haiti itself has been objectified by political manipulations as well as in news coverage for too long to count.

Many of the classes I currently teach focus on writing. In such contexts, embodiment may be viewed as problematic instead of enabling. Composition classes are not generally classes that students want to take, and they are classes whose objective is to teach the amorphous skills of "critical reading" and "writing" rather than specific subject matter. Therefore professors' focus sometimes (often?) has revolved around discipline—on getting students to appear on time, focus, pay attention—typical physical constraints. Thinking about writing in terms of embodiment, however, may productively refocus such concerns on the writing self as involving a body possessed of an idea, bent to express that idea through an interaction with technology of some kind.[16] More specifically, writing classrooms can offer possibilities for unraveling stereotypes of "the other" in general, and when focused on Haiti, for unmaking the monolith that is the product of centuries of manipulation by the powerful. Concerns with embodiedness and liberation may also apply simultaneously to structures and practices of teaching and learning and to ongoing consequences of colonialism and imperialism.

Obviously it is necessary to think, teach, and write about race and ethnicity in a way that does not reinforce otherness. But how is this possible in settings in which all or the majority of students and the professor are not Haitian and/or do not have direct experience of Haiti? In such situations, rather than taking steps toward undoing a process that has been centuries in the making, that process may be inadvertently reinforced. There needs to be some approach to identification that does not adopt/take on/appropriate another's experiences, that avoids unconsciously transferring one's assumptions. In this case, we might consider the imagination as a powerful tool for practical resistance. Inviting students to de-objectify, dis-integrate "otherness" through performance can offer a way to use the imagination not to appropriate "otherness" but to more deeply understand how the process of othering takes place. This approach makes use of the unique possibilities of improvisation in the classroom. As Joni L. Jones writes,

> Improvisation insists that the students invent a reality. That invention is inevitably shaped by their experiences, their biases, their prejudices, and their fears—but it must also go beyond those limitations, because the invention necessarily exceeds the students' stereotyped understandings of an other. (185)

And in terms of process-based writing pedagogy, it makes sense to think about writing in terms of improvisation—indeed, *as* improvisation.

In one experiment, I began by asking students to do a "word association" in which they named all the things that came to mind when they thought of Haiti, and put these on the board. As the list began to take shape, it contained terms such as "poverty" and "hunger," as well as other, sometimes more nuanced but consistently negative views. When students realized this fact (a student in one class exclaimed, "We need something good in there!"), I took that as a cue to move to the next part of the project.

Let's return to *the object*—the discarded object, the object as an emblem of social value—now seen through the lens of performance. The object is no longer inert, still, but rather infused with time and place. It's no longer a thing into which human beings have vanished in the service of creating commercial value. It is now, instead, a site at which lived experience is richly available. It can now tell stories.

As I'd perused the shelves of the thrift store in St. Thomas, I'd found things that had made their way from the shores of Haiti to this other island, perhaps through the peristalsis of tourism. A small purse someone had beaded with the image of a vèvè; a wooden box on which someone had carved the word "Haiti." I couldn't know whose hands had made these things, but someone undeniably had picked up a needle and small glass beads, a fine-pointed chisel and a block of wood. In class, I took out the wooden box with "Haiti" written on the lid and showed it to the class. (I've since seen one like it for sale walking up to the Citadelle, and one in the possession of a friend who attended a conference in Port-au-Prince.) I told my part of the story (how I found this object and why I brought it home), and invited students to actively imagine themselves as observers of some part of this object's history. Who made it? Why? Where are they? What surrounds them? I asked students to write a few paragraphs in which they pictured themselves coming upon this person working, to record the scene and what they thought or felt in those imagined moments.

The purpose of such exercises cannot be to know "the truth," insofar as it is knowable. It is not, through imaginatively calling into being this perhaps completely unknown world, or a world known only through stereotypes, to "appropriate" the story of this imagined person—who really existed, or exists, whose hands may at this very moment be sewing or carving letters into wood. Or cooking. Or touching a child's face. It is, rather, to begin the process of de-objectification by humbling oneself before the un- or imperfectly known.

I read with interest the recent debates over cultural appropriation, in particular the arguments of some white writers who stated that they should have access to any and every experience under the sun—and not just imaginative access, but the *right to capitalize on* these imagined experiences. These arguments struck me as classic white privilege. (What do you mean, some doors are closed to me? the white writer cries, stunned at being told that something is outside their grasp.)[17] The point is so obviously not that you must write about precisely what you know (as others have pointed out), but rather that when you approach what you do not know, you don't act like you *do* know. You respond with questions and curiosity rather than entitlement and authority, with the sense that your assumptions may well be utterly mistaken, and that the world you thought you actually did know is also probably far more nuanced (intersectional) than you realized.

When studying Haiti, it may be important, depending on who you are, to forget everything you thought you knew. Through a process of studying Haitian history, Haitian life as narrated by Haitian people, images of Haiti offered by outsiders, and theories of consumer culture and travel and tourism, we return to the meaning of an anonymous tourist's souvenir with new ways of perceiving. After a journey through concepts of performance and ideas about how history is written, the object itself can be transformed as we are transformed. Thus the value of the discards of a consumer culture—and with them, the co-created notion of human beings as discards, of entire cultures themselves as valueless—is reconfigured.

And each of my students wrote something different in response, sometimes incorporating a meditation on their own lives, sometimes simply picturing the scene, inevitably with an awareness and interest that transformed their prose into a kind of poetry. *He sat on a little balcony,* one student wrote. *A house partly torn apart painted bright green. Down the street, two rows of the same houses, all painted diverse vibrant colors. It had just finished raining, puddles are scattered across the ground and you can smell humidity in the air. The man is sweating, his forehead glistening. His calloused hand grips the chisel as he carves patterns onto the dark wood.*[18]

Syllabus

Haiti: Subject/Object

Course Description

Haiti scholar Michael Dash once wrote, "Haitians are meant to be marveled at, studied, converted, rehabilitated and ultimately controlled." The purpose of this course is to examine how that process of objectification has taken place and to help overturn it using dynamic methodologies and a transdisciplinary series of texts. Over the course of the semester, we will travel to the roots of Western concepts of freedom and race, to the origins of injustice and the centuries-long reinscription of power relations that continue to serve colonial and neocolonial interests. What is at stake, for example, in the marginalizing mantra, "Haiti is the poorest country in the Western Hemisphere"? How are notions of social and cultural value created in societies that have been shaped by histories of enslavement? And how can new narratives of Haiti—and marginalized "others" in general—be created, revealed, disseminated? The answers to such questions can help us both to understand the multivalent nature of oppression, and to develop tools to combat it.

Course Objectives

Consistent with the English Department's general objectives, the student will demonstrate, through a wide variety of forms of evaluation, that they are making progress in their ability to:

- Critique and analyze themes in the history, literature, and daily life of Haiti, with a particular focus on ways in which judgments related to social and cultural value are generated.
- Implement different critical approaches relevant to the study of Haitian history, culture, and society, including the origins of stereotypes, cross-national economic disparities and inequalities, and issues of race, gender, sexual orientation, and class, and demonstrate awareness of how to effectively apply these to class readings and projects.
- Interpret fiction and nonfiction texts focused on Haiti using strategies from literary theory and Cultural Studies as well as lenses provided by other disciplines, including but not limited to Performance Studies, history, and the social sciences.
- Produce analyses of relevant themes through written responses, discussion, and presentations.

- Recognize and use effective research methods, and appreciate the value of appropriately and ethically managing information.
- Use methodologies drawn from Performance Studies and Critical Pedagogy to employ imaginative strategies to achieve insights into the relevant texts and phenomena.
- Implement effective strategies for collaborative work among students, including those with disabilities.

Sample Course Outline and Time Distribution

Taking into consideration the results of a diagnostic essay to be administered on the first day of class as per departmental protocol, the selection of specific themes/texts and precise organization of the course will be determined by the professor.

Unit I: Stories about Haiti: Perceptions and Preconceptions

SAMPLE ASSIGNMENTS

- What terms, concepts, and stereotypes do students associate with Haiti? Create a list on the board or in some commonly accessible forum in order to get a sense of the perceptions of Haiti that students bring to the course.
- How are stereotypes created? How can they be dismantled? To begin to answer these questions, students experiment with writing and performing dialogues in which they portray a gender they do not identify with or a different age group. They then critique their portrayals, discussing how and why they notice that they have absorbed or incorporated "otherness" in this sense. They also examine how their ideas about the other group have shaped their reactions to people they perceive as belonging to it. The results of this project will be applied in discussion to the images of Haiti that students encounter in the texts, both in this section and over the course of the semester.
- After reading sections of *Why Haiti Needs New Narratives,* consider Roxane Gay's story "All Things Being Relative." Do you think Gay is offering a "new narrative" of Haiti in this story? Why or why not?

SAMPLE TEXTS

Cécile Accilien, "Congratulations! You Don't Look Haitian: How and When Does One Look Haitian?"

From Antonia Darder et al., *The Critical Pedagogy Reader*
Paul Farmer, from *The Uses of Haiti*
Roxane Gay, "Gracias, Nicaragua y Lo Sentimos" and "All Things Being Relative"
J. Michael Dash, *Haiti and the United States: National Stereotypes and the Literary Imagination*
Richard Schechner, "Fundamentals of Performance Studies"
Gina Athena Ulysse, *Why Haiti Needs New Narratives: A Post-Quake Chronicle*

Unit II: Retelling the Story

SAMPLE ASSIGNMENTS

- Research a historical figure in Haiti and write an essay or story that describes how you think this person would respond to life in Puerto Rico in the present day.
- Retell the story of the first encounter between the Taíno and Christopher Columbus and his men after reading Columbus's narrative and parts of *1491*, and studying the pilot chart of the North Atlantic.
- Research the conditions experienced by Haitian immigrants to the Dominican Republic, Puerto Rico, or the United States during the twentieth and/or twenty-first centuries.

SAMPLE TEXTS

Excerpts from Charles Arthur and Michael Dash, eds., *Libète: A Haiti Anthology*
Marlon Bishop, "The Other Border: Unauthorized Immigration to Puerto Rico"
Excerpts from Christopher Columbus's account of his first voyage
Selections from Edwidge Danticat, *Haiti Noir*
Laurent Dubois, *Haiti: The Aftershocks of History*
Jeremy Matthew Glick, *The Black Radical Tragic: Performance, Aesthetics, and the Unfinished Haitian Revolution*
David Howard, *Coloring the Nation: Race and Ethnicity in the Dominican Republic*
C.L.R. James, *The Black Jacobins: Toussaint Louverture and the San Domingo Revolution*
———. *Toussaint Louverture: The Story of the Only Successful Slave Revolt in History. A Play in Three Acts*

Charles C. Mann, *1491: New Revelations of the Americas Before Columbus*
Eugenio Matibag, *Haitian-Dominican Counterpoint: Nation, State, and Race on Hispaniola*
National Geospatial-Intelligence Agency, Pub. 106, "Atlas of Pilot Charts North Atlantic Ocean (Including Gulf of Mexico)"
Edward Paulino, *Dividing Hispaniola: The Dominican Republic's Border Campaign Against Haiti, 1930–1961*

Unit III: Castoffs and Treasures

SAMPLE ASSIGNMENTS

- a) Examine an object that has been discarded by a community in which you live (the university, your neighborhood, etc.) List the reasons why it might have been discarded. Then imagine other possible uses it might have. Finally, recreate/reposition the castoff object so that it becomes "useful." b) Examine the work of the Atis Rezistans movement. Now that you have spent time studying Haitian history and culture, what would you argue makes this work uniquely Haitian?
- Analyze "The Effluent Engine" from the perspective of Karl Marx.

SAMPLE TEXTS

Images of the work of Atis Rezistans
Peter Corrigan, *The Sociology of Consumption*
N. K. Jemisin, "The Effluent Engine"
Linda Kachadurian, "Haiti in the Time of Trash: Recycling, Rebuilding, and Remaining Joyful Five Years after the Earthquake"
Karl Marx, *Capital, Vol. 1*
William Rathje and Cullen Murphy, *Rubbish! The Archaeology of Garbage*

Unit IV: Travel, Tourism, and (De)objectification

SAMPLE ASSIGNMENTS

- Write the story of a tourist object/souvenir from Haiti, considering its relationship to the larger sociohistorical contexts in which it circulates. The object is much more than a static thing—it has history,

it exists within the flux of time. Imagine your way into the life span of this object. Who made it? Why? Where are they? What surrounds them? Write a few paragraphs in which you picture yourself coming upon this person working. Record the scene and what you think or feel in those imagined moments.
- Consider how a conversation between Roxane Gay and Zora Neale Hurston might take shape. What do you think each would want to tell, and ask, the other?
- Critically evaluate the Royal Caribbean website on Labadee using the ideas put forth by Dean MacCannell in his chapter on "painful memory."

SAMPLE TEXTS

Archival news articles on Haitian tourism
Roxane Gay, "The Harder They Come"
Zora Neale Hurston, *Tell My Horse: Voodoo and Life in Haiti and Jamaica*
Royal Caribbean, "Cruise to Labadee, Haiti"
Dean MacCannell, "Painful Memory," from *The Ethics of Sightseeing*

Notes

1. As Eugenio Matibag points out, Trujillo's *antihaitianismo* had a personal component—he wore "pancake makeup" to hide dark skin "inherited from Haitian ancestors." See *Haitian-Dominican Counterpoint: Nation, State, and Race on Hispaniola*, 164. And Edward Paulino notes that "[a] metaphorical massacre continues today. The attempt in 1937 to physically eliminate a heterogeneous Haitian-Dominican community in the Dominican Republic is evident where Dominicans of Haitian descent . . . struggle to be seen and acknowledged as legally part of the Dominican nation and its identity. Their group is the only one deemed incompatible with traditional Dominicanness." See *Dividing Hispaniola: The Dominican Republic's Border Campaign Against Haiti, 1930–1961*, xviii.

2. As Ernesto Sagás writes, as a result of *antihaitianismo*, Dominicans of the "lower" classes do not see themselves as "black" (125). To be Dominican, he argues, is not to be Haitian—"In the Dominican Republic, the 'other' is represented by references to blackness in what is an intrinsically Afro-Caribbean nation" (Sagás 127). David Howard notes, "Haitians are the scapegoats in Dominican society" (30).

3. Dash writes, "The imaginative constraints we have examined [in analyzing the relationship between Haiti and the United States] form an inflexible rhetoric of power or a paralysing self-consciousness that not only distances the Other but sadly, inescapably imprisons the Subject as well" (135). See also my argument on whiteness and property in *Wounds of Returning: Race, Memory, and Property on the Post-Slavery Plantation*.

4. See also Cécile Accilien, "Congratulations! You Don't Look Haitian: How and When Does One Look Haitian?"

5. James wrote a play dramatizing the Revolution that premiered in London in 1936 with Paul Robeson in the role of Toussaint Louverture. After being lost for decades, the text of the play was republished in 2013 in a well-reviewed scholarly edition. Jeremy Matthew Glick provides an analysis in *The Black Radical Tragic: Performance, Aesthetics, and the Unfinished Haitian Revolution* (2016).

6. See www.zoranealehurston.com/books/tell-my-horse/.

7. See, for example, Horace Sutton, "The Pleasures of Haiti" (8 June 1947), and Henrietta Brackman, "Haiti's Hospitality; The Island's Rich Folklore Tradition Is One of Its Many Attractions" (4 November 1956).

8. www.royalcaribbean.com/cruise-to/labadee-haiti

9. The chapter entitled "Painful Memory" in *The Ethics of Sightseeing* helps to illuminate the layered realities of places inhabited by tourists and travelers.

10. For example, William Rathje and Cullen Murphy's *Rubbish! The Archaelogy of Garbage* contains a chapter that describes the value of discards to understanding culture (Chapter 3, "What We Say, What We Do").

11. Pilot charts are available at msi.nga.mil/MSISiteContent/StaticFiles/NAV_PUBS/APC/Pub106/106mar.pdf. The chart of the North Atlantic (from 5 degrees N latitude to 67 degrees N latitude, thus covering the western coast of Europe and the British Isles; the western coast of Africa; the Caribbean; and the northern part of South America) illustrates that nothing north of Ireland would have reached the Caribbean, but from the Bay of Biscay on the south are areas that are upwind and upcurrent of the north coast of South America, and these currents sweep along the whole north coast of Hispaniola.

12. Approaches to writing the histories of the Americas increasingly foreground the lives of the people who were there before the horrors of the colonial experiment began, such as Charles C. Mann's *1491: New Revelations of the Americas Before Columbus* and James Wilson's *And the Earth Shall Weep: A History of Native America*.

13. See, for example, Linda Kachadurian, "Haiti in the Time of Trash: Recycling, Rebuilding, and Remaining Joyful Five Years after the Earthquake." Images of the work of Atis Rezistans can be found online, for example, in Rafael Camacho's "*Photo Essay*: Atis Rezistans: Preserving Haiti's Anticolonial Resistance"; Miami Design District's "Atis Rezistans: The Remix"; and Atlas Oscura's "Atis Rezistans."

14. The story is available online in *Lightspeed Magazine*.

15. Particularly Chapter 3, "Objects, Commodities, and Noncommodities." For Marx's theory of the commodity fetish, see *Capital, Vol. I*, Chapter 1, "Commodities," Section 4, "The Fetishism of Commodities and the Secret Thereof."

16. Discussing how we might use a Performance Studies–inspired pedagogy in the classroom, Ryan Claycomb asks, "How are our own bodies on display and what does this have to do with teaching writing? How are students' bodies in play not only in the classroom itself, but also outside the classroom during the act of writing? How might we imagine an embodied liberatory pedagogy of writing?"

17. See, for example, Lionel Shriver's speech entitled "Fiction and Identity Politics."

18. I am not able to credit this student from my INGL 3014-120 (Fall 2016) course at the University of Puerto Rico, Recinto de Río Piedras, by name, as they submitted their response anonymously.

Works Cited

Accilien, Cécile. "Congratulations! You Don't Look Haitian: How and When Does One Look Haitian?" *Haiti and the Haitian Diaspora in the Wider Caribbean*, edited by Philippe Zacaïr, University Press of Florida, 2010, pp. 153–170.

Adams, Jessica. *Wounds of Returning: Race, Memory, and Property on the Post-Slavery Plantation*. University of North Carolina Press, 2007.

Arthur, Charles, and Michael Dash, editors. *Libèté: A Haiti Anthology*. Markus Wiener, 2009.

"Atis Rezistans." www.atlasobscura.com/places/atis-rezistans. n.d. Accessed 20 June 2019.

"Atis Rezistans: The Remix." *Miami Design District*. n.d. www.miamidesigndistrict.net/blog/entries/301/atis-rezistans-the-remix. Accessed 20 June 2019.

Bishop, Marlon. "The Other Border: Unauthorized Immigration to Puerto Rico." Latino USA, National Public Radio. 2 Jan 2015. www.latinousa.org/2015/01/02/border-unauthorized-immigration-puerto-rico. Accessed 20 June 2019.

Brackman, Henrietta. "Haiti's Hospitality; The Island's Rich Folklore Tradition Is One of Its Many Attractions." *The New York Times*, 4 November 1956.

Camacho, Rafael. "*Photo Essay:* Atis Rezistans: Preserving Haiti's Anticolonial Resistance, *NACLA Report on the Americas*, vol. 50, no. 2, 8 June 2018, pp. 188–193.

Claycomb, Ryan. "Performing/Teaching/Writing: Performance Studies in the Composition Classroom." *Enculturation: A Journal of Rhetoric, Writing, and Culture*, vol. 6, no. 1, 2008, http://enculturation.net/6.1/claycomb. Accessed 14 April 2017.

Columbus, Christopher. *The Four Voyages*. Translated by J. M. Cohen, Penguin Classics, 1992.

Corrigan, Peter. *The Sociology of Consumption*. SAGE, 1997.

Danticat, Edwidge, ed. *Haiti Noir*. Akashic Books, 2011.

———. *Haiti Noir 2: The Classics*. Akashic Books, 2014.

Darder, Antonia, Marta P. Baltodano, and Rodolfo D. Torres. *The Critical Pedagogy Reader*, 3rd ed. Routledge, 2017.

Dash, J. Michael. *Haiti and the United States: National Stereotypes and the Literary Imagination*. Macmillan, 1988.

Dubois, Laurent. *Haiti: The Aftershocks of History*. Henry Holt, 2012.

Embree, Zack. *Atis Rezistans: Art Making and Community Making in a Ghetto of Port-au-Prince*. 2013. https://vimeo.com/67073900. Accessed 20 June 2019.

Farmer, Paul. *The Uses of Haiti*. Common Courage Press, (1994) 2003.

Gay, Roxane. "All Things Being Relative." *Ayiti*. Grove Press, (2011) 2018, pp. 85–89.

———. "Gracias, Nicaragua y Lo Sentimos." *Ayiti*. Grove Press, (2011) 2018, pp. 91–94.

———. "The Harder They Come." *Ayiti*. Grove Press, (2011) 2018, pp. 79–83.

Glick, Jeremy Matthew. *The Black Radical Tragic: Performance, Aesthetics, and the Unfinished Haitian Revolution*. New York University Press, 2016.

Howard, David. *Coloring the Nation: Race and Ethnicity in the Dominican Republic*. Signal Books, 2001.

Hurston, Zora Neale. *Tell My Horse: Voodoo and Life in Haiti and Jamaica*. Harper Perennial, (1938) 2008.

James, C.L.R. *The Black Jacobins: Toussaint Louverture and the San Domingo Revolution*. Vintage (1938), 1989.

———. *Toussaint Louverture: The Story of the Only Successful Slave Revolt in History. A Play in Three Acts*. Edited by Christian Høgsbjerg. Duke University Press, 2013.

Jemisin, N. K. "The Effluent Engine." *Lightspeed Magazine,* March 2018, Issue 94. www.lightspeedmagazine.com/fiction/the-effluent-engine. Accessed 20 June 2019.

Jones, Joni L. "Teaching in the Borderlands." *Teaching Performance Studies*, edited by Nathan Stucky and Cynthia Wimmer. Southern Illinois University Press, 2002, pp. 175–190.

Kachadurian, Linda. "Haiti in the Time of Trash: Recycling, Rebuilding, and Remaining Joyful Five Years after the Earthquake." *ReVista: Harvard Review of Latin America*, vol. 14, no. 2, Winter 2015, pp. 50–52.

MacCannell, Dean. Chapter 11, "Painful Memory." *The Ethics of Sightseeing*. Oakland: University of California Press, 2011, pp. 167–81.

Mann, Charles C. *1491: New Revelations of the Americas Before Columbus*. Vintage, 2005.

Marx, Karl. *Capital, Vol. 1: A Critical Analysis of Capitalist Production*. Penguin Classics, (1867) 1992.

Matibag, Eugenio. *Haitian-Dominican Counterpoint: Nation, State, and Race on Hispaniola*. Palgrave Macmillan, 2003.

National Geospatial-Intelligence Agency. Pub. 106. "Atlas of Pilot Charts North Atlantic Ocean (Including Gulf of Mexico)." 2002 edition. msi.nga.mil/MSISiteContent/StaticFiles/NAV_PUBS/APC/Pub106/106mar.pdf. Accessed 30 June 2019.

The Official Website of Zora Neale Hurston. "Tell My Horse." www.zoranealehurston.com/books/tell-my-horse/. Accessed 28 June 2019.

Paulino, Edward. *Dividing Hispaniola: The Dominican Republic's Border Campaign Against Haiti, 1930–1961*. University of Pittsburgh Press, 2016.

Rathje, William, and Cullen Murphy. *Rubbish! The Archaeology of Garbage*. The University of Arizona Press, 2001.

Royal Caribbean. "Cruise to Labadee, Haiti." www.royalcaribbean.com/cruise-to/labadee-haiti. Accessed 28 June 2019.

Sagás, Ernesto. *Race and Politics in the Dominican Republic*. University Press of Florida, 2000.

Schechner, Richard. "Foreword: Fundamentals of Performance Studies." *Teaching Performance Studies*, edited by Nathan Stucky and Cynthia Wimmer. Southern Illinois University Press, 2002, pp. ix–xii.

Shriver, Lionel. "Lionel Shriver's Full Speech: 'I Hope the Concept of Cultural Appropriation Is a Passing Fad.'" *The Guardian*, 13 September 2016.

Stucky, Nathan, and Cynthia Wimmer. "Introduction: The Power of Transformation in Performance Studies Pedagogy," *Teaching Performance Studies*, edited by Nathan Stucky and Cynthia Wimmer. Southern Illinois University Press, 2002, pp. 1–32.

Sutton, Horace. "The Pleasures of Haiti." *The New York Times*, 8 June 1947.

Ulysse, Gina Athena. *Why Haiti Needs New Narratives: A Post-Quake Chronicle*. Wesleyan University Press, 2015.

Wilson, James. *And the Earth Shall Weep: A History of Native America*. Grove Press, (1998) 2000.

11

Rethinking Latinx Studies from Hispaniola's Borderlands

JOHN RIBÓ

In recent years Transnational Hispaniola has emerged as an important framework in contemporary Dominican Studies. Building on the work of Silvio Torres-Saillant, Lauren Derby, and Ginetta Candelario, scholars led by April J. Mayes, Yolanda Martín, and Kiran Jayaram have institutionalized this transnational turn in a number of ways. Mayes, Martín, and Jayaram organized Transnational Hispaniola conferences in Santo Domingo, Dominican Republic, in 2010, New Brunswick, New Jersey, in 2012, and Port-au-Prince, Haiti, in 2016; the Latin American Studies Association expanded its Haiti/Dominican Republic section in 2011; and the Caribbean Studies Association created a Transnational Hispaniola section in 2016. Though the bicentenary of Haitian independence in 2004, the earthquake in Port-au-Prince in 2010, and the Dominican Constitutional Tribunal's Sentencia 168-13 in 2013 all contributed to this transnational shift in Dominican Studies, this framework has proven generative well beyond these events. Transnational Hispaniola reevaluates how Haiti and the Dominican Republic, as two parts of one island connected by culture, history, and ecology, form a complex borderland at the crossroads of the Greater Antilles and at the heart of the emergence of modernity/coloniality in the Americas, a borderlands that Junot Díaz calls "Ground Zero of the New World," and that Torres-Saillant describes as "the land where blackness first acquired its modern significance" (Díaz, *Brief Wondrous Life* 1; 8).

Despite this groundswell of Dominican Studies scholarship approaching Hispaniola transnationally and arguing for the island's centrality in global histories of empire, race, slavery, and abolition, Latinx Studies has been slow to include Haiti.[1] The absence of Haiti in Latinx Studies is part of the systemic silencing of Haiti and the Haitian Revolution and has specific disciplinary explanations as well. If one assumes, for example, that Latinx Studies focuses exclusively on the cultural and linguistic legacies of Spain in the Americas, then the exclusion of Haiti from Latinx Studies appears logical. This has not, however, been the discipline's historical trajectory; nor are Latinxs the cultural, linguistic, or biological offspring of Spain alone. Latinx Studies emerged from the strategic alliance of Chicanx and Puerto Rican civil rights movements of the 1960s. From the creation of the first university curricula in the field, to the permanent addition of "Spanish/Hispanic" to the US census in 1980, these efforts deployed imperfect yet strategically useful umbrella terms to build coalitions of diverse constituencies. These coalitions have had the goal of winning legal rights and giving agency, visibility, and voice to people whose life chances have been diminished by the effects of coloniality. As a nation shaped by neocolonial relations and with a sizable US diaspora, Haiti shares much within the peoples and cultures that fall under a more inclusive definition of Latinx Studies.

In this essay, I provide close readings of two cultural products: an episode of the television series *Orange Is the New Black* titled "Power Suit" (2016), and *Forget* (2010), the debut album of Dominican American musician George Lewis, Jr., a.k.a. Twin Shadow. My readings of these two texts demonstrate how transnational approaches to Hispaniola can help rethink Latinx Studies from the Haitian-Dominican border, and, in doing so, enact a much-needed shift in the field toward including Haiti and its diaspora in discussions of US Latinx cultural production and lived experiences. If, as many scholars have argued, the Haitian Revolution is a foundational event of modernity/coloniality not only for Haiti, the Dominican Republic, and Hispaniola, but more broadly, for the Caribbean, the Americas, and indeed the world, then Latinx Studies must take the Haitian Revolution's complex historical legacies into account. Transnational approaches such as those conceptualized by Mayes, Martín, Jayaram, Torres-Saillant, Derby, and Candelario, which focus on Hispaniola and which include Haiti and its revolutionary history as fundamental objects of inquiry of Latinx Studies, promise to catalyze constructive debates within the field's ongoing discussions of ethnicity and race. These contribute to more inclusive representation in syllabi, curricula, and scholarship of Afro-Latinxs in general, and of Haitian Americans and Dominican Americans specifically. Such curricula provide more historically nuanced and culturally specific understandings of racial formations across the islands of the Caribbean and their diasporas in the US.

The project of rethinking Latinx Studies from Hispaniola's borderlands is part of an ongoing, intersectional, transnational, and collective undertaking that is indebted to the work of many people active in Dominican, Haitian, and Latinx cultural production and studies. Since the late 1990s, Edwidge Danticat and Junot Díaz have been perhaps the most visible leaders in efforts to reach out to broad audiences to raise awareness of the 1937 massacre of Dominicans of Haitian descent and of Haitian migrant workers on the Dominican-Haitian border, and of the continued precarity of these populations today.[2] Before Danticat and Díaz, the poems "Haïti" (1978) by Dominican poet Sherezada "Chiqui" Vicioso and "Parsley" (1983) by African American poet Rita Dove explored relations between the neighboring nations of Hispaniola in verse. Since the early 1990s, Dominican-Haitian relations have played an important, if often obfuscated, role in the contemporary Dominican fiction written in English of Julia Alvarez, Loida Maritza Pérez, Angie Cruz, Nelly Rosario, and Ana Maurine Lara. Contemporary Dominican artists such as Josefina Baez, David Pérez Karmadavis, and Sherezade García, as well as writer, critic, and curator Alanna Lockward, have made important contributions through art and exhibits exploring Hispaniola's transnational connections. Alvarez, Danticat, and García have also collaborated with historian Edward Paulino on Border of Lights, a project that since 2012 has commemorated the anniversary of the 1937 massacre on both sides of the Dominican-Haitian border and in diaspora through ceremonies, gatherings, testimonials, and art projects.

Part of a larger global trend that Paul Jay terms "the transnational turn in literary studies," Transnational Hispaniola has been the object of study of a rich community of scholars (1). This community includes foundational figures of contemporary US Dominican Studies such as Silvio Torres-Saillant, Ramona Hernández, and Lauren Derby. Additionally, well-established scholars of Dominican culture, literature, and history such as Ginetta Candelario, Maja Horn, Edward Paulino, María Cristina Fumagalli, Milagros Ricourt, and Néstor E. Rodríguez have contributed to the vibrancy of the discipline. The Transnational Hispaniola collective named this approach and fought for its recognition. This collective includes April J. Mayes, Yolanda Martín, and Kiran Jayram, as well as Carlos Ulises Decena, Yveline Alexis, Arturo Victoriano, and the many presenters and organizers who made three international conferences possible. Finally, there is an emerging generation of academics including Lorgia García-Peña, Anne Eller, Karen Jaime, Dixa Ramírez, Rachel Afi Quinn, Brendan Jamal Thornton, Raj Chetty, Omaris Zamora, Diego Ubiera, Jeannine Murray-Román, Sophie Maríñez, and Abigail Lapin Dardashti. These scholars—and certainly many others still—labor to articulate counter-narratives to dominant scripts of Dominicanness written by the Trujillo and Balaguer regimes and reinforced by US imperial hegemony. These alternative articulations of Dominicanness take into account the often-overlooked historical specificities and cultural practices of the Dominican people as well as the long history of transnational connections between the Dominican Republic and Haiti on the island and in the greater diaspora.

While the two primary objects of analysis of this essay—"Power Suit" and *Forget*—form part of this growing corpus of cultural production of Transnational Hispaniola, both can pass and hide in plain sight in US popular culture. As mainstream, collectively produced cultural products that do not mark or market themselves as explicitly and exclusively Dominican, the Dominicanness of this episode of *Orange Is the New Black* and of Twin Shadow's first full-length album can be overlooked, can pass unremarked by mainstream Anglo-American audiences. Keeping in mind the lessons of Michel-Rolph Trouillot, "Power Suit" and *Forget* serve as powerful examples of the work teachers must do to provide context for students learning about cultures and histories as subject to silencing as those of Hispaniola and its diasporas.

Despite these similarities, "Power Suit" and *Forget* feature very different approaches to representing Dominicanness. From the outset, "Power Suit" presents conflicting insider and outsider views of Dominican identity that both root Dominicanness in blackness via Haiti. In contrast, *Forget* never explicitly mentions the Dominican Republic, Haiti, or Hispaniola, and yet its imagery, its themes, and its conclusion nevertheless evoke the long transnational history of racial terror in the Americas. Despite these different approaches to representing Dominicanness, both "Power Suit" and *Forget* emphasize how in the US black and brown people, Haitian, Dominican, and otherwise, must operate within racial formations and economies of incarceration borne out of slavery and reactionary responses to abolition. Within these complex historical legacies of the transatlantic slave trade, Haiti's unique revolutionary charge as the only nation in the world founded through slave revolt provoked three primary reactions: celebration, vilification, and silencing. I argue in the pages that follow that "Power Suit" and *Forget* offer different visions of Dominicanness that loosely correspond to these three prototypical responses to the Haitian Revolution and that figure Haiti as the celebrated, vilified, or silenced other of Dominican blackness.

"Power Suit"

Since its debut in 2013, the Netflix original series *Orange Is the New Black* has been a popular success integral to the streaming service's emergence as an important producer of video content in the contemporary media landscape. A fictional dramedy loosely based on Piper Kerman's 2010 best-selling memoir of the same title, the series takes place in the minimum-security wing of the fictional Litchfield Penitentiary. Focalized through the fish-out-of-water narrative of the blonde, white, upper-middle-class, bisexual protagonist Piper, the show features an ensemble cast that consists largely of female actors of color. While Piper's story remains central throughout the series, episodes often focus on supporting characters to reveal in flashbacks how they came to be inmates, family members of inmates, or employees of the institution.

Scholars have been divided in their reception of *Orange Is the New Black*. Sarah Artt and Jane Schwan introduce their special issue on the series for *Television and New Media* emphasizing that the show has received "equal shares of praise and blame" (468). Jane Caputi applauds the series for representing women "regularly erased in the mass media" while simultaneously recognizing it as "a reflection of the disproportionate over representation of marginalized women incarcerated in what activists call the prison industrial complex" (1131). Anna Marie Smith lauds the show's "brilliant multicultural female ensemble acting of Shakespearean quality" while lamenting its "reassuring and self-immunizing message for white liberals and progressives" supposedly "hip enough to see right through the privileged white narcissism" (277, 280). More insightfully still, Smith explains that these contradictions are key to the series' success:

> Mass cultural products like *Orange* have become much more sophisticated, plural, and self-contradictory; they are endowed with multiple entry points and promote scores of parallel reception tracks. Their target audience is no longer the homogeneous nation, but the mashups of niche market audiences by the dozens. *Orange* is a successful show because it can be almost all things to almost all people: softcore porn for the male homophobe; confirmation of racist and ethnic slurs about irresponsible and work-shy black women and Latinas for white cultural racists; and a limited but accurate archive of sex positive lesbian history. (277)

"Power Suit," the second episode of the show's fourth season, epitomizes this ability to appeal to conflicting "niche market audiences" in how it represents Dominicanness through references both to Dominican counterculture and to racist stereotypes. While the episode offers to my knowledge the most substantial treatment of Dominican culture in US television, its official plot summary—"The newcomers stir up ethnic and domestic conflicts, but Maria sees an opportunity"—frames the episode as an allegory for white anxiety about Dominican immigration to the US. The "newcomers" are an influx of mostly Dominican inmates who arrive at Litchfield after the state privatizes and sells the penitentiary to MCC, a corporation that overcrowds the prison to maximize profits. In the episode, Maria, one of the original Litchfield inmates who is Dominican, takes advantage of this demographic shift to challenge the protagonist Piper's dominance in the prison yard's pecking order; to put it simply, Dominican immigrants challenge Anglo-American hegemony. Though the entire episode deserves analysis, I focus here on two reflexive moments at the beginning of the episode that reframe *Orange Is the New Black*, at least for this one episode, as a Dominican television show and that exemplify the show's ability to appeal simultaneously to conflicting sectors of its diverse audience. In the first moment, the episode performs a Dominican restaging of its opening credit sequence. In the second, Anglo-American prisoners discuss Dominican "newcomers" as the latest wave of Latinx immigrants to be reduced to racist clichés.

When teaching television, I prefer to assign screenings of episodes as homework so that students consume the media as they normally would in a comfortable setting. At the beginning of class, I ask that they share their general reactions as a warm-up to lower their affective barriers and to expose students to the variety of responses different people can have to the same television show. Finally, I lead the class in a close analysis of a short excerpt. This multistep viewing experience from screening, to open discussion, to close analysis models for students different kinds of viewing that take place when analyzing television. One of my favorite pedagogical strategies when teaching television is to lead students in a close reading of the opening credit sequence and theme song of a show. Although audiences tend to take these first moments of a show for granted, opening credit sequences and theme songs often set the stage for television series by evoking the dominant themes, tones, and subject matter of a show through suggestive sights and sounds. *Orange Is the New Black* follows this model, setting a series of sepia-toned, cropped close-ups of real, former female inmates including the author Piper Kerman to "You've Got Time," an original song composed for the series by independent musician Regina Spektor (Dunne). The sequence parallels the structure of the show; as images of real, formerly incarcerated, disproportionately black and Latina women flash across the screen, the theme song's lyrics call on viewers to "Remember all their faces. Remember all their voices."

The first scene of "Power Suit" effectively restages this opening sequence as a Dominican remix. Immediately after the opening credits, a medium shot tracks down a crowded hallway revealing a long line of frustrated female inmates in tan uniforms waiting with towels, toothbrushes, and toilet paper to use an overcrowded restroom. Similar to the women in the opening credits, none of the women in this scene are regular or featured cast members of the show; rather they are extras who represent the anonymous incarcerated masses in the US. Over the din of the crowd, women sing in Spanish. At the end of the tracking shot the camera slows to rest on three unknown women in orange uniforms clapping, harmonizing, dancing, and laughing, oblivious to the annoyance of their neighbors.

The song the women sing is "El blue del ping pong" by Rita Indiana & Los Misterios, a musical group led by queer Dominican performance artist, writer, and musician Rita Indiana Hernández; "Los Misterios" refer to the luases, or divinities, of Dominican *vudú* (Vodou). "El blue del ping pong"—or ping-pong blues—describes the singer's lesbian desire for her lover through a playful chain of extended metaphors tangentially related to ping-pong. The song echoes themes from a piece about table tennis Hernández included in her collection of literary vignettes *Ciencia succión* (2002) and comes from the group's first and only album to date, *El Juidero* (2010). For the album, Hernández collaborated with filmmakers to create videos for many of the songs. Notably, the lyrics and video of *El Juidero*'s sixth track, "Da pa lo do" allegorize Dominican-Haitian relations.[3] The song and its video advocate for solidarity among the peoples of Hispaniola built on recognition of the common heritage the neighboring nations share, not only as two parts of one island, but also as two peoples with deep, connected roots in the African diaspora and in Afro-Caribbean spiritual practices.[4]

From these brief descriptions of "El blue del ping pong" and "Da pa lo do," it should be clear that these intertextual references to Rita Indiana & Los Misterios in "Power Suit" evoke an artist whose work transgresses taboos of Dominican culture in its open celebration of Vodou, same-sex desire, and Haitian-Dominican solidarity. Introducing this episode of *Orange Is the New Black* with a procession of anonymous, female inmates that culminates with three Dominican women unabashedly enjoying themselves together while singing "El blue del ping pong" reframes the show within a specific countercultural expression of Dominicanness and sends a coded message to specific "niche market audiences" familiar with Rita Indiana and her work. Furthermore, if the audience misses this first reference in the opening scene, the episode reinforces its intertextual link to "El blue del ping pong" by Rita Indiana & Los Misterios by playing the original official track over the end of the final scene and closing credits, effectively bookending the episode within the soundscape of a Dominican musician, writer, and artist who sings in Spanish and identifies as a queer, Afro-diasporic practitioner of Dominican Vodou. For informed, Spanish-speaking audience members, these references to Rita Indiana in "Power Suit" evoke a contemporary Dominican icon who challenges machista, heteronormative, negrophobic, anti-Haitian notions of Dominicanness.

The problem, of course, is that many viewers who do not speak Spanish and who are unfamiliar with Dominican culture may not recognize "El blue del ping pong" and may not know who Rita Indiana is or what her art represents. For this portion of its audience, "Power Suit" addresses the complex multiplicity of Latinx cultures in a short conversation between series regulars Angie Rice and Leanne Taylor, two Anglo-American inmates who are best friends and become associated with the white supremacist faction of the prison's population over the course of season four. The conversation takes place just before a general meeting of all inmates called by the warden. Angie and Leanne sit near the front of the auditorium and gaze back at the multitude of black and brown women behind them. As Angie looks back over her shoulder at the crowd, she cracks an inane racist joke with a smirk:

> Angie: There's [sic] so many Mexicans now it's like a Home Depot parking lot.
> Leanne: Dominicans. If you're gonna be racist, you gotta be accurate or you just look dumb.
> Angie: Is [sic] Dominicans the ones that wear gold chains and smoke cigars and swim to Florida?
> Leanne: No.
> Angie: Is it the coffee and the coke and the "Hips Don't Lie."
> Leanne: No. They talk a lot, and play baseball, and are always like "I'm super not-black" even though Haiti's the exact same island.
> Angie: That's right. Yeah, I hate them.

The dialogue comically critiques Anglo-America's ignorance of US Latinx communities at the same time as it provides reductive, racist glosses of Mexican, Cuban, Colombian, and Dominican cultures. The conversation ironically plays on tensions between ignorance and knowledge, between broad generalizations and granular taxonomies at work in the epistemological underpinnings of racism. Though Angie hates all Latinxs equally, she cannot distinguish them well enough to keep her stereotypes straight, an ignorance that, according to the more knowledgeable Leanne, renders Angie's racism less effective. Leanne coaches Angie to be a better racist by providing the "correct" stereotypes and concluding with one of the most common clichés about Dominicans: that we deny our blackness. For these racist Anglo-American characters, Dominicanness is inextricably linked to blackness via Haiti. Within the white supremacist framework of their conversation, linking Dominicanness to blackness via Haiti serves multiple purposes. It denigrates and thus dehumanizes Dominicans. It undermines negrophobic, anti-Haitian Dominican nationalism. And, in a prison divided among feuding Black, white, and Latinx contingencies, and in which the Dominicans are the largest subset of Latinx inmates, it destabilizes power relations and questions loyalties, because despite their love of Rita Indiana and their dark skin, the female Dominican characters of *Orange Is the New Black* do not overtly identify as black or African American.

The tension between these two moments in the episode—the intertextual references to Rita Indiana, on the one hand, and the conversation about Latinx stereotypes, on the other—exemplifies the contradictory dynamic of *Orange Is the New Black* that Anna Marie Smith describes. The show defines Dominicanness from conflicting insider and outsider perspectives. For fans of Rita Indiana, the episode frames itself as participating in countercultural practices that blur borders of race, gender, sexuality, and nation in the Dominican Republic and its diaspora. For those less versed in Dominican culture, the show provides a cursory gloss of Dominicanness in a set of stereotypes spouted by characters who are self-avowed racists. Despite the seemingly diametric opposition of these two sources, both the oeuvre of Rita Indiana and the racist banter of Angie and Leanne define Dominicanness as inextricably linked to blackness via Haiti.

This seeming contradiction—that both the insider and outsider, both the progressive and retrograde definitions of Dominicanness in "Power Suit" define Dominican blackness via Haiti—makes sense within the historical relations triangulating Haiti, Dominican Republic, and the US. In her groundbreaking book *The Borders of Dominicanidad*, Lorgia García-Peña writes that

> "fear of Haiti"—the overwhelming concern that overtook slave economies like the United States and Spain following the slave revolt that began in 1791 and led to Haitian independence in 1804—is foundational to the production of US notions of race and citizenship. Fear of Haiti dominated the young and robust, slavery-driven US economy and determined the Empire's relationship to the two Hispaniola republics. (7)

García-Peña goes on to explain that the Haitian Revolution transformed nineteenth-century Hispaniola into the home of neighboring abolitionist black republics and thus "an international locus for black resistance and liberation as well as the object of fear in the antebellum United States" (8). The conflicting definitions of Dominicanness in "Power Suit" correspond to this duality of nineteenth-century Hispaniola. Haiti, as both "locus for black resistance" and "object of fear," underwrites both Rita Indiana's celebration of Afro-Dominican culture as well as Angie and Leanne's white supremacist vilification of Dominican blackness.

Teaching Haiti in Dominican and Latinx Studies through this episode of *Orange Is the New Black* requires providing students the analytical tools to think critically about the visual and aural techniques of the show, and the contextual knowledge to understand the historical legacies and the cultural references that the show evokes. Although the sequence could be planned in a variety of ways, I recommend four units to provide students critical context. (See the end of this chapter for a sample syllabus and suggested readings.) These units focus on the history of Hispaniola, film analysis, the work of Rita Indiana Hernández, and finally the episode of *Orange Is the New Black*.

For the historical unit, I pair two articles: "Haitians, Magic, Money: Raza and Society in the Dominican-Haitian Borderlands, 1900–1937" by Lauren Derby and "Transnational Hispaniola: Toward New Paradigms in Haitian and Dominican Studies" by April J. Mayes, et al. Derby historicizes anti-Haitian, anti-Black Dominican nationalism while Mayes, et al. provide concrete models for imagining Hispaniola transnationally and Dominicanness otherwise.

For the unit on film analysis, students read Timothy Corrigan's *A Short Guide to Writing About Film* in conjunction with a screening of Raoul Peck's documentary *I Am Not Your Negro*. Corrigan's text offers useful terminology, strategies, and examples of film analysis, while Peck's film draws astute parallels between the histories of cinema and of diasporic blackness in the Americas.

For the unit prior to screening and discussing "Power Suit," students listen to the entirety of the album *El Juidero* by Rita Indiana & los Misterios, screen the video for "Da pa lo do," and read Karen Jaime's "'Da pa' lo' do": Rita Indiana's Queer, Racialized Dominicanness." Though Rita Indiana Hernández's literary works are increasingly available in English translation, her music and music videos appear exclusively in Spanish. In addition to excellent analysis, Jaime's article includes helpful English translations of portions of the lyrics of "Da pa lo do." Additionally, during class discussion I would encourage Spanish-speaking students to translate any other lyrics and answer any other questions their classmates may have to bridge this language barrier.

The scaffolding of these three units sets the stage for the screening and discussion of "Power Suit." Together the materials of these four units provide students the historical knowledge, cultural context, and analytical tools necessary to critically engage this episode of *Orange Is the New Black* and to understand its insightful commentaries on Haiti's fundamental role in the historical formation of Dominican identity.

Forget

I often find it useful to lead with something students know in order to teach them something they do not; this method validates their knowledge while empowering them to learn, and most importantly, to teach themselves. Teaching Haiti through "Power Suit" leverages the popularity of *Orange Is the New Black* to expose students to film and television studies, to the histories and cultures of Hispaniola, and to exciting and important cultural products that are less well known, such as Rita Indiana. Once this groundwork has been laid, it only makes sense to continue building upon this foundation with an even more challenging object of study. In 2010 Dominican American musician George Lewis, Jr., released *Forget*, his first album under the moniker Twin Shadow. He has since released three more full-length albums, signed to the major label Warner, and toured extensively in the Americas and Europe. Born in the Dominican Republic and raised in Florida by his Jewish American father and Dominican American mother, Lewis's formation as a musician spans genres and blurs the borders of US popular music. In an interview with Jesse Ship for the now-defunct music website *Spinner*, Lewis explains,

> I tried to sing for a metal band when I was 16 but I got kicked out because I was too "not metal." Race has definitely played a factor in my non-acceptance in the music world, and it probably played a huge factor in me being kicked out of the metal band. I don't feel it much these days. But I do admit, being a black dude and playing this kind of music is definitely a bit of a novelty. (Ship)

In recounting these experiences, Lewis critiques how racism is encoded into musical genres; "not metal" here clearly means not white. The irony, of course, is that the roots of metal are firmly planted in rock and roll, which is inextricably linked to the African diaspora. In the racialized codes of US popular music genres, however, Lewis is reduced to an incongruous "black dude," a description that effectively silences African Americans' contributions to US popular music as well as Lewis's complex identity. Though Lewis identifies as black and pinpoints race as one possible cause of his exclusion from this teen metal band, gender, by his own admission, also likely played a part. In the same interview, Lewis confesses that he identifies with "a more effeminate type of nature," explaining that growing up with sisters he always enjoyed fashion and having his hair styled. Lewis's professed penchant for the effeminate resonates as well in the musical influences on display in Twin Shadow's *Forget*, which in sounding like a moody cross between Prince's *Purple Rain* and 1980s new wave synth pop hearkens back to a moment three decades earlier when androgynous, gender-bending acts ruled the popular airwaves.

The intersection of race and gender that Lewis intimates in this interview plays a key role in the themes of *Forget*, an album that consists of 11 tracks that trace a hazy narrative of an illicit, failed romance haunted by race. The relationship between an anonymous first-person protagonist and his beloved is introduced in the first song, "Tyrant Destroyed," which opens with the beloved promising to "never let another black boy break [her] heart" and ends with the protagonist's fears that "Any fair skinned boy could take [her] home." While the track announces the importance of race as a key subtext to the album's doomed romantic drama, it does so only by deploying ambiguous innuendo. It suggests that the couple's relationship is interracial while also disallowing the listener from definitively identifying either the protagonist or the beloved in racialized terms.

Though these two indeterminate references in the first track are the only explicit allusions to race on *Forget*, the album's lyrics repeatedly evoke the threat of racial terror in a series of haunting images of flight and pursuit interspersed throughout the record. In the second track, "When We're Dancing," the protagonist escapes an abusive encounter with his beloved only to realize, "The search party's out. Yes, they're hunting your name." In the album's fourth song, "Shooting Holes," the protagonist and his lover flee together leaving "tracks," pursued by "hounds." Finally, on the sixth track, "Yellow Balloon," when the couple meets in secrecy in the woods, the protagonist warns his beloved, "If you hear your momma coming, get away from me." These images are symbolically loaded. The racially ambiguous protagonist fleeing search parties armed with dogs evokes the pursuit of runaway slaves. Coupled with the implied interracial romance between the protagonist and the beloved, these images also recall the many lynchings in the US justified by the supposed threat of miscegenation. Always subtle and never foregrounded, these descriptions of chases and escapes interspersed throughout *Forget* nevertheless conjure up the long, violent history of racial terror of the Caribbean and the Americas.

The relationship between the protagonist and the beloved is doomed from the start, and as the album progresses and the romance eventually fails, the landscape of the lyrical imagery grows increasingly bleak. The downward spiral culminates in the final, eponymous track, "Forget." Though deceptively simple, terse, and repetitive, the song's lyrics present the album's final evocative image of the troubled history of racial terror in the Caribbean and the Americas by menacingly weaving the threads of the album together into a rope. The song opens by repeating the two lines of its chorus: "They'll give us something; they'll give us so much to forget, or enough rope to deal with it." The song never explains who "they" are, but within the context that the imagery of the album establishes, I read this unidentified third-person pronoun—this faceless, nameless, collective subject repeated throughout the chorus—as the haunting personification of the anonymous yet ever-present menace of violently policed regimes of race, gender, and sexuality.

"They" embodies the gaslighting, paranoia-inducing contradictions of living as a subject whose life chances are materially diminished by racialized, gendered, and sexed hierarchies so embedded, encoded, and enmeshed in the fabric of society as to seem "natural" and thus invisible, anonymous, and depersonalized. In the song's two verses, the negative effects of this racial terror manifest psychologically and somatically as insomnia, nightmares, fevers, and heartache. The options available to counter these symptoms offer little solace: either forget in order to survive, or face the noose, whether it be of one's own or the lynch mob's making. Faced with these stark possibilities, the first-person protagonist of Twin Shadow's *Forget* heeds the titular command to forget "all of it," "everything," "everyone," to forget in order to survive. And yet the audience has the album, however cloaked in silence it may be, as a record, as a testament of the willfully forgotten trauma of racial terror.

Teaching Haiti through Twin Shadow's *Forget* presents challenges. The album offers only oblique connections to Haiti through subtle references to hemispheric histories of racial terror. Yet I find that when given the opportunity, students rise to these kinds of challenges. After teaching units on the history of Hispaniola, film analysis, Dominican popular culture, and *Orange Is the New Black*, I recommend presenting Twin Shadow's *Forget* to students enigmatically, suggesting that the album is connected to the themes of the previous units without explaining how. In preparation for class, students listen to the album, read the lyrics, and conduct research outside of class in pursuit of connections between the album and Hispaniola. In class, students share the connections they found first in small groups and then as a whole class. Certainly not all students will be convinced or satisfied by such an exercise, but it models important lessons and practices. Asking students to find their own connections between a cultural product and the themes of a class demonstrates that critical analysis and research require creativity. It also underlines the need to connect elusive clues to expose pervasive biases that shape the world, an essential lesson to the generation of Black Lives Matter.

Never Forget

As I write this conclusion, a jury in North Charleston, South Carolina, deliberates the fate of former police officer Michael Slager, who on April 4, 2015, shot and killed an unarmed 50-year-old African American man named Walter Scott. The details of the shooting are chaotic but at the same time, by now, somehow rote. Slager stopped Scott for a broken brake light. Scott fled on foot. Slager pursued. The two men struggled. Slager fired his Taser. Scott fled again. Slager fired eight shots from his pistol, hitting Scott five times in the back. Slager handcuffed the arms of Scott's wounded, dying body and left him bleeding, face-down, in a field.

The only record, the only testament of this shooting, was a smart phone video filmed by Feidin Santana, a Dominican immigrant who accidentally happened upon the scene. In an interview with NBC's Matt Lauer, Santana admitted that as he filmed the video and after he came forward publicly to share it with Scott's family, he feared for his own life. In describing his decision to film the shooting as the tragedy unfolded, Santana explained, however, that "[t]here were just the three of us in that moment . . . I just wanted [Scott] to know that he was not by himself" (Kim).[5]

Although Feidin Santana could not save Walter Scott, he stood as a witness in solidarity to record Scott's tragic death so that at the very least Scott's family might know the truth, so that at the very least that truth might not be silenced and forgotten. What a sad gift to give. And yet that fateful moment Santana describes before the shooting began in which those three men stood in that North Charleston field, together and at odds, forms part of more than 500 years of racial terror in the Americas that originate in the colonial encounter on Hispaniola. Five hundred years of history tell me that it is possible, but unlikely, that justice will be done. Junot Díaz eloquently argues that in Trump's America "the joyous destiny of our people" is "to bury the arc of the moral universe so deep in justice that it will never be undone" ("Under President Trump"). Perhaps one way to start is to stand in that field with Walter Scott and Feidin Santana and never forget.

Syllabus

Course Description

Latinx Studies is often framed as a transdisciplinary field of scholarly and cultural production preoccupied with historicizing and theorizing borders. This class applies this framework to Hispaniola—the Caribbean island shared by Haiti and Dominican Republic—to interrogate the ethno-racial, cultural, linguistic, and geographic borders of Latinx Studies itself. The course has two primary objects. First, it aims to provide students the knowledge and skills necessary to understand the pivotal role that Hispaniola played in the history of race in the Americas and to observe how that history permeates popular culture today. Second, the class invites critical reflection on why Haiti has historically been excluded from Latinx Studies and how this exclusion of Haiti from Latinx Studies parallels other forms of exclusion and violence people of African descent have faced throughout the Americas.

Unit 1: The History of Hispaniola's Borderlands

    Derby, Lauren. "Haitians, Magic, and Money: Raza and Society in the Haitian-Dominican Borderlands, 1900 to 1937." *Comparative Studies in Society and History*, vol. 36, no. 3, 1994, pp. 488–526.

    Mayes, April, et al. "Transnational Hispaniola: Toward New Paradigms in Haitian and Dominican Studies." *Radical History Review*, no. 115, Winter 2013, pp. 26–32.

Unit 2: Film Analysis

    Corrigan, Timothy. *A Short Guide to Writing about Film*. Pearson, 2015.
    I Am Not Your Negro. Directed by Raoul Peck. Velvet Film, 2016.

Unit 3: Rita Indiana & Los Misterios

    "Da pa lo do." *YouTube*, uploaded by engelleonardo7, 19 October 2011, www.youtube.com/watch?v=Y72XAybPTnU.

    Jaime, Karen. "'Da pa' lo' do": Rita Indiana's Queer, Racialized Dominicanness." *Small Axe*, no. 47, July 2015, pp. 85–93.

    Rita Indiana & Los Misterios. *El Juidero*, Premium Latin Music, 2010.

Unit 4: "Power Suit"

    "Power Suit." *Orange Is the New Black*, season 4, episode 2, Netflix, 17 June 2016, www.netflix.com/watch/70242311?trackId=14170287&tctx=0%2C0%2Cccdeb7c6-5432-4b5f-8344-2ffba6050d8a-502316538.

Unit 5: Forget

    Twin Shadow. *Forget*, Terrible Records, 2010.

Suggested Readings

Candelario, Ginetta E. B. *Black Behind the Ears: Dominican Racial Identity from Museums to Beauty Shops*. Duke University Press, 2007.

Chetty, Raj and Amaury Rodríguez, editors. *Dominican Black Studies*, special issue of *The Black Scholar*, vol. 45, no. 2, 2015.

Daut, Marlene. *Tropics of Haiti: Race and the Literary History of the Haitian Revolution in the Atlantic World, 1789–1865*. Liverpool University Press, 2015.

Fumagalli, Maria Cristina. *On the Edge: Writing the Border between Haiti and the Dominican Republic*. Liverpool University Press, 2015.

Maríñez, Sophie. "The Quisqueya Diaspora: The Emergence of Latina/o Literature from Hispaniola." *The Cambridge History of Latina/o American Literature*, edited by John Morán González and Laura Lomas, Cambridge University Press, 2018, pp. 561–582.

Mayes, April J., and Kiran Jayaram. *Transnational Hispaniola: New Directions in Haitian and Dominican Studies*. University of Florida Press, 2018.

Paulino, Edward. *Dividing Hispaniola: The Dominican Republic's Border Campaign Against Haiti, 1930–1961*. University of Pittsburgh Press, 2016.

Ramírez, Dixa. *Colonial Phantoms: Belonging and Refusal in the Dominican Americas, from the 19th Century to the Present*. New York University Press, 2018.

Ricourt, Milagros. *The Dominican Racial Imaginary: Surveying the Landscape of Race and Nation in Hispaniola*. Rutgers University Press, 2016.

Suárez, Lucía M. *The Tears of Hispaniola: Haitian and Dominican Diaspora Memory*. University Press of Florida, 2006.

Thorton, Brendan Jamal, and Diego Ubiera. "Caribbean Exceptions: The Problem of Race and Nation in Dominican Studies," *Latin American Research Review*, vol. 54, no. 2, 2019, pp. 413–428.

Notes

1. Spanish is a gendered language in which the default gender for collective adjectives is the masculine. For example, if there is a group of multiple female Latinas and just one male Latino, then they are all described as Latinos. The "x" in Latinx Studies challenges this idea that the masculine is the default, includes women and LGBTQ people, and represents gender as more complex and gradated than a male/female binary. Other common options for gender-inclusive terminology for the field include Latino/a, Latina/o, and Latin@ Studies.

2. For more on Danticat and Díaz's collaborations, see Russ.

3. The song's title renders the Spanish phrase "Da para los dos" (There's enough for the two) in Dominican vernacular.

4. For scholarship on "Da pa lo do" and its video, see Jaime and Quinn.

5. Kim, Run Kyung. "Feidin Santana, Bystander Who Recorded Walter Scott Shooting: 'I'm Still Scared.'"

Works Cited

Artt, Sarah, and Anne Schwan. "Screening Women's Imprisonment: Agency and Exploitation in *Orange Is the New Black*." *Television and New Media*, vol. 17, no. 6, 2016, pp. 467–472.

Border of Lights. 2016, www.borderoflights.org.

Caputi, Jane. "The Color Orange? Social Justice Issues in the First Season of *Orange Is the New Black*." *The Journal of Popular Culture*, vol. 48, no. 6, 2015, pp. 1130–1150.

Corrigan, Timothy. *A Short Guide to Writing about Film*. Pearson, 2015.

Derby, Lauren. "Haitians, Magic, and Money: Raza and Society in the Haitian-Dominican Borderlands, 1900 to 1937." *Comparative Studies in Society and History*, vol. 36, no. 3, 1994, pp. 488–526.

"Da pa lo do." *YouTube*, uploaded by engelleonardo7, 19 October 2011, www.youtube.com/watch?v=Y72XAybPTnU.

Díaz, Junot. *The Brief Wondrous Life of Oscar Wao*. Riverhead, 2008.

———. "Under President Trump, Radical Hope Is Our Best Weapon." *The New Yorker*, 21 Nov. 2016, www.newyorker.com/magazine/2016/11/21/under-president-trump-radical-hope-is-our-best-weapon.

Dunne, Carey. "Move Over Dove. *Orange Is the New Black* Celebrates Real Women." *Fast Company*, 20 August 2013, www.fastcodesign.com/1673132/move-over-dove-orange-is-the-new-black-celebrates-real-women.

García-Peña, Lorgia. *The Borders of Dominicanidad: Race, Nation, and Archives of Contradiction*. Duke University Press, 2016.

I Am Not Your Negro. Directed by Raoul Peck. Velvet Film, 2016.

Jaime, Karen. "'Da pa' lo' do'": Rita Indiana's Queer, Racialized Dominicanness." *Small Axe*, no. 47, July 2015, pp. 85–93.

Jay, Paul. *Global Matters: The Transnational Turn in Literary Studies*. Cornell University Press, 2010.

Kim, Run Kyung. "Feidin Santana, Bystander Who Recorded Walter Scott Shooting: 'I'm Still Scared.'" *Today*, 9 April 2015, www.today.com/news/feidin-santana-bystander-who-recorded-walter-scott-shooting-i-m-t13671.

Mayes, April, et al. "Transnational Hispaniola: Toward New Paradigms in Haitian and Dominican Studies." *Radical History Review*, no. 115, Winter 2013, pp. 26–32.

"Power Suit." *Orange Is the New Black*, season 4, episode 2, Netflix, 17 June 2016, www.netflix.com/watch/70242311?trackId=14170287&tctx=0%2C0%2Cccdeb7c6-5432-4b5f-8344-2ffba6050d8a-502316538.

Quinn, Rachel Afi. "El rostro negro dominicano y la Quisqueya *queer* de Rita Indiana Hernández." *Nuestro Caribe: Poder, Raza, y Postnacionalismos desde los límites del mapa LGBTQ*, edited by Mabel Cuesta, Editorial Isla Negra, 2016, pp. 254–269.

Rita Indiana & Los Misterios. *El Juidero*, Premium Latin Music, 2010.

Russ, Elizabeth. "'A Hispaniola Conspiracy': Edwidge Danticat and Junot Díaz Performing (in) the Caribbean Public Sphere." *Reimagining the Caribbean: Conversations Among the Creole, English, French, and Spanish Caribbean*, edited by Valérie K. Orlando and Sandra Messinger Cypess, Lexington Books, 2014, pp. 121–140.

Ship, Jesse. "Twin Shadow Can't 'Forget' Musical Non-Acceptance Due to Race." *Spinner*, 19 January 2011, www.shipwrckd.com/2014/11/twin-shadow-cant-forget-musical-non-acceptance-due-to-race-spinner/.

Smith, Anne Marie. "*Orange* Is the Same White." *New Political Science*, vol. 37, no. 2, 2015, pp. 276–280.

Torres-Saillant, Silvio. "One and Divisible." *Small Axe*, no. 29, June 2009, pp. 4–25.

Trouillot, Michel-Rolph. *Silencing the Past: Power and the Production of History*, Beacon Press, 2015.

Twin Shadow. *Forget*, Terrible Records, 2010.

12

Teaching Haiti and the Dominican Republic

Cultural Representations of Haitian Immigrant Experiences

ANNE M. FRANÇOIS

Portrayals of Haitian immigrants in mass media are often one-dimensional, a fact that has resulted in the perpetuation of clichés and stereotypes. By contrast, many diasporic writers, filmmakers, artists, and intellectuals present far more complex and layered representations of Haitian immigrants in their works. In this essay, I discuss a course on diasporic representations of Haitian immigrant experiences in literature, painting, films, and music of Haiti and the Dominican Republic, an interdisciplinary course that is focused on the humanities but relevant to a variety of fields, including global studies, migration studies, area studies, and cultural studies.

In a course that addresses Haiti in the context of the Dominican Republic, it is imperative to give students an overview of the political history of these two countries that share the island of Hispaniola in the Caribbean Sea. As the first and only Black republic in the Western Hemisphere, Haiti holds huge historical importance and has inspired revolutionary movements worldwide against slavery, racial oppression, and economic exploitation. Although different in many aspects from Haiti, the Dominican Republic is historically and culturally connected to its neighbor. However, the relationship between these nations has been difficult and at times violent, in part due to disputed issues of borders and migration.

The first unit of the course, on literature, enables students to sharpen their critical thinking skills as they examine issues of immigration policies, borders, loss of cultural identity and language, cultural alienation, racial discrimination, ethnicity, and globalization. Traumatic experiences of racial, political, and economic oppression on the part of Haitian immigrants, as well as their resistance in the face of hegemonic powers, are represented in poetry, short stories, and novels. One focal point of this section of the course is the Parsley Massacre, an ethnic purge carried out in October 1937 on the orders of Dominican dictator Leonidas Rafael Trujillo. Trujillo, fearing an influx of Haitian immigrants into the Dominican Republic, ordered the deaths of thousands at the border based on a language test. Haitians, along with Dominicans who looked dark enough to be Haitian, or who could not roll the "r" in *perejil*, the Spanish word for "parsley," were murdered.[1] The Parsley Massacre remains an important trope in the Haitian imaginary. Novelists and poets can provide invaluable historical and cultural context for students; Haitian novelists Jacques Stephen Alexis and René Philoctète, for example, describe the trials of their characters escaping the massacre in their novels *General Sun, My Brother* (*Compère Géneral Soleil*) and *Massacre River* (*Le Peuple des terres mêlées*), respectively. Haitian American author Edwidge Danticat, from a later generation of writers, revisits the same historical event in her story "Nineteen Thirty-Seven," included in her collection entitled *Krik? Krak!*

The title *Krik? Krak!* is of utmost significance because it underscores the importance of the oral tradition in Haitian culture. The phrase "krik krak" invokes a call-and-response interaction between storyteller and audience. It is metaphorically a call or an engagement between the text and the reader. Telling stories is cathartic for immigrants dealing with displacement and other types of suffering, and storytelling sustains Haitian culture, as well as the lives of individual Haitians, serving as a collective means of preserving and transmitting the oral tradition to the next generation of storytellers.

The stories in *Krik? Krak!* portray Haitian immigrants in different contexts. In addition to "Nineteen Thirty-Seven," the collection includes "Children of the Sea," which features the protagonist fleeing Haiti's political instability and reaching the shores of Miami in a risky boat. The last story in the collection, "Caroline's Wedding," depicts the struggle of two young women, children of Haitian immigrants, in their attempt to negotiate US and traditional Haitian cultures. They are described in a state of in-betweenness, not quite belonging to either culture. An examination of "Caroline's Wedding" enables students to reflect on and draw conclusions about identity crises and cultural alienation experienced by immigrants facing displacement or a sense of non-belonging. An analysis of the relationship between a Haitian traditional mother and her US-born children can help shed light on generational conflicts and the complex issue of respectability as shaped by cultural expectations and gender socialization.

After reading *Krik? Krak!*, students can be invited to examine the characters in relation to the following themes: "boat people," wet feet policy, political refugees, economic migrants, hybrid identity, cultural alienation, and orality. The instructor can further expand class discussion by bringing in the context of global immigration policies, travel bans, and family separations. Through these texts, the instructor can create space for open debate and discussion, including the possibility that politicians might be able to propose fair immigration policies. The instructor can separate the class into two groups and have each group present its arguments for and against immigration. Another activity is to have students make cross-cultural comparisons by sharing their attitudes or those of their communities about storytelling. The focus of the activity might be on the importance and/or the absence of oral traditions in their own cultures. If time permits, after reading "Nineteen Thirty-Seven," the instructor can consider a comparative examination of textual references from the perspective of intertextuality and paratext, putting Danticat in dialogue with another work on the Parsley Massacre, such as Rita Dove's narrative poem "Parsley." The divisional structure of the poem metaphorically illustrates the social and cultural separation between Haitians and Dominicans. While comparing texts, students and the instructor can reflect on the use of language as a powerful tool of domination and a symbolic form of violence used to create psychological borders that subjugate, separate, and divide in concrete physical terms as well. Within the wider context of migration and immigration, they can also analyze the extent to which language may determine social and geographical boundaries lived by Haitian immigrants.

A novel that provides an effective cultural point of reference for this course is Danticat's *The Farming of Bones*, which depicts the story of Amabelle Désir, a young Haitian female servant in the Dominican Republic whose dream of marrying the cane cutter she has met is cut short by genocidal violence. This narrative provides an opportunity to analyze the representation of female agency through Amabelle, who plays a subservient role as well as that of a heroic protagonist fighting for survival.[2] Danticat creates a more inclusive cultural and representational narrative space by exploring a migration experience of Haitian women in the Dominican Republic. Male writers have traditionally focused on male characters and neglected to represent the experiences of women migrants in their fiction, and the importance of integrating female voices in narrative spaces should be emphasized.

The Haiti/Dominican Republic Interface

Dominican literature does not generally give much attention to the 1937 massacre, which exacerbated border issues between Haiti and the Dominican Republic that continue to this day. Lucia Suárez notes:

> In contrast to a Haitian tradition of disclosure of misery and violence, the politics of silence—or rather—denial have been dominant in Dominican memory. . . . In general, it would seem that Dominican literature has traditionally ignored the violence and strife the country continues to experience. Instead it has focused on romantic, myth forming stories. This is substantiated by the position of authors like Julia Alvarez. For example, at a book tour presentation at Duke University in 1998, Alvarez stated flatly that she was not interested in reviewing violence through her work. . . . (7–8)

Nevertheless, Alvarez does briefly refer to the massacre in her novel *How the Garcia Girls Lost Their Accents* (1992). Dominican American novelist Junot Díaz also mentions the massacre in *The Brief Wondrous Life of Oscar Wao* (2007). And in his collection of short stories *Drown* (1996), Díaz alludes to tensions between the Dominican Republic and Haiti when the protagonist Yunior, an inner-city Afro-Dominican immigrant youth living in the Dominican Republic and then New Jersey, is compared to a Haitian by his brother Rafa because of his dark skin. Yunior tells us,

> Back in the capital he rarely said anything to me except shut up, pendejo. Unless, of course, he was mad and then he had about five hundred routines he liked to lay on me. Most of them had to do with my complexion, my hair, the size of my lips. It's the Haitian, he'd say to his buddies. Hey Señor Haitian, Mami found you at the border and only took you in because she felt sorry for you. (5)

In this passage, the antagonist at once expresses his hatred of his brother and associates Haitian migrants with poverty. This passage may be interpreted as reflecting Díaz's criticism of prejudicial attitudes toward race and national identity in the Haitian-Dominican context. However, although Díaz criticizes the Dominican government's anti-Haitian policies, at the risk of angering Dominican authorities, his fiction does not focus in a significant way on Haiti.

Another text that sheds light on the lives of Haitian immigrants in relation to the Dominican Republic is Alvarez's *How the Garcia Girls Lost Their Accents,* which depicts the lives of the four Garcia sisters—Carla, Sandra, Yolanda, and Sofia—who immigrated with their family to the US to escape reprisals for their father's involvement in a failed coup against the Trujillo regime. Like the protagonists in Danticat's story "Caroline's Wedding," the Garcia girls have to negotiate a new culture and a new landscape and adopt a new language, in addition to confronting racism in the US.

One of the characters, Yolanda, returns to the Dominican Republic after 29 years in search of her lost origins. (The search for origins is a common trope in Caribbean literature.) Upon her return, Yolanda reflects on her childhood, which was influenced by two Haitian maids, Pila and Chucha. In depicting Chucha, who survived the Parsley Massacre, Alvarez focuses on the darkness of her skin and her practice of Vodou. Pila, a teller of ghost stories, disappears after being accused of stealing from the family (219). The author's depictions of both Haitian maids' skin color in contrast to Yolanda's is used to reinforce Yolanda's attraction to whiteness and to underscore an atmosphere of racial bias. An approach rooted in postcolonial theory helps students analyze ways in which history, race, class, gender, culture, economics, and politics come together to shape the experiences of Haitian im/migrants. As they consider particular texts, students can pay close attention to issues of representation, absence, and voicelessness within specific social, historical, and political contexts.

Both Junot Diáz and Edwidge Danticat have advocated for better treatment of Haitian immigrants in the Dominican Republic. As social activists, they have worked together to oppose the 2013 Dominican law that stripped the Dominican-born children of Haitian immigrants of their rights as Dominican citizens, leaving them stateless, without political or legal protection. Students can read an interview that Richard André conducted with Danticat and Díaz entitled "The Dominican Republic and Haiti: A Shared View from the Diaspora" in which they discuss this issue, with the two authors answering questions such as, "What do you think most Haitians/Dominicans don't understand about the other side?"[3] As part of this discussion, students should be encouraged to conduct research on the issue of statelessness and write short essays examining immigration policies among the US, Haiti, and/or the Dominican Republic.

The second unit of the course focuses on painting, which is an engaging way to help students learn about historical ties among Haiti, the Dominican Republic, and the United States, including about issues such as economic exploitation on sugar cane plantations. For example, the Haitian painter Philomé Obin (1892–1986) depicts Haiti's struggles and resistance before, during, and after the US Occupation of Haiti (1915–1935) in a series of paintings titled *Débâcle des Cacos 19-6-15* (circa 1947), *Crucifixion de Charlemagne Péralte pour la Liberté* (1970), and *Trois générations (Avant L'Occupation, Pendant L'Occupation, Après L'Occupation)* (circa 1981). In a painting titled *Grand'mère me disait que la riv. massacre était en sang* (circa 1975), Ernst Prophète (1950-) represents the bloody imagery of the 1937 massacre of Haitians in the Dominican Republic. Other

Haitian painters focus on representations of plantation landscapes and cane cutters, as well as the US Occupation. For instance, Haitian painter Ulrick Jean-Pierre (1955–) represents the peasant as a figure of resistance against the Occupation in his painting titled *Le caco* (*During the American Occupation*, 1986). In this painting, a young, muscular peasant stands proudly with his machete, high in the mountains, ready to defend his pride and his land. Jean-Pierre also addresses the issue of exploitation and profits related to sugar cane in his landscape painting titled *Awareness of Exploitation*. In this painting, the artist focuses his attention on the unequal power dynamics between an overseer, who is dressed in white and wearing a colonial hat, and the half-naked and clearly malnourished children who are cutting the cane. The motif of sugar cane can be used as a point of departure to encourage students to develop presentations on the economies of Haiti and the Dominican Republic, past and present. For example, students might conduct research on the conditions of Haitian immigrants working in the *bateys*, or Dominican cane plantations.

The third unit of the course focuses on films and videos. An effective documentary for class discussion in this unit is "Haiti and the Dominican Republic," from the PBS documentary series *Black in Latin America* by Henry Louis Gates, Jr. This segment examines historical, political, social, and cultural relationships between Haiti and the Dominican Republic and describes differences between the two countries. Students can choose a specific topic highlighted in the documentary and write a response or a short essay about it. Bill Haney's *The Price of Sugar*, which focuses on Haitian immigrants in the bateys, is another effective documentary to use in the classroom. Students should also be encouraged to watch a selection of Dominican movies at home, including *One Way Ticket* (*Un pasaje de ida*), directed by Agliberto Meléndez (1988), which narrates the tragic story of a group of Dominicans who die while trying to reach the United States by cargo ship. The film is based on the deaths by suffocation of Dominican migrants aboard the *Regina Express* in 1980, an event that was covered in the world news at the time. A discussion topic arising from the film is the differential treatment of immigrants based on their geographic origins and the political situations in their home countries, as well as stereotypes about immigrants in the nation they are entering. Raoul Peck's *Haitian Corner* (1981) provides a powerful representation of the experiences of a male Haitian immigrant to the United States, escaping the dictatorship of Baby Doc; the film highlights cultural and social differences between life in Haiti and the diaspora, including gender socialization. The instructor can assign students to monitor current news on Haiti and the Dominican Republic and then share and discuss what they have learned with the class as a whole. Students can also be paired to review each other's homework assignments and report on the ensuing conversations in class discussion.

The fourth unit focuses on music. The expressive poetics of music offer a potent teaching tool about Haiti and the Dominican Republic. For example, the instructor can play songs by the Haitian American musician Wyclef Jean, and students can be assigned to conduct research on his early career with The Fugees, a contraction of "Refugees." The significance of this name can itself be the focus of class discussion. Students can further analyze the lyrics of one of Jean's albums, for example *Masquerade*, to investigate ways in which his immigrant experience is reflected there, as it is more directly in his memoir *Purpose: An Immigrant Story*. A comparative analysis may be conducted between the lyrics and the memoir. The work of Dominican immigrant musicians such as rappers Black Point and Don Miguelo can also be used to good effect in the classroom.

The crisis on the Haitian and Dominican border is a microcosm of global issues that affect millions of people worldwide—of wars, displacements, ecological catastrophes, and poverty, among many other calamities. In the US and other Western countries, many politicians have tried to dismiss the plight of migrants and immigrants by employing exclusive and racist discourses. In the face of these problems, a course that uses literature and the arts to consider Haiti and the Dominican Republic together, while not shying away from the historic and current tensions that have shaped the dynamic between these nations, can prompt students to think deeply and in detail about what borders mean. Foregrounding the experiences of Haitian immigrants in this context helps students analyze how nations go about constructing concepts of belonging/non-belonging, for example, and how individuals describe what it feels like to live within uncertain borderlands.

Lesson Plan

Course Description

In this course, the figure of the Haitian immigrant will be our guide. Over the course of the semester, we will explore the journeys of immigrants as we read stories, consider visual media (videos, documentary films, and other fictions), and listen to music from Haiti and the Dominican Republic. These materials will introduce us to important historical and socioeconomic ties among Haiti, the Dominican Republic, and the United States. This course is designed to help you discuss immigration and border conflicts as worldwide issues that affect millions of people today.

Learning Objectives

1. Students will be able to understand and discuss the geopolitical history of Haiti and the Dominican Republic.
2. Students will be able to analyze major themes related to Haitian immigration in works of fiction, as well as character and plot development.
3. Students will be able to understand and explain issues arising from linguistic and cultural differences related to immigration.

Sample Lesson Plan for a 40-minute class discussion of Edwidge Danticat's short story "Caroline's Wedding"

a. 5 minutes. Warm-up session. Write on the board, "What is an immigrant?" Have students discuss this question in pairs, then have students volunteer to share responses with the class as a whole.
b. 5 minutes. The teacher **reviews** essential vocabulary and key words on the board with the students.
c. 5 minutes. The teacher does a **comprehension check.** What have you learned? Discuss with your partner (2 minutes) and identify initial details on the board.
d. 10 minutes. The teacher **divides** students into small groups and has them work with the text to identify the different structural elements of the short story and then to discuss **its major themes**, such as immigration policies, generational conflicts, and gender socialization.
e. 10 minutes. The teacher transitions to a whole class discussion for **cross-cultural comparisons**. The teacher asks students to reflect on and discuss the following questions:

- What are some of the ways in which the two sisters, Caroline and Grace, negotiate their Haitian and US identities?
- The theme of immigration is prevalent in the story, and the narrator, Grace, is excited about becoming a US citizen. Why is becoming a citizen important to Grace? What are some of the advantages that US citizenship can provide in the context of the story?
- How does food demonstrate a connection to culture?

f. 5 minutes. **Assessment**: The teacher asks students to volunteer to recap two main points of the day's lesson.

Notes

1. In *From Sugar to Revolution*, Myriam Chancy writes about "passing the parsley test and the consequences of failing it" (82).
2. For more on strong female characters in Haitian literature, see Beverly Bell's *Walking on Fire*.
3. The interview was published in the Summer 2014 issue of *Quarterly Americas* and is available online at www.americasquarterly.org/content/dominican-republic-and-haiti-shared-view-diaspora.

Works Cited

Alexis, Jacques Stephen. *General Sun, My Brother*. Translated by Carrol F. Coates, University Press of Virginia, 1999.

André, Richard. "The Dominican Republic and Haiti: A Shared View from the Diaspora." Interview with Edwidge Danticat and Junot Díaz. *Quarterly Americas*, Summer 2014. www.americasquarterly.org/content/dominican-republic-and-haiti-shared-view-diaspora. Accessed 1 August 2019.

Alvarez, Julia. *How the Garcia Girls Lost Their Accents*. Algonquin Books, 1991.

Bell, Beverly. *Walking on Fire: Haitian Women's Stories of Survival and Resistance*. Cornell University Press, 2002.

Candelario, Ginetta E. B. *Black Behind the Ears: Dominican Racial Identity from Museums to Beauty Shops*. Duke University Press, 2007.

Chancy, Myriam. *From Sugar to Revolution. Women's Vision of Haiti, Cuba, and The Dominican Republic*. Wilfrid Laurier University Press, 2012.

Danticat, Edwidge. *Krik? Krak!* Vintage Books, 1996.

———. *The Farming of Bones*. Soho Press, 1998.

Danticat, Edwidge, and Junot Díaz. "The Dominican Republic's War on Haitian Workers." *The New York Times*, 20 November 1999.

Díaz, Junot. *The Brief Wondrous Life of Oscar Wao*. Riverhead Books, 2007.

———. *Drown*. Riverhead Books, 1996.

Dove, Rita. "Parsley," from *Museum*. Carnegie Mellon University Press, 1983.

Gates, Henry Louis. "Haiti & the Dominican Republic: An Island Divided." *Black in Latin America*, PBS, April 1991.

Haney, Bill. "The Price of *Sugar*." Uncommon Productions, 2007.

Jean, Wyclef, with Bozza Anthony. *Purpose: An Immigrant Story*. It Books/Harper Collins. 2012.

Meléndez, Agliberto. One Way Ticket (*Un pasaje de ida*). Producciones Testimonios, 1988.

Paravisini-Gebert, Lizabeth. "Bitter Sugar: Teaching the Caribbean Plantation Through the Arts." *Reimagining the Caribbean: Conversations Among the Creole, English, French, and Spanish Caribbean*, edited by Valérie K. Orlando and Sandra Messinger Cypess, Lexington Books, 2014, pp. 103–119.

Peck, Raoul. *Haitian Corner*. Volkenborn/ZDF, 1989.

Philoctète René. *Massacre River*. Translated by Linda Coverdale, New Directions Books, 2005.

Súarez, Lucía M. *The Tears of Hispaniola: Haitian and Dominican Diaspora Memory*. University Press of Florida, 2006.

Contributors

Cécile Accilien is chair of the Department of Interdisciplinary Studies and professor of African and African Diaspora Studies at Kennesaw State University. She is the author of *Rethinking Marriage in Francophone African and Caribbean Literatures*. She has also coedited and contributed to two collections of essays, *Revolutionary Freedoms: A History of Survival, Strength and Imagination in Haiti* and *Just Below South: Intercultural Performance in the Caribbean and the U.S. South*; she cowrote *English-Haitian Creole Phrasebook* and *Francophone Cultures Through Film*. She is currently working on a book on Haitian popular cinema.

Jessica Adams is the author of *Wounds of Returning: Race, Memory, and Property on the Postslavery Plantation* and coeditor of *Guantánamo and American Empire: The Humanities Respond*; *Just Below South: Intercultural Performance in the Caribbean and the U.S. South*; and *Revolutionary Freedoms: A History of Survival, Strength, and Imagination in Haiti*. She also coedited a scholarly edition of Arna Bontemps's novel of Haiti, *Drums at Dusk*. Her essays, short stories, poetry, and creative nonfiction have appeared in a variety of journals. She is assistant professor of English in the College of General Studies at the University of Puerto Rico, Río Piedras.

Alessandra Benedicty-Kokken is research coordinator/senior researcher at the Research Center for Material Cultures at NMVW (National Museum for World Cultures) in the Netherlands, working under the aegis of Wayne Modest and Stijn Schoonderwoerd. She also teaches at Utrecht University's Gender Studies Program and the City College of New York. From 2009 to 2019, Benedicty-Kokken served as assistant professor and was promoted to associate professor of Caribbean and Postcolonial Studies and French at the Graduate Center (City University of New York) and the Division of Interdisciplinary Studies at the City College of New York. She is series editor for Brill's Caribbean Series and a book reviews editor for the *Journal of Haitian Studies*, as well as a member of the FACE Foundation's French Voices selection committee. Her most recent publications focus on human rights history and notably the relationship between Africana and Jewish intellectualisms, Martinican contemporary arts, and the novels of Igiaba Scego and Abdourahman Waberi. She is author of *Spirit Possession in French, Haitian, and Vodou Thought: An Intellectual History*; second editor with Kaiama L. Glover of *Revisiting Marie Vieux Chauvet: Paradoxes of the Postcolonial Feminine*, a special issue of *Yale French Studies*; and co-editor with Kaiama L. Glover, Jean Picard Byron, and Mark Schuller of *The Haiti Exception: Anthropology and the Predicament of Narrative*.

Anne M. François is a former professor of French at Eastern University. She holds a BA in French, a Masters in French culture and civilization, and a PhD in Francophone studies from New York University. She is the author of *Rewriting the Return to Africa: Voices of French Caribbean Women Writers*. Her primary areas of interest are the Francophone Caribbean, West African and Afro-Latino literatures and films, and Haitian Creole. She has also contributed chapters to three volumes of essays, *Reimagining the Caribbean: Conversations among the Creole, English, French and Spanish Caribbean*; *French Women Authors: The Significance of the Spiritual (1400–2000)*; and *African Caribbeans: A Reference Guide*. She has translated a short story, "Une histoire de danse et de pluie," by Louis-Philippe Dalembert in *Calabash (A Journal of Caribbean Arts and Letters)*.

Régine Jean-Charles is associate professor of Romance languages and literatures and African and African diaspora studies at Boston College, where she teaches classes including Black Feminisms 101, Francophone Women Writers, Haitian Literature and Film, Paris Noir, and Where #blacklivesmatter Meets #metoo. Her scholarship and teaching on world literatures in French include work on Black France, Sub-Saharan Africa, Haiti and the Haitian diaspora. She holds a BA from the University of Pennsylvania and an AM and PhD from Harvard University. She has received fellowships from the Ford Foundation, the Mellon Mays Foundation, and the Woodrow Wilson Foundation. Her first book, *Conflict Bodies: The Politics of Rape Representation in the Francophone Imaginary* examines theoretical, visual, and literary texts in order to challenge how rape culture is represented and theorized. Her essays have appeared in *American Quarterly, Callaloo, French Forum, Journal of Haitian Studies, Meridians, Research in African Literatures*, and *Small Axe*, among others. She is currently working on books about feminist ethics in contemporary Haitian literature and about Haitian girlhood in literary and visual texts.

Elizabeth Langley is assistant professor of Spanish and French at Fort Hays State University. She received her PhD in Romance studies from the University of Miami where she also served as the inaugural graduate student teaching fellow in the American Studies program. Her philosophy of teaching centers on the classroom environment, use of technology, and lifelong learning. Her teaching and research interests include literature and visual art of the Americas; translation, memory, and resistance studies; as well as second language acquisition and pedagogy.

Valérie K. Orlando is professor of French and Francophone literatures in the Department of French and Italian at the University of Maryland, College Park. She is the author of six books: *The Algerian New Novel: The Poetics of a Modern Nation, 1959–1970*; *New African Cinema*; *Screening Morocco: Contemporary Film in a Changing Society*; *Francophone Voices of the "New Morocco" in Film and Print: (Re)presenting a Society in Transition*; *Of Suffocated Hearts and Tortured Souls: Seeking Subjecthood Through Madness in Francophone Women's Writing of Africa and the Caribbean*; and *Nomadic Voices of Exile: Feminine Identity in Francophone Literature of the Maghreb*. She co-edited with Sandra M. Cypess the volume *Reimagining the Caribbean: Conversations among the Creole, English, French and Spanish Caribbean*.

Agnès Peysson-Zeiss is the coordinator of the Intensive Language sequence in French at Bryn Mawr College. She has researched the works of the Algerian Francophone writer Assia Djebar and published a number of articles on her polyphonic texts, particularly on the Algerian Quatuor. She has examined the forms of metalanguage used by Djebar to rewrite women's history and her way of marking a new approach to her-story through songs, dance and the feminine gaze. Her most recent projects deal with graphic novels and resilience, examining how the arts can fill the void trauma leaves behind and allow people to survive. She is also involved in virtual civic engagement, focusing on women's rights issues in the DRC, translating, with her students, blogs written by women in a Media Center for Women in Bukavu, South-Kivu DRC, to post them and disseminate their stories. Her articles on those two topics are forthcoming.

John Ribó is assistant professor of English at Florida State University and the 2018–2019 recipient of a McKnight Junior Faculty Development Fellowship. His work has appeared in *Chiricú Journal*, *The Journal of Haitian Studies*, *Cuban Studies*, and *ASAP/J* and will be included in the forthcoming *Bloomsbury Companion to Edwidge Danticat*, edited by Jana Evans Braziel and Nadège T.

Clitandre. His current book project, *Haitian Hauntings*, draws upon Haitian, Dominican, Puerto Rican, and Cuban literature, visual arts, music, and media to demonstrate that the Haitian Revolution was foundational not only to the racial formations of the Hispanophone Caribbean and its diasporas but also to the emergence of popular genres that dominate global culture today.

Joubert Satyre joined the French Studies Department at the University of Guelph in 2003. He received his PhD in Francophone literature from l'Université de Montréal in 2003. His areas of research include French Caribbean literature, Haitian literature, and the Baroque. He wrote the chapter on Caribbean literature in *Introduction aux littératures francophones*. He has published Émile *Ollivier: cohérence et lisibilité du baroque* and edited *Horizons multiples de la littérature haïtienne contemporaine*. His articles have been published in journals including *Canadian Literature, L'Esprit Créateur, Présence Francophone, Horizons/Théâtre, Nouvelle Revue Francophone, Journal of Transnational American Studies*.

Darren Staloff is professor of early American history at the City College of New York, CUNY. He received his PhD from Columbia University and a postdoctoral fellowship to the Omohundro Institute of Early American History and Culture. He has been awarded scholarships from the National Endowment for the Humanities as well as the James Madison Program in American Ideals and Institutions at Princeton University. His scholarly interests focus on political and intellectual history in early America and the Atlantic littoral. In addition to various essays, he is the author of two books, *The Making of an American Thinking Class: Intellectuals and Intelligentsia In Puritan Massachusetts* and *Hamilton, Adams, Jefferson: The Politics of Enlightenment and the American Founding*. His current research project is an overview of the Enlightenment in early America.

Bonnie Thomas is associate professor and convener of French studies at the University of Western Australia. She teaches all levels of French and has published widely in the field of Francophone Caribbean literature in journals such as *Small Axe, The International Journal of Francophone Studies* and *The French Review*. She is also the author of *Breadfruit or Chestnut?: Gender Construction in the French Caribbean Novel* and *Connecting Histories: Francophone Caribbean Writers Interrogating Their Past*.

Don E. Walicek is professor in the College of Humanities at the University of Puerto Rico, Río Piedras Campus, where he holds a joint appointment in English and linguistics. He earned a B.A. in anthropology and an M.A. in Latin

American studies at the University of Texas at Austin. The University of Puerto Rico awarded his doctorate in English linguistics. His areas of academic interest include creolistics, sociolinguistics, sociohistorical linguistics, and cultural studies. He has published widely on the social history of language and language contact in the Caribbean, and served as editor of the Caribbean Studies journal *Sargasso* for more than a decade. He and Jessica Adams are co-editors of *Guantánamo and American Empire: The Humanities Respond*. In 2019, he was a Fulbright Scholar at the Center for Inter-American Studies at the University of Graz, as well as a fellow of the American Council of Learned Societies.

Sophie Watt is lecturer in French studies at the University of Sheffield. She studied history as an undergraduate at the University of Paris VII and holds a master's degree and an interdisciplinary PhD in modern French history and literature from the University of Iowa. She joined the Department of French at the University of Sheffield in 2011. Her research interests include the production and writing of history, discourse analysis, postcolonial theories of textuality and neocolonial historical inquiry, and her work specifically analyzes the construction of minority identities within the broader contours of French national identity and traces ethnic prejudices inherent in republican ideology and language.

Index

Adams, John, 7, 119–36
Adams, John Quincy, 7, 119–36
Albanel, Véronique, 142, 146–52
Alleyne, Mervyn, 93–115
American Studies, 115, 183–200
Amistad, 124, 127–31
Antillanité, 36
Aristide, Jean-Bertrand, 135–65

Baker, Andy, 172, 178, 180
Barlet, Olivier, 168, 180
Battle: metaphoric, 24; of the Nile, 126
Bellerive, Jean-Max, 174, 176
Belonging, 35–37, 46, 100, 108, 112, 130, 214, 236, 240, 245
Black, 71, 72, 74, 191; English speakers, 112; nation, 22; republic, 4, 28, 186; women, 17, 28, 225
Black Jacobins, The, 151–53, 156, 205
Black Lives Matter, 233
Blackness, 22, 191, 195, 199
Bonaparte. *See* Napoleon
Border, 215, 217, 220–23, 237, 240–46; conflict, 242
Borderlands, 220, 221–37, 245
Borderlines, 208
Bouqui, 55, 56, 60–62
Bouqui Au Paradis, 7, 51–66
Boutroue, Joël, 175

Camp Corail, 173, 175
Caribbean Discourse, 49, 56

Cédras, Raoul, 140, 141, 151, 180
Césaire, Aimé, 34, 42, 49
Chamblain, Louis-Jodel, 141
Chronique de la dérive douce, 35, 46, 50
Citizenship, 18, 134, 197, 202, 229, 246
Clinton, Bill, 141, 148, 149, 163n6, 163n12, 174, 176
Clinton, Hillary, 171
Collectif NON, 141
Coloniality, 100–104, 110, 116, 174, 221, 222
Constant, Emmanuel, 141
Creole, 6, 7, 25, 42, 43, 52–54, 63, 65n6, 65n8, 185, 186, 238; cultures, 2; languages, 92–116
Critical Discourse Analysis, 137, 146, 157, 161, 165
Cultural alienation, 239–41

Danticat, Edwidge, 6, 8, 16, 21, 27–30, 34, 38, 41, 43, 46, 49nn9–10, 116, 183, 192, 215, 223, 238, 240, 243, 246, 247, 252
Debray, Régis, 138, 142, 147–49, 152, 162, 164
Decolonial turn, 101, 107
DeGraff, Michel, 93–95, 102, 104, 107, 115, 116
Dejean, Yves, 108, 116
Deleuze, Gilles (and Félix Guattari), *Mille plateaux*, 36, 49
Derby, Lauren, 222, 223, 230, 235, 237
Dessalines, Jean-Jacques, 53, 75, 119, 135, 153, 154

De Villepin, Dominique, 142, 146, 157, 162
Díaz, Junot, 221, 223, 224, 237, 238, 242, 243, 247
Discourse-Historical Approach, 138, 146, 161, 165
Displacement, 240–45
Documentary, 17, 19, 21, 22, 25, 167, 169, 170, 175, 177, 178, 191, 230, 244, 245
Duvalier, Jean-Claude, 27, 64, 139; dictatorship of, 26, 140, 144, 145, 149, 151, 154, 156, 163n1
Duvalierism, 156, 159

Écrivain *engagé*, 34–46
Education, 3, 52, 65n1, 94, 95, 102, 109, 110, 113, 116, 180, 198, 199, 209; in Haiti, 93
Emergency Economic Recovery Program (EERP), 141, 148, 149
Epistolary, 167, 171; exchange, 172–74
Ethnodrama, 54, 55
Exceptionalism, 29, 33, 94, 115, 116, 183, 184, 186, 187, 198n1, 199, 200
Exile, 34–40, 43–46, 48, 50, 141, 145, 183, 251

Fatal Assistance, 166–80
Feminism, 15, 33; black, 15, 22, 23, 28, 32, 250
Folklore, 6, 8, 53, 55, 61, 63–66, 218, 219

Getino, Octavio (and Fernando Solanas), 167, 168, 178, 180. *See also* Third Cinema
Glamour aid, 174, 175, 178
Glissant, Edouard, 1, 2, 10n1, 11, 34, 36–38, 43, 44, 46, 49n11
G184, 144, 146, 151
Goudougoudou, 166
Grammar (of Kreyòl), 100, 102, 107, 115
Guattari, Félix (and Gilles Deleuze), *Mille plateaux*, 36, 49

Haiti: and 2010 earthquake, 8, 16, 19, 21–23, 33, 34, 37–39, 166; Haitian Revolution, 4, 6, 7, 11, 16, 24, 25, 28, 31, 37, 39, 73, 98, 101, 119, 21, 123, 128, 131, 134, 135, 153, 186, 187, 205, 215, 218, 219, 222, 229, 236; Haitian Studies, 27, 28, 33, 49, 50, 63, 154, 156, 158, 160, 164, 183, 185–88, 192, 199, 250, 252; Haitian women, 6, 16, 18–30, 31–33, 77, 164, 206, 241
Haïti kenbe la!, 6, 37, 40–43, 45, 46, 49nn8–9, 50

Identity, 2, 26, 28, 74, 93, 100, 108, 115, 146, 184, 185, 192, 195, 217, 218, 224, 230, 231, 239–42, 247, 251, 253
IMF (International Monetary Fund), 140, 141, 148, 149, 157, 160, 163n4, 168, 172
Indiana, Rita, 227–31, 235, 237, 238
Indigenous, 36, 74, 102, 103, 189
Interdisciplinary, 7, 18, 20, 29, 93–116, 183–85, 204, 239, 249
Interim Haiti Reconstruction Commission (IHCR), 172
Intersectionality, 1–11, 16, 18, 22, 26, 212, 222

Jackson, Andrew, 119–36
Jacmel (painting school), 75
Jacmel (town), 98, 126
Jefferson, Thomas, 119, 120, 134n2, 136

Kerman, Piper, 225, 226
Kreyòl, 15, 28, 42, 52–55, 63, 92–116, 185, 202

Laferrière, Dany, 32, 34, 35, 41, 46, 49n9, 50, 178
Language, 17, 22, 28, 36, 42, 43, 52–54, 62–64, 74, 75, 185, 186, 191, 201, 208, 230, 239–42, 251, 253; Creole, 92–116, 138, 145, 147; and power, 150–52, 171; and aid, 175–77; policy, 93, 94, 108, 109, 111, 114
Latinx Studies, 235
Lavalas Party, 139

Le Monde, 2, 44, 47, 50, 75, 138, 146, 147, 149–52, 158, 162, 163
Les Editions Mémoire, 6, 35
Libération, 138, 139, 146, 147, 149, 150, 152, 158, 159, 162, 210, 229
Linguistics, 2, 7, 42, 43, 52, 92, 95–97, 99, 101–4, 110, 113, 153, 161; socio-, 99, 103, 108, 195, 199, 253
Littérature engagée, 34, 36
Louverture, Toussaint, 76, 119–27, 131, 134n2, 136, 154, 215, 218–20

Macoutes, 139, 141, 159, 163
Malice, 55, 56–67
Mémoire d'encrier, 6, 35–38, 40, 45, 49, 50
Miami, 8, 83, 145, 151, 164, 183–88, 190, 192, 193, 195, 199, 218, 219, 240, 251
Mille plateaux, 36, 49
Monstration, 188
Moyo, Dambisa (*Dead Aid*), 167, 174, 178, 180

Nader, Joséus, 172
Napoleon, 120, 126, 127, 153
Native American, 73, 83
Neoliberalism, 163
Non-belonging, 240, 245
Notebook of a Return to My Native Land, 42, 49

Orality, 241
Orange Is the New Black, 9, 222, 224–31, 233, 235, 237, 238

Passion Haïti, 35, 36, 40, 42, 43–47, 49, 50, 77
Peck, Raoul, 8, 158, 166–80, 235, 237
Philippe, Guy, 151
Philosophie de la Relation, 1, 11, 36, 37, 49. See also Glissant, Edouard
Poetics of Relation, 46, 49; and concept of relation, 36, 43. See also Glissant, Edouard
Postcolonial Creolistics, 93, 94–96, 102, 107

Post-racial, 131
Poto mitan, 15–33
Préval, René, 39, 141, 171, 179n1, 180n1

Quasi-War, 125, 126

Race, 1, 120, 124, 131, 134, 135, 145, 184, 185, 190, 195, 199, 202–21, 223, 229, 231, 232, 242, 243
Refonder Haïti?, 37, 38–40, 46, 47, 49
Relation, 1, 3, 44, 46; "world of," 9
Ricœur, Paul, 169, 180
Rigaud, André, 74, 76, 90, 126, 135

Saint-Éloi, Rodney, 6, 34–50
Santana, Feidin, 234, 237
Scott, Walter, 234, 237
Shipping, American, 125
Solanas, Fernando (and Octavio Getino), 167, 168, 178, 180. See also Third Cinema
Structural Adjustment Program (SAP), 140, 141, 160, 163n4, 164
Supreme Court, 129, 130

Teshome, Gabriel, 168, 178, 180
Theatrical devices, 54–62, 64
Third Cinema, 167, 168, 178, 180
Topos (topoï), 47, 148, 149, 161
Torres-Saillant, Silvio, 191, 195, 199n4, 200, 222, 223, 238
Toussaint Louverture. See Louverture
Transcultural modernities, 168, 180
Transnational, 4, 8, 9, 183, 184, 187, 192, 198, 252; Hispaniola, 221–36
Treaty of Mortefontaine, 126
Treaty of 1795, 130
Twin Shadow, 9, 222, 224, 231, 233, 235, 238

Ulysse, Gina Athena, 11, 33, 50, 136, 197, 198, 220
USAID, 139–41, 148, 165, 167, 170

Visibility, 23, 183–99, 222
Vodou, 23, 54, 55, 61–66, 68–91, 227, 243, 250

West Africa, 55, 63, 64, 95, 100, 101, 106, 107, 130, 250

World Bank, 140–42, 148–60, 163n4, 164, 171, 172, 180n6
World Is Moving Around Me, The, 32, 34, 41, 49n9, 50, 178

XYZ Affair, 126

www.ingramcontent.com/pod-product-compliance
Lightning Source LLC
Chambersburg PA
CBHW031805220426
43662CB00007B/534